PEER POWER

Unite, Learn and Prosper • Activate an Assessment Revolution

Paul Bloomberg

Barb Pitchford

Kara Vandas

Eric Bjornstad • Lisa Cebelak • Lori Cook • David Horton
Rachel Carillo Fairchild • Rupa Chandra Gupta • Gary Giordano
Katherine Smith • Sarah Stevens • Isaac Wells

MIMI & TODD
PRESS

For information about this title or to order other books and/or electronic media, contact the publisher:

Mimi and Todd Press
4629 Cass St. #292
San Diego, CA 92109
www.mimitoddpress.com

ISBN: 978-1-950089-00-0

Printed in the United States of America

Program Director: Paul Bloomberg
Publishing Manager: Tony Francoeur
Production Editor: Sarah Stevens
Associate Editor: Leah Tierney
Copy Editor: Terri Lee Paulsen
Typesetter: Van-Garde Imagery, Inc.
Indexer: Maria Sosnowski
Cover Designer: Paul Hamilton, III
Marketing Manager: Donnie Luehring

The author royalties of Peer Power will be donated to the non-profit organization CASEL.

The Collaborative for Academic, Social, and Emotional Learning (CASEL) is a trusted source for knowledge about high-quality, evidence-based social and emotional learning (SEL). CASEL supports educators and policy leaders and enhances the experiences and outcomes for all PreK-12 students.

Dedication

This book is dedicated to the committed educators that are engaged in their profession and committed to students and their learning. We admire you and believe in you. Thank you for making a difference.

Contents

Acknowledgments vii

About the Authors .xi

Introduction xvii

Part I: **Growing Empowered Learners**

Chapter 1   Unite, Learn, and Prosper! Activate an
Assessment Revolution 3

Chapter 2   What's My Contribution? 13

Chapter 3   The Peer Power Framework 29

Chapter 4   Proving Learning: The Power of Progress. 57

Chapter 5   Expanding Meta-Thinking 79

Part II: **Voices from the Field**

Chapter 6   The Reflective Learning Revolution. 95

Chapter 7   Lifting Language Learning With Peer Power 107

Chapter 8   Igniting Goal Setting With Emerging Readers 123

Chapter 9   The Anthem of Empowerment in Grades 3–5 137

Chapter 10   Learning to Learn With Students for
               Effective Collaborative Conversations 151

Chapter 11   The Case for Problem Solving. 161

Chapter 12   Yes! #PeerPower in Chemistry 171

Chapter 13   Learning for Democracy With #PeerPower. 189

Chapter 14   History Class: A Microcosm of Society 205

Part III: Empower Teams to Empower Learners

Chapter 15   Five Keys to Developing High Impact Teams 235

Chapter 16   Relational Trust: The Glue That Holds Teams Together 241

Chapter 17   Empowering Teacher Teams to Drive Their Learning:
               Transforming Professional Learning with
               Impact Team Inquiry. 249

Part IV: A Call to Action

Chapter 18   Unite, Learn, and Prosper . . .
               Become a #PeerPower Activist! 263

               References 267

               Index 277

Acknowledgments

WHEN WE WERE ASKED WHOM to acknowledge for this book, the first thing that came to mind was "our partner districts, schools, teachers and students!" This book simply would not have happened without the many thought partners we have worked with over the past five years who were willing to take risks and who believe in what we believe in. We are deeply indebted to the students, the parents, the teachers, and the leaders who worked with us to bring the *Peer Power Framework* to life in our schools. Thank you to the following thought partners, true #PeerPower Revolutionaries:

School Districts
- Caldwell School District, Caldwell, ID
- District 31, Staten Island, NY
- Fort Bend Independent School District, Sugar Land, TX
- Jurupa Unified School District, CA
- Norris School District, CA

Schools
- Harvest Valley Elementary, Romoland School District, CA
- James Patterson Elementary, FBISD, Sugar Land, TX
- Lyons Township High School, La Grange, IL

- Michael J. Petrides School, District 31, Staten Island, NY

- Park Middle School, Kennewick School District, Kennewick, WA

- PS 39, District 15, Brooklyn, NY

- PS 112, District 20, Brooklyn, NY

- PS 247, District 20, Brooklyn, NY

- PS 09, District 31, Staten Island, NY

- The Public School 13, District 31, Staten Island, NY

- PS 16, District 31, Staten Island, NY

- PS 20, District 31, Staten Island, NY

- PS 22, District 31, Staten Island, NY

- PS 45, District 31, Staten Island, NY

- PS/IS 48, District 31, Staten Island, NY

- PS 60, District 31, Staten Island, NY

- PS 68, District 31, Staten Island, NY

- PS 69, District 31, Staten Island, NY

- Quail Valley Elementary, FBISD, Sugar Land, TX

- Roosevelt High School, Honolulu, HI

Special Thanks To:

- Damien Hernandez, Jurupa Middle School, CA

- Jessica Drogos, Lyons Township High School, La Grange, IL

- Kelly Miller, Norris School District

- Chantel Mebane, Norris School District, CA

- Stephanie Poggi, PS 20, Staten Island, NY

- Nicole Mancusi, PS 20, Staten Island, NY

- Melissa Brander, PS 22, Staten Island, NY

ACKNOWLEDGEMENTS

- Melissa Cohen, PS 22, Staten Island, NY

- Marie Crumbley, PS 22, Staten Island, NY

- Danielle Di Cupa, PS 22, Staten Island, NY

- Errika Gill, PS 60, Staten Island, NY

- Gina Burt, Park Middle School, Kennewick, WA

- Alexi Albert, Park Middle School, Kennewick, WA

- Amber Dickerson, Park Middle School, Kennewick, WA

- Gerardo Mendoza, Park Middle School, Kennewick, WA

- Johanna Wiens, Park Middle School, Kennewick, WA

About the Authors

Paul Bloomberg

In addition to his role as president of *The Core Collaborative Learning Network*, Dr. Paul Bloomberg partners with schools globally with a mission to strengthen holistic, learner-centered systems. Paul and his colleague Barb Pitchford are co-authors of the best-selling book and learner-centered PLC Model, *Leading Impact Teams: Building a Culture of Efficacy*, published by Corwin Press. He is also the lead author of *The EmpowerED Learner: Student-Centered Assessment Toolkit*, published by Schoolwide, Inc. He serves on the board of Spiire, a nonprofit dedicated to empowering LGBTQ+ thought leaders. Paul has led multiple, successful school turnaround efforts nationally. Prior to consulting full time, Paul was the former director of the nonprofit, TIDES, *Transformative Inquiry Design for Effective Schools and Systems*, and a principal/instructional leader in San Diego County. He has served as a distinguished professional development associate for the *Leadership and Learning Center* founded by Doug Reeves. He has been an academic coach for Denver Public Schools and is an accomplished musician. Paul lives in Brooklyn, NY, with his husband, Tony. They have two sons that reside in San Francisco and Carlsbad, California.

Barb Pitchford

Barb Pitchford is the executive director of professional learning and cofounder of The Core Collaborative. During her 30-plus years in public education, Barb has worked at all school levels—high, middle, and elementary—as a teacher, counselor, assistant principal, and principal. For the past several years Barb has worked for a variety of professional development organizations including the Leadership and Learning Center, where she was recognized as a distinguished professional development consultant. Barb also worked with Corwin Press as a consultant specializing in Visible Learning work. Barb is most proud of the work she led as principal of her last school, which was awarded state recognition as a top-performing school several years running. During that time, she also worked closely with Bob Marzano during the development of statewide standards for Colorado.

Kara Vandas

As an international consultant, Kara Vandas works with districts and schools around the country to implement processes and practices that best support student learning. She is the coauthor of *Partnering With Students: Building Ownership of Learning and Clarity for Learning.*

Kara brings experience from her previous work as the director of teacher effectiveness for the Colorado League of Charter Schools. In doing so, Kara has had the opportunity to support rural, urban, and suburban schools of various instructional models, student populations, and across K–12 systems in order to best implement these powerful practices. She worked to establish an innovative teacher education program for teachers serving high-need students. In addition, Kara worked with Edison Schools, now Edison Learning, to train teachers in effective instructional and classroom management practices. Kara also taught with Edison Schools at two charters in Colorado, where she taught middle school science, reading, and language arts. Her teaching career began at the Denver Street School, an alternative school for high-need youth in Denver, CO.

Eric Bjornstad

Eric Bjornstad is a partner consultant and science and mathematics educator from the Chicago area with over 15 years of experience in the high school classroom. He specializes in creation of phenomena-based science instruction with a focus on formative assessment integration. When not working with students or consulting, he might be spotted captaining an adventurous team of adults with a taste for obstacle races in remote locations throughout the country.

Rachel Carillo-Fairchild

Rachel Carillo-Fairchild is a partner consultant with The Core Collaborative. Rachel brings with her 19 years of education experience: She has been a classroom teacher, mathematics coach, and resource teacher as well as a school leader. Rachel has designed and implemented district-wide staff learning in the areas of English Language Development, working with struggling learners, standards-based education, and formative assessment. She is the author of *How to Reach and Teach English Language Learners*.

Lisa Cebelak

As a national educator, Lisa Cebelak partners with educators to create a positive change by focusing on strengths and a student-centered environment. She addresses the *why* behind research in addition to applying best practices for greatest student impact. At The Core Collaborative, Lisa is a passionate advocate and partner consultant of the IncludED solution of services and through a social justice lens partners with schools to support Impact Teams, literacy at the secondary level, and instructional coaching. She is also a Visible Learning for Literacy consultant, a facilitator for Welcoming Schools with the Human Rights Campaign Foundation, and specializes in working with women in educational leadership.

Rupa Chandra Gupta

Rupa Chandra Gupta is cofounder and CEO of Sown To Grow, a student goal-setting and reflection cloud-based tool used to expand student ownership and agency. She spent the last several years working in the San Jose Unified School District, most recently leading school redesign implementation. She loves working side-by-side with students, teachers, and school leaders to help make every learning interaction awesome. Before working in schools, Rupa spent nearly 10 years consulting at Bain & Company and The Bridgespan Group.

Lori Cook

As a partner consultant with The Core Collaborative, Lori Cook specializes in helping teachers create student-centered math environments. Her passion is partnering with educators to empower *all* students to become problem-solvers who persevere and explore math to make sense of it. Lori supports K–12 teachers and administrators across the country to develop clarity of the standards, as well as enhance instructional practices that foster student ownership of learning.

Prior to consulting, Lori excelled at helping low-performing students and teachers find success. Lori served as an achievement director, team leader, curriculum coordinator, and classroom teacher. In addition to her work with The Core Collaborative, she is a senior fellow with the International Center of Leadership and served as a distinguished professional development associate with the Leadership and Learning Center, founded by Douglas Reeves. Lori has authored chapters for two books as well as written professional development seminars that focus on the deep implementation of state standards.

Gary P. Giordano

Gary Giordano is a seventh-grade social studies and eighth-grade special education teacher at the Michael J. Petrides School in Staten Island, NY. He is a proud James Madison Fellow for New York State, Model Teacher through the NYCDOE Teacher Leader Program, and instructional technology designee and

School Leadership Team chairperson for his school building. Gary also serves as an NYC Junior Ambassadors Educator, where he works with students in taking action on issues aligned to the goals of the United Nations. He enjoys conducting Socratic Seminars with his students and crafting digitally enriched instruction that engages his 21st-century learners while achieving a high standard of historical knowledge. In short, he seeks to develop a love for learning with his social studies scholars.

Gary graduated with his Bachelor of Arts from Wagner College in History and Childhood/Special Education, Grades 1–6. He completed his Master of Arts in Social Studies Education, Grades 7–12 at Teachers College, Columbia University and Master of Science in Educational Leadership at Touro College.

David Horton

David Horton is a national consultant and presenter in the areas of teams, assessment, curriculum design, math/science instruction, and systems. He has served as an assistant superintendent of educational services, a K–12 director of curriculum, instruction, and assessment; coordinator of secondary mathematics and K–12 instructional technology; high school administrator; and high school math and science teacher. David's area of expertise is building systems and structures of organizational leadership that align mission and vision with practice. In particular, David's greatest passion is the study and support of teams and collaborative success. He currently teaches as an adjunct professor with three Southern California universities.

Katherine Smith

Katherine (Katie) Smith serves as a partner consultant for The Core Collaborative. She brings experience concerning social studies instruction, curriculum development, and assessment literacy. She has served as a social studies department chair, high school curriculum coordinator, and an assistant principal of curriculum and instruction in Chicago Public Schools. Since 2009, Katie has worked as the coordinator of assessment and research for a large suburban high school district. She has experience designing and administering district assessments, analyzing district-wide data, and designing strategic professional learning plans to increase student achievement. In the last four years, Katie has implemented Impact Teams as a practitioner, as well as a coach. This experience is included as a case study in *Leading IMPACT Teams: Building a Culture of Efficacy.* Katie lives in Illinois with her husband, Jim, and three vivacious daughters.

Sarah Stevens

Sarah Stevens is the national director of professional learning for The Core Collaborative. During her career, Sarah worked in several areas of school improvement and innovation, serving as an elementary teacher, instructional coach, and director of curriculum. In this role, she led a team of instructional coaches specializing in various efforts including coherent curriculum design, leading Impact Teams, and supporting a 1:1 initiative. Sarah's passion is in system thinking and partnering with adults to create a motivating environment where students come first and teaching makes an impact. She is a coauthor of the *EmpowerED Learner: Student Assessment Toolkit* and lives with her husband, James, and their two children, Deagan and Bria.

Isaac Wells

Isaac Wells is the assistant director of Professional Learning with The Core Collaborative. Prior to his work at The Core Collaborative, he worked for six years as a school improvement specialist and instructional coach for Henderson County Public Schools in North Carolina. In his 10 years as a classroom teacher, he taught the fifth, fourth, and second grades, but it was teaching kindergarten that ignited his passion for early literacy. Now Isaac partners with schools and systems across the country to empower teachers and students to take ownership of their learning. Believing that a strong foundation is key to success for all students, he has chosen to focus on supporting deep and meaningful learning in the primary grades.

Introduction

When we came up with the concept of this book during the summer of 2018, we knew that if we were writing about peer assessment and the power of partnership that we had to practice what we preach. And . . . our *Peer Power* collaboration began. We brought 13 authors together to develop a peer assessment framework that we all believed in. To proclaim that collaborating with 13 other authors was easy would be a flat-out lie. But we knew that we would be stronger together and that we *had* to amplify voices from practitioners, scholars, authors, and students. This book represents thousands of hours of practice, scores of partner schools and teachers experimenting with new ideas, lots and lots of reading and revising our thinking, tons of evidence-based research, and decades of collective experience that combine what we consider to be a powerful, doable, authentic process that recognizes and builds on teacher expertise and children's innate desire to learn. We know that the message is important because we believe in teaching the whole child, an approach that is scarce in today's educational landscape.

We wrote this book for busy educators. It is straightforward and can be swallowed whole, from beginning to end, or read in chunks, based on your interest and need.

Part I: Growing Empowered Learners

The first five chapters are devoted to developing and growing empowered learners through the self- and peer assessment process. Our goal is to grow learners who know where they are going, know where they are at, know and can articulate their next learning step and know why they are learning and *prove* it. Part one dives into dispositional learning, introduces the #PeerPower Framework and explores the integration of social-emotional learning with the metacognitive cycle.

Part II: Voices From the Field

The next nine chapters are devoted to amplifying voices from the field. These chapters were written to give multiple perspectives from teachers, consultants, and authors who are working in the field with a goal of bringing the *Peer Power Framework* to life.

Part III: Empower Teams to Empower Students

This section is devoted to leveraging professional learning communities (PLCs) to do this important work. We know that we have to model the #PeerPower philosophy for our students. They need to see that *we* is smarter than *me*.

Part IV: A Call to Action

The final part focuses on our collective call to action. If we want to activate an assessment revolution, we need to bring our words to life by recruiting other #PeerPower Activists.

Guiding Questions and Twitter

At the end of each chapter we have guiding questions for you and a partner to reflect on. We have included our Twitter handles so we can stay connected and share.

Online Resources

We have too many ideas to contain in the pages of our book, so we decided to develop a website devoted to our cause. The site contains downloadable resources, videos, and more. You can access the website by going to www. PeerPowerRevolution.com and use the password REVOLUTIONARY.

We all learn through experimentation, practice (and more practice), and sharing with one another. Our greatest hope is that you will join our #PeerPower Revolution by sharing your successes and mistakes. We hope that you have fun, take risks, learn a lot, and truly empower students to lead the way.

Part I:
Growing Empowered Learners

Chapters 1–5

Chapter 1

Unite, Learn, and Prosper! Activate an Assessment Revolution

Paul J. Bloomberg

Why a Revolution?

Most revolutions are driven by people and groups inspired by hope, idealism, and dreams of a better world. A revolutionary leader fearlessly advocates radical change. Revolutionary people and ideas challenge the status quo and are willing to upset the natural order to achieve their goals. These revolutionaries work together because they share common beliefs. They attempt to change or overthrow the old order, while the old order strives to maintain its power. Confrontation, conflict, and disruption are often necessary to achieve the ultimate goal in an effort to create a better society for *all* people.

Revolutionary leaders want to change the world. It was a boycott of segregated busses that sparked the civil rights movement in 1955. On January 20, 2017, over 680 demonstrations throughout the United States and in more than 68 countries around the world were held as part of the *Women's March*. Women,

men, and children all over the world rose in solidarity to resist women's oppression and mistreatment. These revolutionaries organized and mobilized for a cause they believed in.

Students are revolutionary leaders too. *Never Again MSD* is an American student-led political action committee for gun control that advocates for tighter regulations to prevent gun violence. The group, also known by the Twitter hashtags #NeverAgain and #EnoughIsEnough, was formed by a group of 20 Marjory Stoneman Douglas High School students in the aftermath of the school shooting on February 14, 2018. The group staged protests, demanding legislative action to be taken to prevent similar shootings in the future. *Never Again MSD* was credited in the *Washington Post* as winning a "stunning victory" against the NRA in the Florida legislature on March 2018 when both houses voted for various gun control measures. The law increased funding for school security and raised the required age to buy a gun from 18 to 21. These revolutionary student leaders are still fighting and organizing for stronger gun control measures nationally.

Activate an Assessment Revolution

The time has come at last to activate an assessment revolution—a #PeerPower Revolution. The evidence is mounting and the time has come to put students at the center. Rick Stiggins (2014), a formative assessment revolutionary, writes in his book *Revolutionize Assessment,*

> Traditional testing practices in the United States are based on instructional and motivational principles that cause many students to give up in hopelessness and accept failure rather than driving them enthusiastically toward academic success. This is one of the reasons why national achievement, as measured by NAEP, has flatlined for decades, our place as a nation in international comparisons of academic achievement remains doggedly and disconcertingly in the middle of the pack, dropout rates remain unacceptably high, the achievement gaps that have troubled us for so long persist, and some of our most

able students fail to reach their true academic potential. Our testing policies and practices, which should be helping us address these realities, are in fact one of their causes. (p. 3)

We know what to do! When students are engaged deeply in the learning process they have to think intensively and think critically. Activating students as owners of their learning is a moral imperative. Martin Luther King Jr. described the purpose of education in a 1947 article in the Morehouse College campus newspaper:

> The function of education, therefore, is to teach one to think intensively and to think critically. But education which stops with efficiency may prove the greatest menace to society. The most dangerous criminal may be the man gifted with reason, but with no morals. . . . We must remember that intelligence is not enough. Intelligence plus character—that is the goal of true education. (King, 1947)

Learners require a complex combination of dispositions, skills, values, and attitudes to be successful lifelong learners. Personal qualities like resilience and the ability to communicate and collaborate become important attributes of a learner's identity. The access to technology, information, and the impact of globalization increases the need for our students to be more culturally and socially aware and also aware of how they learn and what drives their learning. Students need to evaluate and assess their own learning. When students are taught how to be reflective and thoughtful, they do more than just learn content. Students learn knowledge, skills, behaviors, and dispositions that will assist them to actively shape their future. They develop these competencies when they apply knowledge and skills confidently, effectively, and appropriately in complex and changing circumstances. They learn to apply these competencies in their learning at school and in their lives out of school.

When students drive their own learning, they learn how to self- and peer assess, and set goals. Students also need to be challenged and to be involved in productive struggle. It is through this struggle that they experience the trials and tribulations of monitoring their goals. These core practices are taught by cultivating a rich *assessment for learning* culture. It is through the self- and peer assessment process that students are empowered to understand who they are as learners and how they learn best. Students in partnership with teachers and their peers also learn critical life skills: how to give feedback, how to receive feedback, how to collaborate effectively with peers, how to organize their thoughts and ideas to communicate effectively, how to actively listen, and how to develop empathy for one another. Students develop academic mindsets where they build positive attitudes and beliefs about their identities as learners. Since learning is social and emotional, engaging students in the self- and peer review process supports students in strengthening social and emotional habits of mind: self-awareness, social awareness, relationship skills, self-management, and responsible decision-making. We are preparing students for jobs that don't even exist; we are preparing students to contribute positively to our society at large!

Recruit Activists

Like all revolutions, we need to put a charismatic face on our #PeerPower Revolution. That charismatic face is you! Yes, *it is you*: teachers, principals, district leaders, parents, and students!

You are the face of this revolution, and we need your help! It is with your passion and incredible grit that we can create conditions in every classroom to expand student ownership through the self- and peer review process. We need *you* to organize and lead this movement.

We can't start a revolution with a single person; it requires a grassroots organization. We have to build partnerships with one another, and we can't succumb to the temptation of competition. To build an assessment revolution, it isn't about being perfect, it is about taking risks and trying new strategies that we have never tried before. We have to mobilize people with different strengths, and we must build alliances and link with others who are already working on the same cause or one related to it.

We have assembled a network of educators who are already leading our #PeerPower Revolution. The members of The Core Collaborative Learning Network are true revolutionaries—a growing network of students, teachers, principals, district leaders, academics, authors, and coaches who are relentless in the pursuit of student ownership and agency. These #PeerPower Revolutionaries achieve their goal by trusting students to lead the way. They are clear about the goals they set with students, they engage students with feedback from multiple sources, they empower students to self- and peer assess, and they partner with students to set and monitor their goals. These revolutionaries know and believe in the benefits of engaging students in the formative process, and they are experiencing the benefits firsthand in their schools and systems. We are thrilled that these formative assessment thought partners have contributed to the launch of our #PeerPower Revolution!

Eric Bjornstad	Lori Cook	Katherine Smith
Rachel Carillo-Fairchild	Gary Giordano	Sarah Stevens
Lisa Cebelak	Barb Pitchford	Kara Vandas
Rupa Chandra Gupta	David Horton	Isaac Wells

Recruit Intellectuals, Turn to the Science

To activate our #PeerPower Revolution, our cause needs to be supported by intellectuals. Many revolutions ignite with a deeper seminal work, such as Martin Luther King Jr.'s letter to Birmingham. It became a central document of the civil rights movement that defused the opposition and rallied support.

The biggest leap forward in the champion of the formative process came in 1998, when Paul Black and Dylan Wiliam completed a meta-analysis of more than 250 research studies on the topic. Their findings, published as "Inside the Black Box," make a compelling case for embracing the formative process. Black and Wiliam's review concluded that "there is no other way of raising standards for which such a strong prima facie case can be made" (1998, p. 148). "Inside the Black Box" led the way for leaders to define and apply formative assessment in classrooms, not just in the United States but throughout the world.

We stand on the shoulders of giants, and we have had revolutionaries leading this cause for decades. These assessment intellectuals and practitioners have been leading the way, and it is time to join their cause in an effort to put students at the center. There are too many to name, but these #PeerPower Revolutionaries will be vital to our success:

Larry Ainsworth	Gregory Cizek	James Popham
Heidi Andrade	Shirley Clarke	Carol Rolheiser
Judith Arter	Terry Crooks	John Ross
Paul Black	Anne Davies	Lorrie Shepard
Susan Brookhart	Thomas Guskey	Rick Stiggins
Jan Chappuis	John Hattie	Helen Timperley
Steve Chappuis	Margaret Heritage	Dylan Wiliam

These #PeerPower Revolutionaries have taught us best practice and the evidence that supports it. The science is clear, and the benefits are great. Engaging students in the self- and peer review process works to improve student outcomes!

Why is self- and peer assessment so beneficial?

- The self- and peer review process increases responsibility for students' own learning as a result of more opportunities for self-reflection (Cyboran, 2006).

- Students become more skilled at adjusting what they are doing to improve the quality of their work (Cooper, 2006). Involving students in self- and peer review supports the development of metacognitive skills.

- Confidence and efficacy play a role in meaningful self-assessment and goal setting. Ross (2006) points out that when teachers explicitly teach students how to set goals and assess their work accurately, teachers can promote an upward cycle of learning and self-confidence. When students demonstrate mastery, self-efficacy is strengthened (Bloomberg & Pitchford, 2017).

- Collaborative learning increases efficacy. Regularly engaging students in peer assessment gives students the ability to understand their own strengths and learning challenges. Bandura (1994) also concludes that cooperative learning strategies have the dual outcomes of improving both self-efficacy and student achievement (Bloomberg & Pitchford, 2017).

- Hattie's (2009) synthesis on self-reported grading reported a $d = 1.33$ effect of the learning. This effect translates into over three years of learning in one year's time.

- Involving students in the formative process develops and refines critical thinking skills (Cooper, 2006).

- Engaging students in the self- and peer review process can reduce achievement gaps for low achievers (Black & William, 1998; Chappuis & Stiggins, 2002).

- The self- and peer review process impacts mathematics problem-solving ability (Brookhart, Andolina, Zuza, & Furman, 2004).

#PeerPower intellectuals bring compelling theory into action. They provide us the facts that we can use to build our case. These researchers help create a coherent and clear vision that will excite the masses about what the future can hold. Intellectuals can articulate what the new world or system will look like. It is up to us, armed with the research, to envision success.

Real-World Learning

Self- and peer assessment *is* real world and all around us! As adults we write drafts or design plans; we get feedback from people that we trust before we make our work public. Most academic writing involves Peer Review. Peer Review involves subjecting an author's scholarly work and research to the scrutiny of other experts in the same field to check its validity and evaluate its suitability for publication. Peer Review also helps the publisher decide whether a work should be accepted. As a peer reviewer for *Science* magazine, you become a part of a valued community. Scientific progress depends on the communication of information that can be trusted, and the peer review process is a vital part of that system. Journalists from reputable news sources are fact checkers; they are in a constant state of Peer Review. A survey conducted by the Pew Research Center found 64 percent of American adults said made-up news stories were causing confusion about basic facts on current issues and events (Mitchell, Holcomb, & Barthel, 2016). Peer Review in the fine arts world can make or break you. Every time you make your work public, you are inviting critique; as a former musician, every time I performed I had to brace myself for feedback. Athletes rely on coaches to help them improve their skills, become stronger, and play better. They depend on coaches to observe them during practice and games to provide valuable feedback. Coaches, in order to build and lead successful teams, must be diligent in the observation and analysis of their athletes.

We live in a world of review. When looking for a restaurant we go to OpenTable and read the reviews to make decisions of where to eat. Peer Review is the focus of many popular reality shows. On *Shark Tank*, budding entrepreneurs get the chance to pitch their business model to the sharks in the tank—five titans of industry who made their own dreams a reality. "Yelp is about the reviewing experience," CEO Jeremy Stoppelman said. "It is like a blog with a little bit of structure" (Hansell, 2008). The popular site spends most of its energy attracting a small group of fanatic reviewers. It structures its website to motivate people through the praise and attention that their reviews receive from others (Hansell, 2008). The bottom line: self- and peer assessment are real world and give students opportunities to engage in a feedback loop. The ability to give and receive feedback is vital to the success of our students in college and career.

Getting the Message Out

As formative assessment activists, we must embrace all the potentials of 21st-century media. We must start our revolution through the quality of our own ideas. The Internet has given us the ability to publish and reach the masses. We must harness the power of social media to make our case. Throughout this book you will be asked to get the message out about how you are expanding student ownership using the self- and peer review process. Get our message out by blogging, creating video, attending Twitter chats, sharing your learning on Facebook and Instagram, and presenting at state and local conferences. Invite other teachers to join our cause to put students at the center of our assessment revolution. We urge you to celebrate how you partner with students so the world can see and hear how your teams empower students to *drive* their learning!

Leading Impact Teams Facebook Group

- facebook.com/groups/leadingimpactteams

Core Collaborative on Twitter

- @TheSocialCore #PeerPower

Core Collaborative YouTube Channel

- youtube.com/corecollaborative

Guiding Questions:

- How will you celebrate self- and peer assessment in your school?

- What thought leaders have inspired you and why?

- What other teachers will partner with you on this journey?

- How will you get others to join our assessment revolution?

Connect with Paul on Twitter @Bloomberg_Paul

Chapter 2
What's My Contribution?

Kara Vandas

"The world today needs students ready to take on worthy and challenging goals, to fail, to get up, to fail again, and to persist until their goals are realized. We need students who see challenge as an invitation, rather than an impassible roadblock. We need difference makers, legacy builders, and world changers. We can be that for them so they can be that for others."

–O'Connell & Vandas, 2015a

LEARNERS, NO MATTER WHO THEY are or their level of engagement or achievement, make a contribution to the classroom. The question is, what is that contribution? How does it foster or freeze learning? How is their contribution impacting their own ability to future-think, set goals, and reach them? How is one learner's contribution impacting other learners in the classroom?

Remember the movie *Ferris Bueller's Day Off*? Ferris made an enormous contribution to learning on his "day off." He showed all other learners in the school how seriously to take school, how to get out of attending, and how to *live it up* while playing hooky. Have you ever considered the day or week after his big day off at his high school? Rumors would have spread like wildfire, and he would have quickly become every high school boy's idol, setting a clear expectation of what students' contribution at that high school entailed.

Remember the roll call scene from the movie where the teacher, played by Ben Stein, called each student's name over and over for the first several minutes of class? Students were slumping in their chairs, the pace of learning was non-existent, and there may have been a few students drooling while waking from a nap. The movie is a dramatization, no doubt; however, we have to ask ourselves some important questions:

- How do students feel about their contribution to the classroom?

- How do we engage them as active participants?

- How do we make sure that just because they are active, they are learning?

Figure 2.1

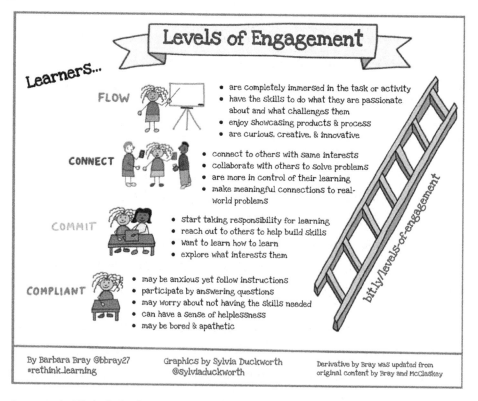

Learn more about the levels of student engagement by Barbara Bray (2018) bit.ly/levels-of-engagement

In thinking more deeply about what we want from student engagement, it may be useful to explore the framework designed by Barbara Bray (2018). She defines engagement as the "degree of attention, curiosity, interest, optimism, and passion that learners show when they are learning." In addition, she includes research on the psychology of learning from the work of Csikszentmihalyi (1990) and Martin-Kniep (2012) to establish a framework for understanding the levels of engagement students experience. The levels begin as compliance and move to commitment, connection, and finally to flow (see Figure 2.1)

Mihaly Csikszentmihalyi (2016) explains,

> *The best moments in our lives are not the passive, receptive, relaxing times. . . . The best moments usually occur if a person's body or mind is stretched to its limits in a voluntary effort to accomplish something difficult and worthwhile.*

If we wish to stretch our student thinking and doing abilities as learners, we must move our students from being compliant to deeply engaged with strategies of their own as learners. Therefore, we are compelled to communicate a new paradigm, to build more equipped learners, because one could argue that Ferris Bueller was strategic, stretched, and pushing the limits. He had a goal, engaged others in the experience, had an impact on others' learning, and reached his goal. The only issue is, he did all those things outside the walls of his school. So the question is, what can we do to engage a learner like him inside the walls of a school?

Empowering Students

The *True North* of an educator (O'Connell & Vandas, 2015) is to empower students with the wisdom and confidence to exceed their expectations. We have no idea what our students will encounter in their lives, what jobs and career fields will be available to them in 30 or 40 years, or what students are capable of if they truly have both wisdom and confidence. That said, we have to think differently about our job. What is our job? Why do we teach? What does it mean to have a teacher? These ideas are changing based on our changing world. When access to information was scarce, teachers could be the fountains of knowledge; but now that information is at our fingertips, what is our contribution to the classroom and what is our students' contribution? In addition to the quote that heads this chapter, educational experts have challenged the contribution and purpose of teachers today:

> "We need to prepare our students for both the present and a vastly different future than exists today." (Costa & Kallick, 2014, p. 6)

> "Powerful learners need to be helped to become more and more independent of their teachers and coaches by learning to take on the skills and sensibilities of the teacher or coach for themselves." (Claxton, 2018, p. 39)

> "The fact is that most schools today do not try to teach for intelligence. Rather than working to change who students are as thinkers and learners, schools for the most part work merely to fill them up with knowledge." (Ritchhart, 2002, p. 7)

In light of these ideas and challenges, let's rethink *our* contribution. Let's embrace the revolution! What is a teacher's contribution to the classroom?

The Truth About Learning

As we work to redefine our role or contribution as educators in the classroom, we may wish to consider some truths about learning that are outlined in *Empower: What Happens When Students Own Their Learning* by John Spencer and A. J. Juliani (2017).

- Truth 1: Every child deserves to own their learning. Teachers can empower student ownership of lifelong learning.

- Truth 2: Every child in your class is someone else's whole world. Empowering students transforms our social/human connections.

- Truth 3: Stories will always shape us. They will always help us learn. Empower students to create and share their own learning stories.

- Truth 4: The only thing you can prepare students for is an unpredictable world.

- Truth 5: Literacy is about learning. And learning is about unlearning and relearning.

- Truth 6: As teachers, we have a huge impact on our students' lives. Empowering our students amplifies that impact.

Now, after considering these truths, let's once again consider *our* contribution as educators in the classroom. Do you agree with the truths provided by Spencer and Juliani? What do these truths mean for your role? Has your thinking changed?

Take a few minutes to define your contribution to the classroom.

My contribution to the classroom and to learning:

How We Communicate

Once we have defined our role, we have to communicate our role to the students we serve. Think of the first days of school each year and consider what we spend our time doing, saying, modeling, and asking students to think about. We asked a group of middle school students to share their ideas with us about the first days of school, and this is what they said:

Questions Posed to Students:

- What do you learn about in the first few days of school?

- What is expected of you as a learner?

- What is your role in the classroom as a learner?

Student Responses:

- The first days of school is all about the rules, rules, rules.

- I learn how she runs the class.

- The first days of school only teach you about what teachers want but not about learning.

- Nothing.

- How to make friends and be successful.

- We learned the basic things from last year.

- The first days of school are boring because every teacher says the same things.

- I forgot.

To be fair, we need to spend time establishing rules and expectations so that we can create a safe and focused learning environment. However, our core business is learning! Are we setting the stage for cultivating a learning community at the onset of the school year? Here are some questions to consider:

- Are we truly helping students understand their role as learners?

- What would students say if we asked them what their contribution to the learning community was?

- Have we come to consensus about what we want from and for our learners?

If not, we may want to reconsider how we create a culture of learning in the classroom. If we want to empower students to take ownership of their learning, we have to talk about learning!

Getting Started

Find Out What Everyone Thinks, Especially Students

We plan, and we prepare, but we rarely ask students what they think about learning. Students are the receivers, the learners, the resisters, the movers, and the shakers, and because of that, we should stop to ask them and *listen*. We need to ask parents too, and we even need to ask teachers and leaders. By doing this simple task, we open our eyes, hearts, and minds to something far beyond what we may have hoped or imagined. John Hattie (2012) has shared much with the education world, but possibly one of his most significant contributions is his insistence that we know our impact. He rarely writes a book or an article or gives a presentation without emphasizing that to increase our effectiveness, we must know our impact on students. This encouragement on his part has led thousands upon thousands of schools to begin looking at their work differently and to begin to ask questions we may have never asked previously. So to get started with teaching students about their contribution as learners, we must begin by asking what they think good learners and student do. We need to ask them what contribution they make to the classroom. In addition, we also may ask parents what they want for their students and what the educators in our buildings believe makes a good student and a good learner.

Consider for a moment what you think, and using the ideas provided, categorize the characteristics listed as that of a good learner or that of a good student.

What is the difference between a good student and a good learner?

- Compliant
- Hard working
- Collaborative with other learners
- Follows directions
- Learns from mistakes
- Has a good memory

- Willing to try, even when it's hard

- Respectful to adults

- Pays attention

- Makes friends easily

- Share ideas with others

- Takes feedback from others

Characteristics of a Good Student	Characteristics of a Good Learner

After finishing the above thinking exercise, it's time to define what you want for your students. What do you want as the contribution of students to the classroom? What is their role? What characteristics do you wish to grow in them? Take time to define five to seven characteristics that would define students' role as learners.

Learners' Contribution to My Classroom
Example: Persistent—is willing to keep working, even when it's hard or the answer is right in front of them.

What Do Others Think?

Once you have interviewed, surveyed, held focus groups, or video recorded responses, use that information to code the types of responses you received. The same tools can then be used throughout the journey to determine progress and next steps until students can clearly and easily communicate their role and contribution to learning grounded in evidence. Our greatest hope is that students will be able to articulate their contribution, but they also must be able to back up their claims with evidence of their contribution to learning.

Develop a Learner Profile

To begin the work of establishing a clear understanding of how learners make a positive contribution to the classroom, consider determining what that might look like as a faculty, using the evidence you collected from other stakeholders as well. What do teachers, leaders, parents, and students want in a skillful, engaged, and contributing learner? What dispositions do we wish them to embody? Ron Ritchhart (2002) describes learner dispositions as the "mechanisms by which we bridge the action-ability gap." He goes on to describe them as more than a desire or inclination to act; they involve values, beliefs, and underlying temperaments, awareness of appropriate actions, motivation to carry on, and the requisite abilities and skills needed to perform. Art Costa (n.d.) describes dispositions as "knowing how to behave intelligently when you *don't* know the answer." It means having a disposition toward behaving intelligently when confronted with problems, the answers to which are not immediately known: dichotomies, dilemmas, enigmas, and uncertainties. With these definitions in mind, we can consider a learner profile, and we may wish to categorize different learner dispositions or attributes we wish to foster and grow in students.

Consider what values, beliefs, attitudes, skills, and knowledge learners need beyond the walls of schools to be successful in their next stage of life. Make a list of what you and your community values or wishes to develop in students. We have included a few ideas to get you started.

Values, Beliefs, and Attitudes	Skills and Knowledge
Belief that mistakes and failure are part of learning	Problem-solving skills

Guy Claxton (2018) provides a suggested set of categories to consider to best establish a group of learner dispositions or powers, as he calls them, that students will develop. His suggested categories include:

- Curiosity
- Attention
- Determination
- Imagination
- Thinking
- Socializing
- Reflection
- Organization

Within each category, he shows how several other dispositions may be put into one group or category. For example, in the category of Curiosity, he includes wondering, questioning, exploring, and experimenting. Why mention the categories? There is a good chance as you work with your colleagues to determine what dispositions you wish to grow and develop in students that you will also have many like terms and connected words or phrases that are raised or shared. How do we then narrow them down? What we want is to define students' contribution to the classroom, and in doing so, we need to teach them a language of doing and way of thinking in a few student-friendly words that reflect what we value in learners.

One idea is to use a strategy called Affinity Diagraming. Using this strategy, after the brainstorm phase, groups categorize the words and phrases that fit together. For example, it is common to have words and phrases like *persist, grit, perseverance, stick to it, keep trying,* and *persistent* all raised by stakeholders. Each is referring to the same outcome for learners but is using a different language to define it. When we all use different words to describe the same dispositions we are hoping to grow in students, students don't necessarily connect them as a similar idea or concept. They then fail to pick up the language of learning we are hoping to instill. To go deep with what we wish students to embody in the classroom, we must develop a shared language of learning. Think of any work, sport, club, or any other organization you have been deeply involved in and have contributed to. There was a shared language, was there not—a group of words, inside jokes, acronyms, and so on that the members of the group used to communicate that outsiders may or may not understand. However, those words established who you were and how you defined yourselves. The same holds true in schools. What do we hold dearly to and use as our language of learning? With this in mind, using an Affinity Diagram allows for a school to establish like terms and then name the categories with a student-friendly descriptor—one that will be used by all stakeholders to establish a way a thinking, believing, doing, and contributing to learning.

Once the words are selected, it is recommended to attach an image or character as well as a definition and list of descriptors (Muncaster & Clarke, 2018). This will support understanding of what the contributions that students can make are and how they can determine if they are using them. Review the following as an example:

Disposition	Definition	List of Descriptors
Be curious	Shift between ideas Or I want to know more.	Ask questions Notice things Look for patterns and connections Think of possible reasons Research Ask "What if . . .?"

Source: Adapted from Muncaster & Clarke, 2018, pp. 3–4.

Making It the Way We Do Business

Learners will not learn a way of speaking and doing in the classroom overnight. In fact, we know that, even when established, learners won't always choose to use positive dispositions toward learning. They won't always make a positive contribution. It's just not that simple. Rather, we need to see this work as growing their capacity to be learners, growing their willingness to take risks, and establishing a safe environment for making mistakes and failing forward. Think of it this way: In areas where we feel a great deal of confidence, we will often be a risk-taker, take on the challenge, and persist until we find success. We have the confidence to stick it out and know that we will prevail because of previous successes. I personally feel this way in classes likes science and writing. However, in areas that we feel a lack of confidence, have had negative previous experiences, or feel unskilled, we often resist the challenge of a new learning experience. For me, it is foreign language. I have had little success in such courses previously, and I am hesitant to want to expose myself to that kind of struggle again. Why? Because I am pretty clueless when it comes to learning languages. I panic, freeze up, and mostly answer with vague, "I don't know" responses. No person on Earth has a growth mindset, as described by Carol Dweck (2006), all the time. We all fall into a fixed mindset at times. Take a second to think about your strongest subject in school and compare it with your least favorite or one that you really struggled in and maybe never overcame. What do you notice about your own emotions related to those two subjects? Which do you feel more inclined to engage in deeper learning in?

Learners in our classrooms are no different, and because of that, we have to think of this work differently as a response. Claxton (2008) offers a framework to keep in mind to establish learners' contributions to the classroom as a way of thinking and doing over time. Take a moment to review the key elements of the framework he outlines and think about your own school. How might each component of the framework impact your thinking and doing at your school?

Framework for Establishing Learner Dispositions

- Learning Rather Than Thinking; Dispositions Rather Than Skills

  - Learning requires more than processing information:

    When it comes to students developing the dispositions of learning, it far exceeds that of just teaching students some thinking strategies, as learning encompasses interaction with others, attitudes toward learning, learning from mistakes, willingness to take on a challenge, and digging into new ideas and content. Therefore, teachers and leaders embarking on this work should understand and provide time and space for students to explore the many facets of learning, and in doing so, develop healthy and positive dispositions toward learning and toward making a contribution to learning.

- Capability Rather Than Attainment

  - Learning how to learn, yet learning never stops:

    Because this work involves building students' capacity to learn and to rely on their dispositions of learning to support their journey, we must be aware that learners are growing and getting better at learning all along the way. They won't always rely on or access the learner dispositions, so the work involves more than a checklist of learner qualities that teachers have taught or will teach; it is rather a journey students have embarked on that involves a supportive system of learning around them. It's not as if we can say, "I taught perseverance last week, and so in the future, students should always use perseverance when faced with a challenge." Then we feel frustrated when they don't choose to stick it out in a difficult situation. It's a capacity thing, and as students have little successes along the way, it will build their capacity for more: more challenge, more grit, more willingness to take on a risk, more success.

- Infusion Rather Than Add-On

  - Culture-change, organic, student-driven:

    There is a time and place to teach the learning dispositions explicitly to students; however, the true power is when students and teachers use it as a way of speaking and doing throughout the process of learning. One assembly on students' contribution to learning or one statement from a teacher, "I told them they needed to own their own learning; they are responsible, but I don't see them being responsible after that," isn't going to get the job done. On the flipside, when infusion is evident, students learn to think of their contribution to the learning of others when goal setting, when they encourage others by using the language of learning they have been taught, when they recognize that getting stuck in learning is just what good learners do because that is growing their skills as learners, then we know they have adopted a way of thinking and doing. When teachers use the language of learning in the classroom in the midst of learning situations, when they recognize times when students need to surface their feelings about their experience as learners, and when teachers ask for feedback from learners to make the next day even more impactful, they have adopted a way of thinking and doing that supports learners. Thus, infusion isn't marked by a one-time event but rather an everyday way of thinking and doing that is shared by all.

- Whole-School Rather Than Just Classroom-Based

  - It is who we are as a community of learners:

    One teacher can have an impact on many students; but together, a community of educators can have an exponential effect on learners.

This is the essence of collective teacher efficacy, because it involves all learners and all leaders. In addition, once students are truly empowered and know and realize their contribution to learning, they become their own teachers and the teachers of others. John Hattie (2012) refers to this as Visible Learning, which happens when students become their own teachers, and teachers see learning through the eyes of students.

Having in mind the framework from Guy Claxton, think about your own school and/or classroom; how closely does your approach and that of your colleagues align? Record your responses in Figure 2.2.

Figure 2.2: Claxton Framework for Implementation

How closely do your practices and processes align? Circle one:	A: Always S: Sometimes NY: Not Yet	What opportunities or next steps should we engage in?
Learning Rather Than Thinking; Dispositions Rather Than Skills	A S NY	
Capability Rather Than Attainment	A S NY	
Infusion Rather Than Add-On	A S NY	
Whole-School Rather Than Just Classroom-Based	A S NY	

Readiness for Empowered Learners

Once you have engaged deeply in this work, be ready! Your learners now have a great and worthy power they have developed as learners. They not only expect to make a contribution, but they also now know they want to, have the skills to do so, and have the power to take learning beyond what we hoped or imagined. Are you ready? It takes some letting go on our part and a willingness for learning to look different, be paced differently, engaged in differently. Our students will begin to trust us more and to expect more from us. They will push back, push forward, and push beyond—and if we stop to think about it, that's just what we want in a prepared learner.

Guiding Questions:

- What is the expectation for learners' contribution to the classroom?

- How is their contribution contributing to building capable, confident learners, prepared for their next steps in learning?

Connect with Kara on Twitter @klvandas

Dig into dispositional learning with
The Empowered Learner Pathway
developed by Kara Vandas!

www.thecorecollaborative.com/the-empowered-learner

Chapter 3

The Peer Power Framework

Paul J. Bloomberg

"What we've discovered is that formative peer assessment, where students are helping each other to improve their work has benefits for the person who receives feedback but also has benefits for the person who gives feedback."

–Dylan Wiliam (Lamb, 2014)

OUR GOAL IS FOR *YOU* and your *team* to be #PeerPower Revolutionaries! So, cultivating and growing empowered learners through the self- and peer assessment process is vital for learners to feel that they are making a contribution to building a classroom learning culture. When teachers explicitly teach students to self- and peer assess, students become empowered to drive their own learning. Putting students in the driver's seat sends a loud, clear message that we trust them and that we believe in them. My mentor, Mimi Aronson, always said that if we listen to students and trust them, they will always lead the way. Without further ado, we are about to dig into the six-stage Peer Power Framework.

The Power of a Peer Coach

Our aim is for students to coach each other in the learning process. Our role is vital because we have to coach student partnerships and groups to have quality academic conversations grounded in valid and reliable feedback. When we create structures for students to coach each other, we create conditions for them to see each other as a valuable resource. In addition, when students coach each other we increase their engagement in the learning process. Hattie and Clarke (2019) discuss enhancing peer feedback through peer coaching by describing four principles of cooperative learning outlined by Slavin, Hurley, and Chamberlain (2003). These principles maximize peer-to-peer feedback.

1. Motivation: Students support their peers because it is in their own interest to do so. Keep in mind that the expectations for cooperative learning must be well structured and taught. When students are motivated, it leads to greater effort.

2. Social cohesion: Students help each other because they care about their partners or group. When students feel they are contributing to one another in a positive way it leads to greater effort.

3. Personalization: Higher-achieving students help lower-achieving students and vice versa. This personalization ensures that students are working at their zone of proximal development.

4. Cognitive elaboration: Requiring students to elaborate and justify their thinking forces students to think more clearly. It also helps them to consolidate their own understanding.

The Phases of Self & Peer Assessment

Black and Wiliam (1998) describes the importance of training students in self-assessment: "If formative assessment is to be productive, students should be trained in self-assessment so that they can understand the main purposes of the learning and thereby grasp what they need to do to achieve." We have found that when teachers abandon self- and peer assessment, it is typically because they have not taught the students strategies to be successful. In addition, self- and peer assessment requires a lot of practice, so it must be a ritual embedded into classroom culture. With extensive practice and feedback, students get better at co-constructing learning intentions and success criteria, giving and receiving feedback aligned to criteria, activating each other as a resource when they are in the learning zone, and using descriptive feedback to revise their work and/ or thinking. Rolheiser and Ross (2001) describe a four-stage model for teaching students to self-assess:

- Define together with students the criteria that will be used to assess the learning.

- Teach students to apply the criteria.

- Give students feedback on the quality of their self-assessments.

- Help students develop individual learning goals and specific action plans.

We have adapted this four-stage framework by adding two extra stages, in an effort to give students extra scaffolding when teaching the peer assessment process. We have found that students need explicit modeling on how to peer assess, so we recommend adopting a peer assessment protocol (Glow and Grow, TAG, Ladder of Feedback, Critique Protocol) to expand peer-to-peer feedback. In addition, we included another stage regarding strategic revision. When students receive feedback from a partner or teacher, they must think about the feedback and then make a strategic decision about revision. In other words, students must actually use the feedback (aligned to the success criteria) from their self- and peer assessment(s) to revise their work and set personal learning goals. Modeling peer assessment, strategic revision, and goal setting for students is essential to be a true #PeerPower Revolutionary.

Gradual Release of Responsibility

Each phase of the Peer Power Framework leverages the gradual release of responsibility. The goal of the gradual release of responsibility model suggests that cognitive work should shift slowly and intentionally from explicit modeling, to joint responsibility between teachers and students, to independent practice and application by the learner (Pearson & Gallagher, 1983a). Each phase will require explicit modeling and will require the teacher to think aloud while teaching each process. You will gradually release the responsibility to the students and then "amp up" descriptive feedback as you continue to coach students through the process. Throughout the rest of this chapter, we will unpack the six phases of peer assessment.

The Peer Power Feedback Framework

Phase 1: Define Success Criteria Through Co-Construction

Phase 2: Apply and Practice Using the Success Criteria

Phase 3: Teach and Model Peer-to-Peer Feedback

Phase 4: Provide Feedback on Feedback

Phase 5: Leverage Strategic Revision

Phase 6: Set, Monitor, and Celebrate CLEAR Learning Goals

The six phases are not quite linear. Many times, after we co-construct success criteria, we often return to co-construction as we refine our understanding about what "success" looks like. As soon as students are clear about the success criteria they can begin moving through the phases. Keep in mind that even when they are moving through the peer review process they can go back and refine and revise the success criteria, especially if there are some key things that they discover as they learn more about the concepts and skills. Feedback is unleashed throughout the process as well. Feedback is ongoing and critical for peer assessment success. Ultimately, students can be moving in and out of the Peer Power phases based on what they need.

The Peer Power Feedback Framework Unpacked

Let's explore the six phases of peer assessment. There are videos in our online resources that will help to illustrate key phases within our framework.

Phase 1: Define Success Criteria Through Co-Construction

The success criteria for products and performances must be defined and clarified with students if we want them to be successful during self- and peer assessment. This stage can be ongoing, since success criteria can be revised and refined when students are in the learning zone.

There are many ways to define success criteria related to a task (product or performance) with students. Using samples of work or doing demonstrations when co-constructing success criteria is critical for achieving clarity. Success criteria without samples of student work and/or demonstrations don't illustrate quality; however, the success criteria paired with samples of student work support the learner in knowing what success actually looks like. For increased clarity, students need to be able to identify the criteria in samples of student work before they start to engage in the evaluation of someone else's work. I once had a student say that he needed a "high-definition image" in his head before he started to work on his project. Clarity is essential for learning.

Co-Construction Steps

At the onset of the learning process, students need to be clear about what they are learning and why they are learning it. This is done through collaborative conversations and by exploring the characteristics of high-quality work. When analyzing samples of student work, many teachers adapt a four-step process outlined by Gregory, Cameron, and Davies (1997) to define success criteria:

> **Step 1: Brainstorm success criteria.** Teachers and students partner together to brainstorm a list of success criteria.

> **Step 2: Sort and categorize.** Once students have generated a list of success criteria, they can sort and organize the criteria into categories. These will eventually become categories on a rubric. This step is also important because of the amount of critical thinking the students have to do to create categories for the criteria. Furthermore, creating categories for the success criteria encourages standards-based dialogue.

Step 3: Revise, refine, and align. During this step teachers can add, revise, and refine the criteria on the checklist or rubric. Wiliam (2018) explains that co-construction of success criteria is not a democratic process. The teacher is in a privileged position with respect to the subject being taught and knows more about the subject than the students do. It is the job of the teacher to ensure that the success criteria are accurate and tightly aligned to the standard. Since students are in the learning zone, the success criteria can be adjusted during the learning process. Success criteria are not static, as students' thinking evolves and the criteria are typically refined based on what students need to be successful.

Teacher teams (Impact Teams or PLCs) also have to align the success criteria across their grade or course. The success criteria should be consistent across the course to ensure equity regarding *what proficiency looks like* and *sounds like*. To increase inter-rater reliability, the team needs to calibrate the success criteria to ensure clarity across their team.

Step 4: Design a rubric or checklist with students. During this step the teacher can guide the students in designing a rubric or checklist using the success criteria they co-constructed with their classmates and teacher. Rubrics can be very specific to a specific project, they can be more general and used across contexts, or they can have a combination of both. When students are in the "learning zone," teachers have found it useful to build a degree of generality when designing rubrics to promote transfer.

For example, the CER (Claim, Evidence, Reasoning) rubric in Figure 3.1 can be used easily across units or across contexts in a social studies course.

Figure 3.1: CER Success Criteria

Success Criteria Co-Constructed With Students	I can teach this	On target	Getting close	Making progress
Claim				
Makes an accurate claim grounded in evidence				
Evidence				
Provides at least 2 examples of evidence to support the claim				
Evidence is from credible sources				
Evidence is from multiple sources				
Citations are used to frame evidence				
Reasoning				
Explains why the evidence supports the claim				
Uses analytical verbs when explaining evidence				
Uses my own words when explaining the evidence				

Another example is a problem-solving checklist that was co-constructed with students in a fifth-grade math class. This checklist can be used across units when students are engaged in problem solving. Success criteria can be removed or added throughout the year depending on what students need.

Effective Problem Solvers:

- Can explain what the problem is asking them to do

- Make connections to what they know about the problem before starting

- Create a plan to solve the problem

- Show all work legibly

- Work is organized

- Label the steps to the process

- Solve problem accurately

- Use multiple representations to justify thinking

Stoplight Rubrics: Your class can design stoplight rubrics based on the success criteria for a product or performance. Students can use the stoplight process to signal possible next steps:

> **Green:** I got this! I can teach a friend.

> **Yellow:** I need some help; I can probably figure it out with a partner.

> **Red:** I need instruction.

Co-Construction Strategies

There are several methods that work when co-constructing and defining success criteria with students. Check out these seven simple strategies to increase clarity with your students.

1. *Analyzing Student Work Samples:* During the co-construction phase, teachers and students examine student work samples to generate a list of criteria. While collaborating with a group or a partner, they can begin to make a list as to what makes the work so effective. It will be important that they annotate the work and label what makes it high quality. Students can analyze exemplars, varied samples of student work, or non-examples with a goal of generating success criteria.

   Exemplars: If students are being asked to write an objective, nonfiction summary, teachers can engage the students in analyzing multiple, exemplar summaries to find out what makes the summaries so effective. Students can brainstorm success criteria based on the characteristics on the student work. Through open-ended questioning, we can also engage students in conversations about quality.

- What made the summary so concise?

- What do you notice about how the summary is organized?

- How do you think the writer chose the vocabulary words used in her summary?

- Why do you think the summary is organized in the same order as the article?

When using exemplars to co-construct, you are engaging students in rich discussion about the author's craft. Furthermore, you are asking students to think critically about the characteristics of high-quality work. The most important part of the co-construction process is that students are justifying their claims about the characteristics of high-quality work using evidence from the work.

In inquiry-based subjects, like math, we typically examine exemplars *after* students have been engaged in investigation and exploration to ensure conceptual understanding. Conceptual understanding is knowing more than isolated facts and procedures. A successful math student understands mathematical ideas and has the ability to use their knowledge in new situations and ultimately apply it to new contexts. We don't want to give away all the strategies in the beginning of the unit because students will often use a strategy and have no idea why it works or how it relates to other math strategies.

Varying Samples of Student Work: Varied samples of student work can also be used to define the success criteria for a product, performance, or strategy. When students have some clarity regarding the expectations, using varying samples of student work increases engagement. We like to pass out samples of student work from *phantom* students. When students compare and contrast the student samples to the exemplars, they can refine their understanding of the success criteria. This usually results in revising the criteria based on what students are discovering during the co-construction process.

Non-Examples: Sometimes using non-examples gets students more involved during the co-construction process. For some reason, students love to pick out things that are incorrect in other people's work—especially the teacher's work. This strategy works best if students know something about the topic.

> *Example: I observed a teacher show a video of students collaborating. In the video students were shouting and talking over one another. Two students in the group weren't participating at all. The students in the video weren't focused on the task at hand. The teacher showed her class the video and the teacher guided her students to co-construct criteria for effective group work based on the non-example shown. The teacher then refined the criteria based on the state's speaking and listening standards.*

2. *Explain and Model:* Teachers can also define success criteria while explaining and modeling during the learning process. For a successful "think-aloud," teachers *explain* each step of the process and then explicitly model how it can be completed. Hattie and Clarke (2019) recommend stopping after each step of the demonstration and asking students, "What did I just do?" The class can generate a list of success criteria as they move through each phase of the demonstration. If the teacher does a clear think-aloud framing the success criteria, students can be capturing the teacher's think-aloud in their notes. Students can share the success criteria they gathered during the think-aloud or demonstration. Then, they can come to consensus by creating a class list of criteria. If older students are taught to take notes during the think-aloud, they will not only gather success criteria but they can also create an exemplar in their notebooks.

3. *Leverage Student Expertise:* Sometimes, after a pre-assessment, it is clear that there are already student experts in the room. A successful student or group of students can explain the processes that they go through to complete a task. Since students are not always precise in their explanation, teachers must support the student thinking aloud by helping to frame each

criterion point. Sometimes teachers use a fishbowl strategy to help showcase student expertise.

> *Example: Students in a second-grade classroom were working to perfect partner talk. They were practicing talking about character traits in their favorite books with a partner. The teacher had two students model effective partner talk for the rest of the class, and then the teacher co-constructed the success criteria with students based on the fishbowl.*

> **Book-talk partners remember to:**

> » *Keep eyes on their partner*
> » *Talk loud enough for your partner to hear*
> » *Use evidence from the text when justifying the character trait*
> » *Take turns sharing*

Leveraging student expertise works great during problem solving when students share out different strategies used to solve a problem. The teacher can support the student by framing each step to the strategy in an effort to co-construct success criteria for different procedures. This strategy also works well in performance-based subjects like art, music, theater, and physical education.

4. **Worked Examples:** As well as providing a clear step-by-step process to how to perform a task or solve a problem, creating worked examples with students increases clarity of the expectations. Providing worked examples for students helps to make processes visible for students and decreases cognitive load. Involving students in analyzing worked examples reduces cognitive load on students so they can concentrate on the processes that lead to the correct answer and not just providing an answer. Using a worked example demonstrates for students what success looks like. A worked example typically consists of a problem statement and the appropriate steps to solving a problem. Using worked examples increases clarity in the many processes or strategies involved in problem solving.

5. *Video Observation:* We have found in many of our schools that video can be one of the most powerful ways to clarify or define success criteria. Using video works especially well when defining success criteria for a student performance.

> *Example: If the students are working toward effective debate techniques, students can watch a video and co-construct the success criteria with their teacher.*

> *Example: A theater class watches a video of a famous scene from a play. They co-construct success criteria based on what made the scene so effective.*

6. *Re-Voice Rubrics:* When students are struggling with one section of a rubric, we have found it useful to have the students reframe the success criteria on the rubric or checklist using their own words. While students go through this process we ask them to annotate a sample of student work to clarify the language on the rubric. When they re-frame the success criteria of the rubric in their own words, then students reinforce the criteria of success.

7. *Use Visual Icons:* During the co-construction process, adding visual icons to the success criteria really helps students to internalize the success criteria. Older kids can look on Google Images for icons that represent the success criteria. Icons provide nonlinguistic representations for the criteria and help students remember the criteria.

Summing Up

Defining criteria with students creates clarity. Teachers and students co-construct success criteria together to increase student ownership. Students must be immersed in lots of samples of student work during the co-construction process so they can make connections between the success criteria and characteristics of high-quality student work. Clarity increases learning.

Phase 2: Apply and Practice Using the Success Criteria

Learning to apply the criteria when students are in the learning zone is critical for students to become successful at evaluating their own learning or the learning of a peer. After the success criteria has been established during Phase 1, students need to be taught how to apply and practice using the success criteria. During this phase, the teacher shows the students how to apply the success criteria to guide their learning. Once students are able to apply the criteria in their own work and find criteria in samples of student work controlled by the teacher, they will be better equipped to give independent, descriptive feedback during peer review.

Annotate: When a teacher showcases her work using a document camera, she can model applying the success criteria out loud for the students through a think-aloud. The teacher can systematically work through the piece—line by line—thinking aloud while applying the success criteria to guide the quality of her work. It is common to color-code the success criteria. The teacher can then highlight or annotate the sample of work based on the success criteria color codes. When using think-aloud to model the self-assessment process, it will be important to stop and ask the students for feedback. They can also be asked to paraphrase the steps you are taking to reflect on the quality of your work.

Teacher: *What did I do to ensure that I was following the success criteria?*

Student: *You used the success criteria like a checklist to monitor your learning.*

Teacher: *How do I know that I included everything into my task?*

Student: *You highlighted evidence that matched the success criteria color codes.*

Teacher: *What do I do when I realize I forgot something?*

Student: *You revise your work by adding it and revise your piece.*

If we want students to create high-quality work, we have to model the expectations associated with the self-assessment process. Students are not wired to be reflective, thoughtful, and self-aware—these habits of mind need to be taught.

Success Criteria Detectives: Once you have established the success criteria, you can have students practice applying the success criteria by having them take on the role of a *success criteria detective.* The role of the detective is to look for clues regarding the success criteria in samples of work controlled by the teacher. Using a wide variety of samples of student work increases clarity of the success criteria during the learning process. Remember, a rubric or checklist is only as powerful as the student work that lays beside it. The student work clarifies the success criteria. You may want to first give the same example or non-example to individual students and guide them to look for each criterion point one at a time. We have found it easier if students work in partnerships to annotate exemplars aligned to the success criteria. We treat students as detectives searching for clues (the success criteria) related to the task. They can highlight, annotate, or color-code the evidence that matches the success criteria.

Collaborative Projects: Another easy strategy when teaching students to apply criteria is for students to partner up to create collaborative projects (products and/or performances) based on the success criteria. Students partner together using the success criteria as a guide while applying the success criteria to their collaborative project. Students can then share their products on the document camera or using chart paper. Students can present their practice projects to the class and use the success criteria while presenting their mini-projects.

Summing Up

Applying and practicing using the success criteria has to be modeled for students. Students need time to practice using the success criteria before they are independent. Using color-codes, visual icons, and/or annotating techniques also support students in applying the criteria. Applying criteria also supports students and teachers develop a shared understanding of the expectations.

Phase 3: Teach and Model Peer-to-Peer Feedback

The purpose of peer assessment is to expand feedback from multiple sources. But first, teams have to adopt a peer-to-peer feedback protocol(s) so students can learn the process. Modeling the self- and peer assessment process is critical to putting students in the driver's seat. Once students are familiar with the success criteria and can apply the success criteria independently, they are ready to practice looking for the success criteria in one another's work. Our ultimate goal is to develop a learner's ability to evaluate work samples using the success criteria. Furthermore, our goal is to build a culture of learning in the classroom where revision is valued and not seen as a punishment. We have had the most luck teaching students peer assessment using a peer-to-peer feedback protocol.

Establish a Peer Feedback Protocol

Glow and Grow

After students have learned the success criteria, they can give positive specific feedback to their peers by giving them a *glow*. Students can then offer a next step aligned to the success criteria by giving their partner a *grow*. The Glow and Grow protocol is effective with primary students.

TAG

The TAG protocol is very similar to the Glow and Grow protocol; however, it has an additional section.

T = Tell your partner something that they did well

A = Ask your partner a question related to the success criteria

G = Give your partner a suggestion using the success criteria

Once these peer feedback protocols are taught to students, the peer feedback structure can be used over and over again. Peer assessment should become a ritual in classrooms. Students get better at peer feedback with practice. Be prepared for the first few sessions to be a bit rocky—but if you stick with it, it will get better with time.

Building the Language of Feedback: When modeling the use of Glow and Grow or TAG, students need to be taught the language of feedback when evaluating one another's work. Many teachers brainstorm feedback stems and frames with students to ensure that the language of feedback is respectful and reliable (see Figure 3.2). The most important part in developing a shared language of feedback is practicing using the stems with students. Our goal is to model what quality feedback looks like and sounds like.

Figure 3.2: Peer Feedback Language Stems and Frames

Admiration	Question
• I like how you ___. • As a reader, it was enjoyable when ___. • I was impressed with ___. • One strength is ___.	• Can you help me to understand ___? • Can you clarify ___? • I wonder why ___. • One question I have is ___.
Clarification	Suggestion
• Could you give me an example for ___? • Can you tell me more about ___? • So far, we have said ___. • Who else could we ask about ___? • Could we agree that ___? • So, you are saying ___.	• One improvement for next time might be to ___. • This is a strategy that may help to ___. • I can teach you a strategy that may help. Let me demonstrate___. • One next step might be to ___. • What do you think you need to strengthen this work?

Modeling Peer Assessment: Demonstration is worth a thousand words! Modeling the Glow and Grow or TAG protocols is crucial for setting clear expectations. Peer feedback protocols can be modeled a variety of ways: the use of a teacher-to-teacher fishbowl, a student-to-student fishbowl, and/or using a video observation.

Teacher-to-Teacher Fishbowl: Just like the student-to-student fishbowl model, two teachers can model the Glow and Grow or TAG feedback protocols with each other. Many teachers will team up and combine their classes so they can model the protocol for their classrooms. The teachers can then lead the class in discussion about what made the peer review quality. Just for fun, the teachers can also model some ineffective ways to give feedback to one another. Debriefing the process will be key to the success. You may even want to develop success criteria for peer review.

Student-to-Student Fishbowl: When students model TAG or Glow and Grow for one another, we empower them to see each other as a resource. Using a fishbowl strategy provides opportunities for students to see the protocol in action. In order for the fishbowl technique to be effective, the teacher may want to frontload the process ahead of time with two students to ensure that the fishbowl demonstration is effective. Be sure to have the students use effective feedback sentence stems or frames. Students will gather around two students modeling the peer review process.

Video Observation: A teacher can record a high-quality model of two students engaged in using a peer feedback protocol, so students have a clear model of what success looks like. While students watch the video observation, the teacher can engage the students in dialogue regarding key points of the process.

Summing Up

Modeling a peer assessment protocol is key! Students must know the expectation so they are involved in the process. Students will get better at self- and peer assessment with practice; practice makes permanence. Remember to use the gradual release of responsibility to turn over responsibility to the students.

Phase 4: Provide Feedback on Feedback

To ensure that self- and peer review is valid and reliable, teachers must give students feedback on the quality of their self- and peer assessment(s). When giving students feedback on their self- and peer assessments, you may want to co-construct a checklist with your students about what makes effective peer assessment (see Figure 3.3).

Figure 3.3: Effective Peer Assessment Checklist

When peer assessing with your learning partner remember to:
- Connect feedback to the success criteria
- Name what your partner did well – be specific
- Use respectful language when giving feedback
- Be honest with your feedback
- Give clear next steps using the success criteria
- Offer clear advice on "how" your partner could strengthen their work; teach them a strategy

When receiving feedback from your partner remember to:
- Write the feedback down
- Ask questions if you don't understand or if you don't agree
- Ask your partner for strategies to make your work stronger
- Say "thank you" for the feedback

Once students get the hang of the process, our greatest hope is that they will engage in the process because they value it—not because they have to do it. There are many ways for teachers to give students feedback on the quality of their peer review. Here are seven different methods to ensure that student self and peer assessment is valid and reliable:

Peer Power Conferences: Nothing beats partnering with students in a conference setting to give feedback on the quality of their self- and peer assessment. Listening in when students are engaged in peer review allows you to give feedback in a timely way. Also, giving feedback on the actual peer review template works well if you don't have time to get around to everyone to listen in. It still will require a quick conference to ensure that students actually understand the feedback. When I confer with partnerships, sometimes I even have other students eavesdrop—especially if they need the same advice.

Process Observer: You can identify a student process observer whose role is to observe the peer review session for quality. Students can use a version of the short checklist from above Figure 3.3 when checking for valid, reliable feedback between students. You can also serve as the process observer. You can rotate between partnerships and give on the spot coaching based on the checklist illustrated in Figure 3.3.

Ed Tech Tools: There are several tech tools that can support you in giving feedback on the quality of your student's self- and peer assessment.

Google Docs or One Drive: If students are using Google Docs or One Drive to give feedback to one another using the comment feature, you can check to see if the feedback is valid and reliable by resolving comments students give each other.

Flip Grid: Flip Grid is a leading discussion platform used by teachers. The good news: It is free! Flip Grid is a great tool for having students reflect orally about their learning. They can even record their peer review session, and other students can give feedback on the quality of their peer review by replying to the video recorded. Of course, they can use the success criteria in Figure 3.3 to lift the level of their response.

Orange Slice: Orange Slice Teacher Rubric and Student Rubric is a Google Docs add-on created by Matt Buchanan to increase teacher efficiency in giving feedback. When using Teacher Rubric to give feedback on student work, fields are automatically highlighted on the rubric or checklist. The rubric or checklist also appears right within the student's document so that the feedback is not separate from the original assignment. Orange Slice also offers a Student Rubric that can be used for peer review. It looks and functions similarly to the Teacher Rubric.

Sown To Grow: With Sown To Grow (www.sowntogrow.com), a new student goal-setting and reflection tool, students can now set and track their goals digitally, and teachers can coach and support them from the sidelines. Over time, students who use Sown To Grow feel more empowered, have a stronger growth mindset, and demonstrate better academic habits. Using Sown To Grow makes it easy for teachers to give students feedback on their reflections after self- and peer assessment; it is also easy to give feedback on the quality of student goals.

Summing Up

Feedback on feedback is critical to the success of self- and peer assessment in the classroom. Teachers need to be explicit in developing assessment literacy. Although it takes time to model, coach, practice, and give feedback on students' self- and peer assessments, the time spent is well worth it. While progress may seem slow and sometimes exhausting, students will quickly move toward independence when they see value in the process.

Phase 5: Leverage Strategic Revision

Revision literally means to "see again," to look at something from a fresh, critical perspective. Strategic revision is an ongoing process of rethinking learning: reconsidering your arguments, reviewing your evidence, refining your purpose, reorganizing your thinking, and reestablishing your focus. Revision is required across all content areas and is vital in advancing disciplinary literacy. Disciplinary literacy is defined as the confluence of content knowledge, experiences, and skills merged with the ability to read, write, listen, speak, think critically, and perform in a way that is meaningful within the context of a given field. Disciplinary literacy becomes increasingly important as students pursue specialized fields of study in K–12 education and beyond. Revision is also a method used to leverage descriptive feedback gathered during self- and peer assessment process.

Why teach students to revise?

- Revision is an important part of the learning process.

- Revising gives students an opportunity to reflect on their learning.

- Revision is closely tied to critical reading; in order to revise student work conceptually, students need to reflect on whether their work reflects the success criteria.

Students need to be taught the value of revision in the learning process because empowered learners revise often. Just like the other #PeerPower phases, modeling and think-aloud is key. You will need to model the revision process using think-aloud so students have a clear understanding of your thought process while revising. You can check for understanding periodically during the think-aloud to see if students can summarize the process as you move through it. You will need to model the revision process with a non-example. Students can take notes on the revision process while you are demonstrating and thinking aloud.

When modeling strategic revision consider the following:

Cultivate a revision mindset. Good learners review their work and revise. Many students have no idea that revision is an essential part of the learning process. When we make mistakes we learn from them and then revise our thinking accordingly. This disposition must be modeled for students, especially students who have not developed this learning disposition.

Explain the revision process explicitly. Provide specific, meaningful goals for the revision by clarifying the success criteria. The success criteria will provide the goal for revision.

Model the revision strategy with think-aloud. This can be achieved by displaying the student work on a chart or screen. Lead a class discussion on how to revise the work based on the suggestions gathered during the self- and peer assessment process.

Provide guided practice with feedback. This can be done in small groups, partnership, or one-to-one through meaningful teacher–student dialogue. Remind students to use the success criteria and feedback gathered from the peer review process when practicing. These collaborative efforts reinforce the understanding that learning is a social process.

Gradually work toward independent mastery by students. To increase independence, co-constructing success criteria for the revision process gives students scaffolding to ensure that revisions are high quality (see Figure 3.4).

Figure 3.4: Success Criteria for Teaching Revision

When teaching revision remember to:
- Model reading the feedback gathered from the peer assessment.
- Think aloud as you process the feedback and make decisions about next steps.
- While thinking aloud, determine a next step based on the feedback.
- Think aloud and frame each step of the process while you demonstrate strategic revision.
- After revising, model reading your work out loud to see if it makes sense.
- Fix up any errors if it doesn't make sense.
- Debrief the revision process with students.

During the revision process students improve reading skills, their ability to observe and listen, and their analytical skills. Student learn to challenge one another's ideas, thus deepening and strengthening their learning. When revising we also empower students to notice patterns of error or habits of organization that undermine creating high-quality work. Developing a critical eye is perhaps the most difficult part of the revision process. But having a critical eye makes you a better reader, writer, and thinker. Students will find that their critical eye works much better when it is focused on a friend's paper than when it is focused on their own; they can be much more objective.

If our goal is to create conditions where students create high-quality work, then giving them time to revise is critical to developing more thoughtful, independent learners.

> *Example: Eric Bjornstad, chemistry teacher at Lyons Township High School and author of Chapter 12 of this book, engages his students in strategic revision of their lab reports after they engage in self- and peer assessment. He gives students extra time to take the feedback and improve their work. His goal is for all students to make progress so revision is crucial for their success. Revision ensures that students are taking the feedback from their lab partner and actually using it to create a stronger lab report. By the way, this is what happens in the real world! In the workplace, researchers and scientists would never publish a paper*

without going through a rigorous peer review. After the peer review, it is the job of the learner to leverage the descriptive feedback to improve the overall quality of the work through strategic revision.

If our goal is for all students to make progress, we must consider increasing time for strategic revision. If we want students to create high-quality work, we must teach them how to revise their work and by using the success criteria to realize success!

Summing Up

Strategic revision must be taught and modeled. Revision is key to disciplinary literacy. When receiving feedback from a teacher or a peer, feedback must be processed and a decision must be made regarding next steps. Students use strategic revision to improve their work.

Phase 6: Set, Monitor, and Celebrate CLEAR Learning Goals

Goal setting is a skill that one must learn to effectively navigate. There are many factors that influence the effectiveness of students' goals. Studies have documented that individuals who write down clearly defined goals are more likely to succeed than those who have vague goals (e.g., I will work on engaging my audience with an effective hook vs. I want to improve my writing). In a study conducted by Ferguson and Sheldon (2010), participants who wrote *why* and *how* they will achieve a goal were more likely to internalize their goals over time and reported greater goal expectancies.

Another component of goal setting is two-fold, whether the student focuses on the process or the outcome of a task. Outcome goals are specific to a task.

Example: I need to get better at pulling key details from the text to support the overall main idea.

Process-oriented goals focus on the procedure or strategy that a student used to work through a specific task. These goals are transferable, meaning you can apply them to multiple situations and/or multiple content areas.

Example: I need to annotate the text for key details while reading. I can also use a self-questioning strategy and use a graphic organizer to track my thinking when determining importance.

Schunk and Rice (1991) found that the best way to promote self-efficacy and achievement is to couple the process goal with progress feedback on how the students use a strategy. Zimmerman and Kitsantas (1999) found that starting from process goals and shifting the focus to outcome goals is beneficial in increasing students' self-efficacy and skills. Ultimately, finding a balance between process and outcome is important.

Example:

What I need to work on:

- *I need to get better at pulling key details from the text to support the main idea.*

How I will learn this:

- *I need to remember to annotate the text for key details while I am reading. I can also use a graphic organizer to track my thinking. My friend Sanai does a great job at finding key details so I am also going to work with her.*

We all are familiar with SMART goals, but many of our schools have been using CLEAR goals as a method for setting and monitoring goals with students. Whether you have students create SMART goals or CLEAR goals, you have to teach how to set goals and create weekly or biweekly goal-setting rituals in your room. Anyone can set a goal—monitoring goals and making goals come to life is the hard part. The CLEAR goal-setting process activates learners as an instructional resource for one another (Economy, 2015).

Collaborative: Goals should be collaborative and set with a friend that can support you in the goal-setting process.

Ask yourself: Who can I collaborate with to meet my goals? Who do I need alongside me? Who are the experts in my classroom?

Limited:	Goals should be limited in both scope and duration.

Ask yourself: When do I start? When do I stop? What obstacles will I have to overcome? How will I know that I am successful? Is there anything I should *not* do to reach my goal?

Emotional: Goals should have an emotional component. Students should be able to explain why the goal is important to them, and it must be relevant so the goal taps into their energy and passion.

Ask yourself: Why am I doing this? How will this goal serve my purpose? How will this goal help other people?

Appreciable: Large goals must be broken down into small goals. Dream big; act small; work hard. Goals must be actionable and name the "how." Focusing on one or two success criteria at a time works great.

Ask yourself: What is the next, smallest obvious action? What other goals can I accomplish on the road to accomplishing this goal? Do I need to learn new strategies to achieve my goal? What strategy could I learn to close the gap? What evidence will I track to monitor my goal?

Refinable: Set goals with a laser-like focus, but when new situations arise, give yourself permission to refine and modify them.

Ask yourself: What can I anticipate changing? What could happen beyond my control that could get in the way of achieving my goal? What matters most? When will I revisit this goal to tweak it? What is most likely to go wrong? What is my Plan A, Plan B, and Plan C?

"A culture of self and peer assessment in my classroom has facilitated a community of collaborative, passionate learners who are truly empowered. Students are knowingly at the center, which has enabled not only their ability, but truly has resulted in eagerness to engage in the learning process. As a result, learning now extends far beyond merely what children "need to learn," but, moreover, allows all students to gauge this conceptually; children are able embrace why this learning is relevant, meaningful, and purposeful. Children are motivated to understand where they are headed in their learning, embrace where they currently reside, look forward to goal- setting and are capable of doing all of the aforementioned with efficacy. Communication and social engagement have improved as motivation to assess and reflect, provide feedback to others, expectations of self, and support of peers have all resulted. Due to the portrayal of criteria for success in the language of the child, success has become the language of the child."
—Danielle Di Capua, Melissa Cohen, and the Fifth-Grade English Language Arts Team at PS 22

Strategies for Promoting Goal Setting

1. **Modeling:** Teachers must model the goal-setting process. It helps if teachers demonstrate a weak model and also a strong model and have students co-construct success criteria for effective goal setting.

2. **Success Stories:** Present specific cases where academic goal setting has enabled students to achieve success.

3. **Video:** Have students observe successful students set, negotiate, and monitor learning goals.

4. **Choice:** Giving students a choice on which learning goal to start with will increase autonomy. Students learn more when they are in charge of the goals they set and monitor.

5. **Examples:** Use student samples of work to show what the next level of learning looks like and the expectations for achievement.

6. **Mastery Experiences:** Provide students with early success opportunities through low-stake, targeted activities to increase sense of competence.

7. **Feedback:** Students should receive timely, specific feedback on their progress.

8. **Collaboration:** Have students work with each other to peer assess using the success criteria. Have students partner as a support mechanism to monitor learning goals.

Summing Up

Goal setting needs to be taught and modeled just like the other Peer Power phases. Anyone can set a goal; it is the monitoring of the goal that is difficult. Therefore, goal-setting rituals need to be established in class to keep goals alive. Goals can be set during all phases of the learning process. We set goals when we are learning something new, and we set goals when we realize that we have not done our best. We also set goals at the end of a learning cycle when we realize we still haven't quite learned it. As students become skilled at assessing their progress toward their goals, teachers partner with students to provide guidance on (1) generating goals based on the success criteria, (2) recording their goals and actions, and (3) monitoring progress in making their goals come to reality.

Collective Vision to Action

Now that you know the six-stage framework, it's time to take collective action. In partnership with your students, it's time to stop thinking about it and start cultivating and growing empowered learners. The biggest benefit to building a revolution is that it gives you an insane amount of energy. Joining our assessment revolution will make you want to wake up early. You may even have a hard time falling asleep at night, or you may wake up in the middle of the night with a great idea on how to get students more involved in their learning. You will become more and more motivated to make a difference because you know that this work really matters. This work will have long-term impact on every life that you touch. You will be making a difference by taking our collective vision to action.

Guiding Questions:

- How can self- and peer assessment create independent learners?
- How can teacher teams create clarity with students?

- Why should teachers co-construct success criteria with students?

- What is the gradual release of responsibility, and how does it relate to the peer review process?

- Why do teachers give feedback to students on their self- and peer assessments?

- How does goal setting improve learning?

Connect with Paul on Twitter @Bloomberg_Paul

Explore Chapter 3 #PeerPower tools on our companion website.

www.PeerPowerRevolution.com

Chapter 4

Proving Learning: The Power of Progress

Kara Vandas

"Our job is to get every kid on a winning streak and keep them there."

–Rick Stiggins

How Do Learners Know They Are Making Progress?
How Do I Motivate My Students?

For many years, we have made clear to students their status or achievement in school. We have been clear with them what grades they have earned, what group of students they belong to (honor roll, college-bound, not college bound, good readers, not such good readers, etc.) and what we assume their future achievement will be by forming ability groups of like-performing students (Hattie, 2009). What is interesting about all of this information is that one of the biggest, most pertinent issues that teachers bring up when asked is students' motivation toward learning (Knight, 2013). It is a common question in professional development, coaching sessions, and in water-cooler conversations among colleagues. In fact, when providing students an instructional coach to work with, the most commonly asked for support is in the area of student engagement and motivation. So we have pretty clear evidence that achievement information isn't that motivating to many students. In fact, we know that labeling students by a performance level is actually quite demotivating and in situations such as this, we find student performance becomes a reflection of the label that has been given to them (Hattie, 2012).

Conversely, the research shows that not labeling actually makes learning go forward, which is reflected in a significantly positive impact with an effect size d = 0.44, which roughly equates to one year's growth in one year's time. If labeling students doesn't motivate students and not labeling them accelerates learning, why do we keep relying on this information to communicate to students about their performance? We don't just communicate it either; often, students are told they have to do this or that, or they will get a bad grade, so grades and achievement are also used sometimes as a punitive measure with the hope that it will provide motivation to students. What is interesting is that when you spend time in primary grade classrooms, you often experience the joy of learning, and motivation is innate, almost contagious. However, it continues to grow or diminish, based on their experience in the classroom. If a person walked into a secondary classroom and every hand went up when a question was asked, we'd probably wonder what the special sauce was that the teacher was using to get that to happen. However, every student wanting to respond to questions and engage in learning happens regularly in primary classrooms. What happens to our learners? School. Grades. Labeling.

What does motivate students? Progress, small and inspiring moments of mastery foster a desire to keep going, keep learning, and go beyond what was previously possible. In fact, we know a lot about how to build students' efficacy for learning, which in turn builds motivation. Now, we need action. *We need to start the revolution: Students knowing and proving their learning!*

The Building Blocks of Self-Efficacy:

Rick Stiggins (2015) once said, "Our job is to get every kid on a winning streak and keep them there." This is the essence of building self-efficacy. When learners get a taste of success, they innately want more. Knowing that to be true, based on the research surrounding self-efficacy (Reivich, 2010), we must explore this concept further: *increased self-efficacy grows motivation.*

Building self-efficacy is rooted in four actionable and doable components: (1) mastery moments, (2) vicarious experiences of others' mastery moments, (3) feedback from others, and (4) mood, attitude, and the upward spiral.

Mastery Moments

Let's think about the words *mastery* and *moment*, because the words paired together are crucial to understanding this concept. It does not refer to total mastery of a concept or skills or winning a championship or competition; rather, it refers to knowing for a moment or in the moment that a small victory was won, an "a-ha" moment occurred, a synapse of brilliance exploded in the brain. It is not that the learners have conquered every standard to be learned for the year; rather, it means that they have conquered one or even part of one standard, and most importantly, they know it. A mastery moment then smacks of progress. Progress is powerful, intoxicating, and breeds the desire for more. In fact, when students attribute success to something that they have done and that they know they can repeat like studying or practicing, they are empowered. When students feel they lucked out, just guessed well on a quiz, or had an underprepared opponent, they build little confidence for next time and even fear the next experience, worrying they have no skills to take on the new challenge.

Furthermore, when we think of those mountaintop mastery experiences, like winning a championship, passing a big test, or winning a competition, we know that millions of mastery moments have occurred to prepare the participants for the mountaintop experience. It is with those mastery moments in hand that they step onto the court, take their seat in the exam room, or get their instrument ready to play. They know they can be victorious because they have each of those mastery moments to stand upon and to rise from.

We often look at those people who have won the championships, competitions, played in the big concert, or aced the test and wonder how they could be so motivated, how could they stick to it so long through many different adversities. The answer is that they have high self-efficacy, built, in part, by millions upon millions of moments of mastery, applied to deeply personal goals that are based in progress.

Let's stop thinking of all the barriers for our students and all the reasons they can't and start believing in the power of moments of mastery building toward mountaintop experiences. What would happen if we did?

Vicarious Experiences Through Models of Success

Have you ever found yourself glued to the TV during the Olympics or riveted by a masterful musical performance? We often sit there, not just being inspired by them but dreaming of what we are capable of doing ourselves. "Could I be a bobsledder? Maybe it's not too late." "Maybe I should learn the guitar; it seems really cool. I bet I could do it. That guy on the stage did, and he looks like he walked right off the street." These are vicarious experiences. We didn't experience success or a mountaintop moment personally but somebody did, and we aren't that different from them. This holds true for learners in the classroom too. They think, "Wow, my buddy just wrote a really good essay or story; I am not so different. I bet I can too." It also works for teachers as learners. When we go to another teacher's classroom and watch a masterful strategy in action, we think, "Oh, that is what that looks like. I can do that." We take their mastery moment back to our own classroom and build off of it to improve our own instruction.

What if we shared mastery vicarious experiences in the classroom by having students share their ah-ha moments with others? How do we empower our students who have mastered a standard or a step in the learning progression to show the way for others? Do students share expertise? Students know all of the achievement levels of others students anyway. They know who is in the high reading group, who aced the test, who always gets good grades. What if they knew the progress of other students?

I will never forget the moment when a student of mine, we will call her Loretta, shared her understanding of animals' ability to adapt to their environment with the class. When she initially raised her hand, many students cringed, others rolled their eyes, some just stared. Loretta was known by all students to be behind the others. She was regularly pulled from class to work one-on-one with a para on all sorts of skills, and my other students knew it. She also spoke more slowly than others. In other words, she wasn't seen as smart, skilled, or able in the eyes of my other students. However, that day, she blew every mind in the room. She slowly explained how animals adapt to their environment, including ideas like mimicry, camouflage, and natural selection. Jaws dropped that day. Loretta had a mastery moment, and everyone knew it. She connected all sorts of key concepts we had been learning. She built the efficacy of every learner in the room that day, and when it came time to work in groups, several students asked for Loretta to be in their group, as she knew what she was doing. This never would have happened one day previously. She also raised the bar for all the students in the class, as their work products improved because they felt the need to raise their own performance, based on the mastery that Loretta had achieved.

How can students build confidence through the mastery moments of others? How can we share these mastery moments? How can students share their expertise with others?

Feedback

Feedback, feedback, feedback—this is all we have been hearing lately in the ether of education. It is a buzz word right now to say the least, and it's right up there with collective teacher efficacy and assessment-capable learners. What does it really mean? In the case of building self-efficacy, it has a really interesting meaning. Specifically, it is the direct persuasion from others into our practices. In other words, it is the messages we hear from others that shape our understanding of ourselves and our learning.

What messages are students sending to one another? I will never forget the day I sat in the back of a ninth-grade algebra class. I was observing in classrooms all around the high school that day. In this class, the students had a particularly motivated and skillful teacher. She cared deeply; you could just tell by the language she used with students and how long she spent providing written feedback on the assessments she passed back that day. However, an interesting interaction played out as she was passing back the tests: students started comparing scores. "How did you do?" "I bombed it, 67 percent." "Of course you did, moron!" "I got a 78 percent—kicked your a--."

As I sat there, watching this play out in row after row of students, I wondered what went wrong. I peered over shoulders of students to notice the abundant comments the teacher had taken the time to write on each student's paper. Not one student stopped to read the comments; they simply looked at the score, made a few comments to their friends, and tossed the papers into their backpacks or binders. I knew the teacher must have been heart-broken and frustrated. I didn't get a chance to talk with her that day and hoped she wouldn't give up. For me, the experience set me on a journey of learning about feedback. Because sitting there that day, I felt she had done a ton of work, written thoughtful comments for each student, and it was an utter waste of time in terms of moving student learning forward. I soon learned about the difference between grades and feedback, and how students react to having a grade posted on their paper, rather than just feedback. In fact, many experts, such as Grant Wiggins (2010) and Dylan Wiliam (2011) advocate for separating the grade and feedback, giving students an opportunity to respond to feedback, grades aside. In addition, I learned of the research of Graham Nuthall (2007), who recorded students' private conversations in the classrooms to determine how feedback is exchanged naturally. From his insightful research, which included a lot of candid, unchecked student conversations, we learned that 80 percent of feedback that students receive in a day is from their peers and 80 percent of the time, it is wrong or inaccurate. Yikes! This is a disaster in any classroom, as students are giving each other the wrong messages. Nuthall also learned that students lack a language of feedback, and instead tend toward being overly nice and general or mean.

Effective feedback moves learning forward. It always, no matter the mastery or proficiency level of the student, provides a next step in learning. The feedback giver doesn't need to know what the receiver should do next; rather, they are a partner to discuss next steps with. So if feedback is the game, and Peer Power is the way, how do we do this better? What would happen if we taught students how to be peer mentors and tutors? What if we taught, modeled, and practiced a language of feedback and peer support?

Mood, Attitude, and Safety: The Upward Spiral

When students experience mastery moments of their own and that of others and when they receive useful feedback, they find themselves on an upward spiral or what Rick Stiggins referred to as the "winning streak." In thinking about this aspect of building self-efficacy, it may be interesting to consider famous winning streaks in history. What would happen if we examined what happened in these winning streaks? What are the common ingredients of these streaks? How did these examples get on an upward spiral?

Think of winning streaks that you are aware of and how that winning streak was realized. Think of sports, music, or industry dynasties and giants like the Boston Celtics, LA Lakers, Chicago Bulls, Triple Crown winners, UConn women's basketball, Michael Phelps, Carl Lewis, Richard Petty, the Yankees, the Montreal Canadiens, the Beatles, Alabama football, Pink Floyd, and Apple iPhones and iPads. How did each of these groups of people or products achieve what they have? They got themselves on a winning streak and kept themselves there.

How can we use these examples to benefit students? One of the things that each of these have is a history of success, they have built it one mastery experience at a time, that win was acknowledged, it was capitalized on, and it propelled the teams, companies, and individuals into the next experience. Can you imagine being Michael Phelps going for gold number 8, 10, or 12? What was on his side of the winning equation? Previous success. This is what we need for students—they need to have success day after day after day, and not without struggle but the tiny moments must be realized that will give them just enough to want more. Many might say, "Yeah, but Michael Phelps has this perfect body for swimming." To that I say, "Yeah, but how many hours, days, and years did he spend in the pool working to achieve the most refined stroke, the most efficient flip-turn, and the best start off the blocks? He certainly didn't roll off the couch and roll into winning gold after gold medal. His body doesn't really matter in those moments; rather, the mastery of each of those skills propelled him forward. He worked and worked and worked. He spent much of his life as a fish, just to get to the top of his game. How many millions of minutes, turn after flip-turn after flip-turn, did he have to practice to get there? Our students need to know that he wasn't born the fastest swimmer in the world. He wasn't born to smash records, and he wasn't born to stand at the top of podium. He was dedicated, teachable, willing to practice the same skills over and over, build off of each mastery moment, and he was willing to take the risk of competing. The risk grew over time, as he became the one to beat; the target was on his back. Did he decide to sit on the couch and eat potato chips? No! He swam and swam, and he swam. Our students must know that a winning streak or the upward spiral will be filled with dreams of success, days of practice, mastery moments to revel in, defeats to learn from, sore muscles, and will prove to show learners just how capable they are. If we put the first three components in place—mastery moments, vicarious experiences of others, and feedback or persuasion from others—we have the opportunity to propel students beyond what they ever hoped or imagined. Are you ready for the journey? Let's look at a few starting points.

Practices to Stop and Practices to Start

As we endeavor to get students on the upward spiral, we must consider what to keep and what we can give up, toss out, and say good riddance to in order to allow our students to prove their learning, and in doing so, build their efficacy and their motivation (see Figure 4.1).

Figure 4.1

Self-Efficacy Building Blocks	Practices to Stop	Practices to Start
Mastery Moments	Stop relying on tests, grades, and scores to define success	Start helping students see progress through the use of success criteria, goal setting, and progress monitoring aligned to success criteria. **What It Might Look Like:** • Student-friendly progress tools, checked on regularly • Celebrating mastery moments (skills and concepts learned, as well as learner dispositions used)
Vicarious Experiences Through Models of Success	Stop grouping students in like-ability groups as the major structure for small-group instruction. Mix it up—regularly!	Start grouping students in heterogeneous groups to learn from one another. Allow students who have reached a level of expertise on a standard or step of a progression to teach others. **What It Might Look Like:** • Students sharing their learning aloud through think-alouds • Students who have mastered a skills or concept being peer mentors for those who are not there yet
Feedback and Social Persuasion	Stop thinking that feedback comes only from teachers; feedback comes from multiple sources including students' peers	Start using peers as feedback partners and mentors; teach all learners how to give and receive feedback in a way that propels learning forward **What It Might Look Like:** • Peer-to-peer feedback based on the success criteria • A balanced approach to feedback, with feedback to and from teacher, self, and peers

Self-Efficacy Building Blocks	Practices to Stop	Practices to Start
Mood, Attitude, and Safety: The Upward Spiral	Stop allowing students to keep their learning quiet and to themselves	Start acknowledging the small moments of mastery. Make sure students know that the small moments of mastery lead to *mountaintop* mastery moments. **What It Might Look Like:** • Student-led conferences • Students moving their own learning forward when they are ready and have proven learning

Putting It Into Practice

When jumping into this work, teachers often feel they are starting from scratch, have to toss everything they have been doing, or have little to start with; however, the opportunities, if we choose to open our eyes to them, are all around us, and many can be built from what we are already doing.

1.   The Language of Feedback

Teachers

First and foremost, we can start with something simple, and yet, quite power-ful. It's our language, the way we talk to our students about our expectations, their work performance, and how they can progress. Before I knew about how to develop learning intentions and success criteria with students, I very much wanted them to know and put into practice that success was built one day at a time. I had many students who had never seen or experienced success in ELA, science, or art, which are all subjects that I taught. I wanted them to know that I wanted them to be successful every day, and that if they were, they would quickly find success in the class overall. The problem was not my intention; it was my language. I used to say, "This is how you get an 'A' today." What I didn't realize is that I was unintentionally showing that I cared about their grade rather than their progress or their learning. I was telling them that I focused on grades and achievement. It is so simple—just one sentence, yet what a powerful sentence it was. I found my students coming to me regularly saying, "Is this good? Is this 'A' work?" I also experienced a small but tough-to-reach group of students that didn't do anything. Looking back, I can see that I was promoting a fear of failure and not building a willingness to take positive risks, dare to be wrong, share an answer, or engage deeply in learning. As the years progressed, along with my understanding of how to set and share expectations with students, I watched the impact that my change in language had on my students. Instead of saying, "This is how you get an 'A' today," I began using phrases like, "Good learners make mistakes," "What progress did you make today?," "Use your success criteria and the exemplars," and "How do you think you are progressing?"

While it might seem so simple, we often communicate misconceptions, judgments, and opinions by our language. With a simple change of moving from deficiency-focused language to growth-focused language, we can see an enormous impact on our students' mindsets toward learning (Claxton, 2018).

Consider the following questions regarding the way we talk about learning (adapted from Claxton, 2006, p. 10):

Beliefs:
- What teacher beliefs and intentions do I convey to students? What do I act as if I believe or value? What am I modeling? Are mistakes, risks, and failures okay?

Expectations:
- What expectations or ground rules have I set in my classroom/school? What language is acceptable or used in the classroom by all?

Intentional Language:
- Who talks about learning and how do we talk? What is our shared language about learning?

- What language or words will we stop using that are deficiency-focused, and how do we change them to growth-focused?

- What does our classroom or school environment tell us?

Learning Opportunities:
- How is time structured and with what effects on learning?

- Who gets to do and decide what?

Students

Our next task once we have worked on our own language is to teach students a language of feedback and the role they will play in the learning of others. Without our work on this, students are left to wonder and to their own skills as communicators when it comes to how they talk about learning with their peers. What follows are a few ideas from experts to get you started in teaching a language of feedback to students.

First, we must establish the role students play in giving and receiving feedback. We must teach students what it means to be a peer expert, mentor, or coach. In other words, we have to co-construct what that looks like and does not look like. Taking a cue from John Hattie and Shirley Clarke's (2019) book *Visible Learning Feedback*, we can use their success criteria for being an effective peer coach.

What makes a good learning coach?
- *They help you reflect against the success criteria.*

- *They don't tell you the answer. Instead, they ask questions and make you think.*

- *They suggest strategies, (e.g., word choice), help you focus on particular elements of the success criteria to improve your learning.*

- *They are specific, helpful, and kind.*

Source: Hattie & Clarke, 2019, p. 98.

A second strategy comes in the form of teaching Feedback Stems and Frames, just as we often use sentence stems and frames in the classroom to support students in writing (O'Connell & Vandas, 2015b, p. 108). Students can be intentionally taught the language and attitudes for giving and receiving feedback through modeling, practice, examples, and non-examples of how to speak and listen during feedback conversations. In the following chart, O'Connell and Vandas have provided several phrases that can be taught to students so they know how to give and receive feedback with peers and teachers.

Feedback Stems and Frames

Giving	Receiving
I noticed that . . .	I appreciate you noticing that . . .
I wondered about . . .	I hadn't thought about that . . .
I was confused by . . .	I heard you say that _____ confused you.
I suggest that . . .	Based on your suggestion, I will . . .
Have you thought about . . .	Thank you, what would you do?
You might consider . . .	I'm not sure what that looks like; tell me more.

Finally, in getting started with students, it is helpful to establish some simple structures for giving and receiving feedback. We recommend choosing one, modeling, practicing, and using it deeply until students know it as their own. See Chapter 3 and Chapter 7 for more ideas in building shared language of feedback with students.

2. Goals Setting & Getting: Focus on Progress— Leverage Student-Used Progress Tools

Let's think about goals differently. We often think of goal setting as something we do each new year to make resolutions about how we'd like to look thinner, stop bad habits, or improve our lives. These goals tend to be big and often vague as well: I will exercise more this year, or I will clean the closets so the house is less cluttered. In a few months' time, as life continues on, we forgo our new goals for just getting on with life or getting our most pressing to-do list done. If such goals don't work for adults, they certainly won't work for students. Students are often asked to set goals for a quarter or semester of learning, which is a long time period, so they revert to goals like, I want to get an "A" in math. Again, these goals are just too big and too vague to be attainable, hold our attention, or have any concrete practices or strategies that will get us there. We have to rethink goal setting and getting.

What we know from research is that if we are clear with students what they will need to learn and prove in order to be successful ahead of the learning, they are more likely to invest in the learning experience with us (Hattie & Donoghue, 2016). In addition, they are more likely to take risks, enjoy the thrill of learning, and more likely to use goal-directed behavior—which speaks strongly to how to go about setting goals with students.

Sharing the Goal of Learning and the Ingredients to Success

First and foremost, we must share with students the overarching goal of learning and pair that with success criteria that provide them a pathway to success. We can sometimes be afraid to put the challenge of learning out there for students, feeling like we have to break all the learning into tiny steps. The truth is that humans love challenge. Kindergartens are excited to know that by the end of year they will be reading books all by themselves, for example. Students in art class are nervous but motivated to know that they will be creating art for a public exhibit. High school students are interested to find out that they will learn to solve complex problems in mathematics using the quadratic equation. It sets the challenge for students. It puts the goal in mind and lets students know we believe in their ability to learn. Give students the large overarching goal of learning.

Once students have the goal, use examples of other anonymous student work, exemplars, worked problems, non-examples, and modeling to show them what success looks like. When students are learning to read, show them other students who have learned to read independently on video or in person. They will see the goal with their own eyes, get excited, and be able to speak to what that learner is doing to be successful. With these examples, exemplars, worked problems, non-examples, and models in hand, ask students to voice what the success criteria would be. Consider these additional methods for co-constructing success criteria with students:

- Show students a finished piece of student work. Ask students to work in pairs to first review the learning intention(s) and then to analyze the student work for how closely it aligns. Ask students to record their ideas and share them with the class to generate success criteria for learning intention(s).

- Provide students with two examples of anonymous student work: one example of high quality and the other of lesser quality. Ask students to compare the two pieces by first noticing the things that are the same to establish basic criteria. Next, they look for things that are different to extend the criteria and explore how quality affects the degree to which the success criteria have been met.

- Use a variety of exemplars that show students different ways to achieve the success criteria and foster creativity. Ask students to notice the differences in the exemplars and highlight the success criteria in each by noticing how each one meets or exceeds the criteria.

- Show multiple versions of one student's work that has progressed over time until they met exemplary. Ask students to notice how the student improved over time, highlighting the success criteria that they achieved in each piece of work.

- Demonstrate how to think through a task and while doing so, ask students to construct success criteria as you go along. Students can also be a part of the modeling of the task.

- In a math or science class, the teacher may begin by modeling and using worked examples of how to solve a problem. Next, the teacher can ask students to verbalize and chart how to finish a partially complete problem, find an error in a problem, or write an explanation for a correctly solved problem. By asking student to articulate the process and problem-solving strategies being used, they are co-constructing what success looks like.

- Explain or show something being done incorrectly and allow the students to explain how it should be done correctly. Collect their responses to establish initial success criteria.

- Revisit existing success criteria after a project or task is completed by asking students to reflect on what could be edited, removed, updated, or revised to better align to the learning intentions and to the quality of the product.

Sources: Adapted from Clarke, 2008; Almarode & Vandas, 2018.

Focusing on Progress Rather Than Achievement

Once we have set goals and clearly communicated learning intentions and success criteria, students are ready to monitor their progress; but we have to provide them tools to do so. Remember the progression from mastery moments to mountaintop experiences? This is how we build our students' efficacy, one mastery moment at a time, working toward the goal of making progress with our learning. Students can have a multitude of mastery moments by checking in on the success criteria they have accomplished and determining their progress and next steps for learning. Educators interested in using such structures may wish to consider the following questions:

- How do I align my pre-assessment to the success criteria and have students use it to determine what they already know and what they need to learn?

- How do I have students use the success criteria to check on their progress regularly?

- How do I align formative assessment and feedback to the success criteria?

- How do I have students revisit the success criteria at the end of a unit or chunk of learning to prove learning?

The following tool in Figure 4.2 has some basic components that can be modified in a thousand ways to create a student-friendly goal-setting and -getting tools.

Figure 4.2: Example Goal-Setting Tool

My Learning Goals	
Where are we going in our learning? We are learning to . . .	How am I doing? Success Criteria: • _____ • _____ • _____ • _____ • _____
Which success criteria do I already know? What's your evidence?	• What is your next step in learning? • What is your goal for that next step? • What strategies will you use to accomplish your goal? • How will you know you're successful?

3.   Portfolios

Portfolios were all the rage several years ago in education, and then they fell out of favor due to workload, coherence of what is or is not included, and storage, just to name a few complications. However, this structure, used well, is a powerful tool to put into the hands of students. The biggest issue was quite possibly that teachers were owning this process, and if we can help students own the process, this strategy can be not only doable but powerful for students to prove their learning, realize their mastery moments, and make plans for future learning. In other words, it can be a significant efficacy builder.

As Paulson, Paulson, and Meyer (1991) stated, "The portfolio is something that is done by the student, not to the student." Students can own this process if it is valued by the teacher, given time and space to grow over time. Therefore, some criteria for effectiveness of student-owned portfolios may be useful. The following are guiding questions that teachers can use to plan, launch, and reflect on the use of learning portfolios as a structure for learning.

Guiding Questions for the Effectiveness of Portfolios:

1. Are students in ownership of the process, the selection of work, the reflection, and so on? How do I continually work to transfer the ownership from teacher-owned to student-owned?

2. Is time and space given for students to regularly update and extend what has been captured in the portfolio? How can I support them in curating their learning?

3. Does the portfolio capture more than work completed? Is the portfolio a reflection of the learning that has transpired, the growth over time? Does it capture feedback, students' thinking, goal setting and goal getting, planning next steps in learning, and learning strategies students have used and transferred into their own learning toolbox?

4. Are students provided regular opportunities to have learning conversations, using the portfolio as evidence, of what they are learning, how they are progressing, and where to next for their learning? Can it be used for a variety of purposes from regular self-reflections, peer review, feedback to the teacher about learning needs, student-led conferences, and so on?

After considering the guiding questions, one may also determine just what components they may ask students to collect and curate in a portfolio. We wish to emphasize learning and progress in this portfolio, so there may be things that one may not typically consider—messy and in-progress work, feedback, and others. This is what we like to call a "messy" portfolio that best represents the ups, downs, ins, and outs of learning. Consider the different following components in Figure 4.3. Is this what you would wish for students to collect and curate? What would your list look like?

Figure 4.3: Artifacts for the Learning Portfolio

1	2	3	4	5
Learning goals, learning intentions, success criteria	Learning maps, work samples, homework, practice, photos, rough drafts, pre-assessment, etc.	Learner strategies aligned to artifact collected	Evidence of feedback that aligns to work samples and shows how it was used to improve learning	Final products, performances, and/or post-assessment

Source: O'Connell & Vandas, 2015b, p. 131.

4. Student-Led Conferences

Student-led conferences are another opportunity for students to prove their learning and own it at the same time. So many times, conferences are lackluster events that parents, teachers, and sometimes students endure. They often provide little information about what students are actually learning and rather focus on behavior, turning in assignments, doing homework, and so on. Little is about what students are or are not learning as a result. The conferences can be painful reminders of that we aren't there yet in students owning, sharing, or proving their learning. What if we changed this scenario? What if we threw tradition out the window? What if we started a revolution?

In a blog written for Peter Dewitt's *Finding Common Ground*, Mary Jane O'Connell and I proposed just such a new scenario (2015b). What if student-led conferences built student efficacy? What if students had control? What would conferences look like if they did? We propose using the three questions that assessment-capable learners can answer about their learning (2012) and adding one additional question, "What's my contribu-

Link to read Peter Dewitt's blog, *Finding Common Ground*

tion?" This provides a framework for students to share their learning and how they impacted the learning of others. It is a frame to build from, and if given the opportunity, students will surely innovate beyond this frame, making the conference even better.

What follows in Figure 4.4 provides suggestions as to how to change up the conference scenario, having students at the helm and allowing them to direct the learning conversation, proving their learning publicly.

Figure 4.4: New Conference Scenario

Question	Students Will Share	Evidence
Where am I going?	Learning goal(s)	Student-friendly learning goals, paired with success criteria
How am I going/doing?	Achievement or progress toward learning goal	Student work samples from beginning, middle, and end of learning cycle, paired with the success criteria
Where to next?	Content and skills still to be learned or ways to deepen learning Strategies used by the learner to move learning forward	Success criteria yet to be met or ways student would like to deepen his or her own learning Strategies that work best for student (notetaking, summarizing, organizing information, peer review, etc.)
What is my contribution?	Students will explain how they contributed to the class's learning	Students explain or share evidence of how they supported others in moving learning forward

Turning Mastery Moments Into Mountaintop Experiences

In this chapter we have laid groundwork for building self-efficacy in students and provided several ideas that can be used by students and teachers to prove learning. Now it's time to activate our #PeerPower Revolution! When we sit down and contemplate what it takes to build stronger learners, we cannot rest on teaching them strategies alone; we have to consider their confidence, their need for progress, the feedback they require to move learning forward, their feedback to us, and their need to realize millions of mastery moments. Those mastery moments they and their peers have achieved will propel them forward, will launch them further, and will equip them to reach those mountaintop moments of graduation, scholarship, going to college, succeeding in math and science—whatever it is they choose to put before them as a goal. We can get them there by realizing one mastery moment at a time.

Guiding Questions:

- How do you leverage the four sources of efficacy with students?

- How will you build a language of feedback with learners in your classroom and school?

- How does your team put focus on progress over achievement?

- How will you turn mastery moments into mountaintop experiences?

- How do you create conditions for students to prove their learning?

Connect with Kara on Twitter @klvandas

Chapter 5
Expanding Meta-Thinking

Paul J. Bloomberg

"So few people are really aware of their thoughts. Their minds run all over the place without their permission, and they go along for the ride unknowingly and without making a choice."

–Thomas M. Sterner, p. 9

What Is Metacognition?

#PeerPower Revolutionaries understand the power of meta-thinking or metacognition during the learning process. Anyone who knows me knows that I like to think and explore new ideas. I also love to think about thinking itself. Over the past decade I have been on a journey to become more self-aware in my personal and professional life. Being self-aware enables you to learn about yourself in a way that no one else can teach you. Self-awareness is important because when we have a better understanding of ourselves, we are then empowered to make changes and build on our areas of strength as well as identify areas in life that we would like to improve. Metacognition expands self-awareness. It is more than "thinking about one's thinking." Dylan Wiliam (2018), one of our favorite

#PeerPower Scholars, explains that metacognition includes knowing what one knows (metacognitive knowledge), what one can do (metacognitive skills), and what one knows about one's own cognitive abilities (metacognitive experiences). In the end, metacognition refers to the mental processes used to plan, monitor, and assess one's understanding and performance.

Strengthening Emotional Intelligence

Engaging students in deep reflection about their own learning is emotionally charged, especially for students who have had an academic life of failure. We must be equipped to deal with the emotions of our students during the learning process. Integrating social and emotional learning (SEL) practices into the learning process is foundational in strengthening a positive learner identity for our students. Learner identity is the perception a person has of themselves as a learner. This perception can be changed over time through both positive and negative experiences. When students have a positive learner identity they are able to make connections and reflect on their emotional and cognitive processes. With practice, they are able to reflect on themselves as learners with an aim of fostering a deep understanding of how their actions, emotions, thoughts, and motives about themselves in learning are interconnected.

Why Is Metacognition Important?

In the mid-1980s, metacognition was initially studied for its development in young children (Baker & Brown, 1984; Flavell, 1985). Then, scholars began to research how experts used metacognitive thinking and how these thought processes could be taught to novices to improve their learning (Hatano & Inagaki, 1986). The bottom line: When we teach and guide students to use metacognitive practices, they can accelerate their learning. In Hattie's (2009) seminal meta-analytic synthesis, *Visible Learning*, he identified strategies emphasizing metacognition and self-regulated learning.

Influence	Effect Size
Self-Regulation Strategies	.52
Strategy Monitoring	.52
Metacognitive Strategies	.55
Self-Verbalization and Self-Questioning	.59
Help Seeking	.72
Evaluation and Reflection	.75
Elaboration and Organization	.75
Transfer Strategies	.86

Considering that a .40 effect size is about one year's growth in one year's time, it is incumbent upon #PeerPower Revolutionaries to make these influences come to life in their classroom. When students activate metacognitive practices, they learn more!

Activate the Metacognitive Cycle

Being a self-directed, independent learner can be challenging for students. The good news: We can teach students metacognitive practices so they become more self-aware of the learning process to strengthen student ownership. The authors of *How Learning Works* describe a cycle of basic metacognitive processes (Ambrose, Bridges, DiPietro, Lovett, & Norman, 2010). If our goal is to empower students to drive their own learning, students have to be able to

- assess the demands of the task,

- evaluate their own knowledge by taking a personal inventory,

- plan their approach,

- monitor their approach, and

- reflect and adjust their plan as needed.

Many students have trouble accurately assessing their own learning and performance, and they fail to adapt their approaches to new situations. When we teach students how to activate these basic metacognitive processes, we are able to amplify student agency. In addition, when teachers guide students to leverage the metacognitive cycle they can also integrate SEL strategies into content instruction with a goal of strengthening emotional intelligence.

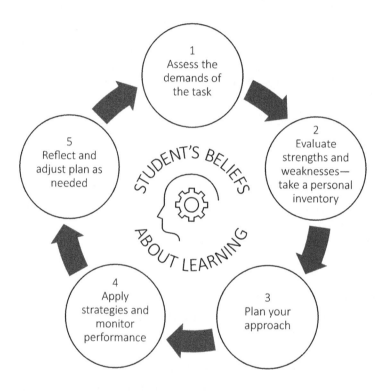

The Metacognitive Cycle: Adapted from *How Learning Works* (Ambrose, Bridges, DiPietro, Lovett, & Norman, 2010, p. 193).

Phase 1: Assess the Demands of the Task

At this stage the student assesses the demands of the task. This is usually the hardest part for students. They typically don't take enough time on the front end of the learning process to really understand the demands of the task. Students need to be taught *how* to assess the task, and they will need feedback at this stage before it becomes a habit. Here are some questions that you can teach students to ask themselves during this stage:

- What is the goal of the task?

- What is the teacher's goal in having me learn this material?

- What questions do I have that I want to learn more about?

- Have I done something like this before? How is this similar or different?

- What habits of mind do I need to activate to be successful?

Emotional Connection: During this stage of the metacognitive cycle, emotions flare up. If this is a difficult or challenging task, students may feel anxious or fearful. If these emotions are in play, students will need to learn how to recognize these emotions, express them and ultimately regulate them since emotions affect actions. In this case, if a student feels anxious, they may want to shift their emotional state to a feeling of excitement for a new challenge. When we are faced with a challenge, good learners must activate a perseverance mindset. They may have to try multiple approaches before they succeed. If they think the task is easy, they may feel overconfident and make silly mistakes. This will require them to strive for accuracy, slow down and make sure that they are careful.

Fix-Up Strategies:
- Use an app like the *Yale Mood Meter* (www.moodmeterapp.com) to help strengthen emotional intelligence with students. Students can check in with their emotions when moving through the metacognitive cycle. When they use the mood meter they (1) plot their feelings, (2) describe why they have their feelings, (3) select a strategy to shift their feelings if they desire, and more.

- Co-constructing success criteria for successful completion of the task helps to mitigate for negative emotional responses during this stage. The success criteria can become a roadmap for successful task completion (see Chapter 3). In time, students will be able to construct success criteria independently, but it will need to be modeled and guided first.

- Teaching students to use the success criteria as a checklist to guide their work during the learning process will give students a scaffold that they need when learning new concepts and skills.

- Explore non-examples with students to help build understanding about what *is not* acceptable. This strategy strengthens understanding of the assessment criteria and also increases student engagement.

Phase 2: Evaluate Strengths and Weaknesses – Take a Personal Inventory

At this stage, students take a personal inventory. They have to evaluate their own strengths and weaknesses relating to the task. They have to determine if they have the knowledge and skills necessary to be successful. Keep in mind that students who have weaker knowledge and skills are less able to assess their abilities than students with stronger skills (Dunning, 2007). We have all had times where we miscalculated our abilities and didn't give enough time to a project or assignment and realized that we were in over our head. If students have difficulty evaluating their own strengths and weaknesses relating to the task, it gets in the way of goal attainment. Students can ask themselves these questions when taking a personal inventory:

- What do I already know about this topic or task?

- What strategies do I know that may work to achieve my goal?

- I am still learning _____, and I don't feel confident yet.

- If I did something like this before, how could I do a better job this time?

- What questions do I have? What do I need to learn to be successful?

Emotional Connection: When we engage in self-evaluation of our own knowledge and skills and are asked to identify our own strengths and weaknesses, it is a humbling experience. Keep in mind that students need to feel safe so they feel comfortable being vulnerable. When we allow ourselves to be vulnerable we must keep in mind that feelings of shame, self-doubt, fear, and anxiety crop up. We have to learn how to deal with these emotions during the learning process. How can we create learning environments where students feel safe to be honest about the knowledge and skills they have? Safety is a major source of efficacy, and our ultimate goal is to strengthen student efficacy.

Fix-Up Strategies:

- Teach students to self-question using the guiding questions from above.

- Create a T-Chart with students. In one column they jot down their strengths and in one column they jot down their weaknesses and/or what they are concerned about relative to the task at hand.

- Teach students how to *ask for help*. Asking for help should be admired and applauded; asking for help is actually a brave thing to do. Many teachers use a stoplight rubric aligned to the success criteria to strengthen "help seeking."

- Self-assessment will be critical at this stage; they will need to be taught how to evaluate their strengths and weaknesses. Of course, this will need to modeled and practiced so learners make this a habit. This has a .72 effect size (see the table above).

Phase 3: Plan Your Approach

If students are compromised during the first two phases of the metacognitive cycle, it has a domino effect on the plans they create to accomplish the task. If they have not assessed the task correctly, students will create plans that aren't well matched. Also, many students don't even think about designing a plan before they start. To build *planning* capacity with students we can guide students to create action plans with benchmarks so students learn how to break down complex tasks into manageable chunks. Ultimately, students need to create their own plans and timelines. Co-constructing success criteria for high-quality planning will scaffold the learning for students who need it. Also, putting emphasis on the planning part of projects will be key until planning becomes a habit. Students can ask themselves these questions when making learning plans:

- What strategies will I deploy to be successful with this task?

- How will I sequence the strategies needed for success?

- What tools or resources will I need to be successful? (manipulatives, highlighters, notes, sticky notes, etc.)

- How much time will I need to accomplish this task?

- How will I organize my thinking?

- Where should I sit? How should I prepare my workspace so I can learn more?

- Who can I collaborate with to achieve my goal?

Emotional Connection: If students don't have a strategy toolkit to draw from during the planning phase, they often quit or give up before they even start. Some students *fly* through this phase because they have the knowledge and skills to be successful and, to be quite honest, making a detailed plan slows them down. Each student is different and each student may need something different; they will need to experiment with different planning techniques before they determine a "good fit." The following strategies can support the planning process:

Fix-Up Strategies:

- Students can visualize or sketch a plan before they start. Keep in mind that the plans that students make don't have to be detailed.

- Students can list the strategies that they want to use and then number them in the sequence that they will deploy them.

- Students can collaborate with one another to create *action plans* before they start. After all, this is what happens in the real world—we support one another when dealing with complex tasks, assignments, or projects.

- Have students complete an *advanced organizer* during the planning phase. An *advanced organizer* is a tool used to introduce the lesson topic and illustrate the relationship between what the students are about to learn and the information they have already learned. You can populate the organizer in advance to reduce information overload. Students can select key strategies from a strategy bank that you prepare in advance, and you can help make connections to prior knowledge for students who need extra scaffolding.

Phase 4: Apply Strategies and Monitor Performance

After creating a plan of action, students must deploy learning strategies in the appropriate sequence. During this stage they have to monitor their performance. We will want to ask students to engage in self-verbalization and self-questioning during this phase. If we want students to self-regulate their learning, they need to be able to talk through their plan while doing it. We teach them to self-verbalize by teaching them to think out loud while they are working through their plan. Modeling a think-aloud during this phase will be critical if we want students to do the same. Students can ask themselves these questions during this phase:

- Is this strategy working? How do I know?

- What strategies aren't working? What could I deploy instead?

- Am I using trial and error to make decisions about what to do next?

- Do I need to make a midcourse correction? Who can I learn from if things aren't turning out the way that I want?

Emotional Connection: When applying strategies and monitoring our own learning we sometimes feel like self-verbalizing or thinking aloud may slow us down *or* that it is only a technique that struggling students use. For some students, it may even feel unnecessary altogether. Research is quite clear that if we self-verbalize and monitor our learning during the learning process we learn more. The Visible Learning effect size for self-verbalizing is .59 (Hattie, 2009). How can we create a classroom culture where monitoring our own performance is just as valued as the grade that we get at the end? Sometimes learners feel like it is not efficient to monitor their learning, because they have been rewarded in the past for getting to the end quickly. They feel impatient and disrespected because this feels like an unnecessary step to them.

Fix-Up Strategies:
- Teach students to self-assess. Use the questions from above to guide self-assessment. Self-assessment will have to be modeled by the teacher or other students.

- Teach students to *annotate* their work and to jot down their thinking on *sticky notes*; this will make their thinking visible and support this phase.

- Teach students to self-verbalize or think through the strategies they are deploying out loud.

- Students will need to experiment with different ways to monitor their learning; what works for one student may not work for others. The key to making this stage come to life is for students to have autonomy and choice in the way that they learn best.

Phase 5: Reflect and Adjust Plan as Needed

During this phase, students will need to be taught how to reflect on their progress and adjust their plan as needed. Many students will not adjust their plan if they feel that it will be too time-consuming, or if they have to start over. Sometimes students will use an inefficient strategy because they are familiar with it, and they are reluctant to try a new strategy for fear of failure. Students need to be taught *how* to reflect. They should reflect using the success criteria and reflect on the cognitive strategies they deployed while learning. Students can ask themselves these questions during this phase:

- To what extent did I accomplish the goals of this task?

- How does what I learned today relate to prior learning?

- What worked well? What did I need to change?

- To what extent did I use tools and resources needed?

- What did I learn? I used to think ___. Now I think ___.

- If I were my teacher, how would I describe the quality of my learning?

- If I have to do something like this again, what do I want to remember?

- What habits of mind or disposition did I have to activate most?

Emotional Connection: We have all been in a situation where we were trying to solve a challenging problem and our strategy didn't work. We feel frustrated, anxious, and even angry. If our plan is working we sometimes gloat, brag, or become overly confident. All of these emotions crop up and sometimes all at the same time. What can we do to help students validate their emotions? How can we help them to move through difficult situations with grace? How do we teach them that we are only as strong as our weakest link and it is our job as learners to help everyone succeed? Developing a *revision mindset* will be vital for student success.

Fix-Up Strategies:

- Teaching students to rely on one another during this phase is critical to their success. Students can use the "phone a friend" strategy so they activate each other as a learning resource.

- Have students create a *Plan A* and *Plan B*—this way they have a backup plan ready if their first plan doesn't work out for them.

- Strategic revision is crucial during this phase, and they have to be able to speak to their revisions. Use Google Docs or sticky notes to make revisions easy for students.

- Use guiding questions to scaffold the reflection process (see above questions).

- Have students share out multiple ways that they accomplished the task. This is important so students know that there isn't just one way to accomplish their goal. Have students share their approach and frame each step of their thinking. Have the other students jot down the steps the student used.

In the End

Actively deploying metacognitive skills supports students in developing a positive learner identity, particularly their perception about their *ability* to learn. Students with a healthy learning identity see themselves as learners, and they know that they have control over learning outcomes. They are more inclined to seek out challenge and take responsible risks. *Meta-thinking* can be taught and is crucial if we want students to be self-directed, lifelong learners. "Reflecting critically on one's own learning is emotionally charged, which is why developing such skills takes time, especially with students that are accustomed to failure" (Wiliam, 2018). Creating time and space for students to engage in meta-thinking is an absolute for #PeerPower Revolutionaries. Expanding student agency, the belief that students have to influence the world around them, is the reason that #PeerPower Revolutionaries are relentless in their pursuit of developing self-regulated, self-directed learners!

Guiding Questions:

- How do you teach students meta-thinking?

- How could you use the metacognitive cycle with students?

- How can SEL and peer assessment be taught together?

- What is one practice that you would like to strengthen?

Connect with Paul on Twitter @Bloomberg_Paul

Part II:
Voices from the Field

Chapters 6–14

WANT TO MAKE A DIFFERENCE but don't know how? Collaborating with like-minded people with a collective goal of expanding student ownership and agency is how we learn more. If we are serious about starting an *Assessment Revolution*, collaboration will be key to our success. After all, we are #PeerPower Revolutionaries!

1. Collaboration with like-minded people provides an avenue to bounce ideas off of others with no hidden agendas.

2. Collaboration provides a sense of community.

3. Collaboration holds us accountable to trying new ideas connected to our goal.

4. Collaboration supports us in scaling this profound work.

5. Collaboration around key learning goals helps our schools become true learning organizations.

6. Collaborating with others helps us to communicate our shared competencies. It allows us to share what we are doing well and what we need support with.

Since our book is a collaborative project by 13 authors, the true essence of #PeerPower, the next nine chapters have been written to offer you different perspectives of the #PeerPower Framework in action. These perspectives illustrate the use of the framework in different grade levels and content. Connect with them on Twitter to collaborate and learn more!

Chapter 6

The Reflective Learning Revolution

Rupa Chandra Gupta

"We do not learn from experience. We learn from reflecting on experience."

–John Dewey

READ THE FOLLOWING TWO WRITTEN reflections from real students regarding what they must do to improve in their learning:

1. *I don't know what I did wrong, I tryed [sic] my best to get a perfect score, but I didn't.*

2. *The Strategies that worked the best for me was reading and re-reading the poem and the infographic. I just had to think about what related in both the infographic and the poem.*

The difference is palpable. We know the second student is significantly more likely to connect the dots between actions and outcomes, while the first seems destined to feel frustrated, be unsure of what to do next, and perhaps give up.

In this chapter, you will learn the unparalleled importance of reflective learning, what quality student reflection looks like, and simple, concrete protocols that will deepen metacognitive skills in your classroom. Together, we can kick-start the reflective learning revolution and build better prepared, lifelong learners!

Why Reflective Learning Matters

Most educators agree that student reflection on learning is a positive academic process that can enhance student engagement and success. Forms of reflection have been embedded in classrooms for decades, but they have often been narrowly applied by content or circumstance. Journal writing seems less appropriate for math or science classrooms. Deliberate reflection on behavior comes with negative infractions, but not when students are positively contributing to the community.

The latest learning science research, however, has illuminated the importance of metacognition (the awareness and understanding of one's own thought processes) in learning. Metacognition is especially powerful when it focuses on **learning strategies** or specific actions that a learner takes to improve or challenge themselves.

A comprehensive literature review from the University of Chicago Consortium (Farrington et al., 2012; see Figure 6.1) demonstrated that "students learn more effectively when they monitor their own learning processes, determine when they are having difficulty, and adjust their behavior and/or strategies to tackle the task at hand."

Figure 6.1: Noncognitive Factors in Student Learning

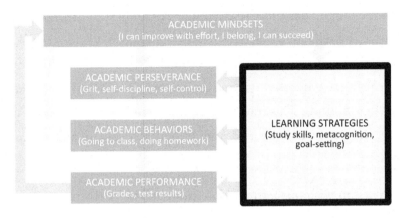

Adapted from "Teaching Adolescents To Become Learners. The Role of Noncognitive Factors in Shaping School Performance: A Critical Literature Review" (Farrington, et al. The University of Chicago Consortium on Chicago School Research. 2012)

The researchers compare this process of metacognition to "the thermostat of a furnace, which continually monitors the temperature in a room and responds by adjusting the output of heat. In the absence of this self-regulation, students are apt to give up prematurely, before fully mastering the work at hand, and gain less understanding from the time they do devote to learning" (Farrington et al., 2012). The analysis ultimately concluded that "all students can benefit from classroom instruction that builds metacognitive skills and learning strategies, such as monitoring, planning, and self-regulating" (Farrington et al., 2012).

I support school-wide implementations of student-led goal setting and re-flection all over the country, and the power of getting this right is profound. When students embed regular goal setting and reflection, they earn significantly higher grades in school (Rohanna, 2018) and improve their academic mindset and outlook (Soroten, 2016)—all in a way that benefits students who are the most behind. **Building these skills has the potential to close equity gaps!**

Reflective learning is not just a nice-to-have in classrooms. It's a must-have.

So What Does Quality Reflection Look Like?

Interestingly enough, despite the extended research supporting the power of metacognitive and reflective practice, very little has been written to describe what quality reflection looks and feels like. For goal setting, many educators use the SMART goal framework as a starting point (Specific, Measurable, Achievable, Relevant, Time-Bound). This frame is helpful as students think about upcoming steps, but it does not include a checklist of how to evaluate and process performance to date.

In partnership with our national Educator Advisory Board, my organization developed a set of success criteria to define this process more concretely.

Success Criteria: A high-quality reflection includes:

- An assessment of **performance** *(Where am I falling on the rubric? What's my grade? This can be determined by self-assessment or restate a peer or teacher's assessment.)*

- An assessment of **emotional response** *(How do I feel about where I am? Proud because I improved? Disappointed because I didn't meet or exceed expectations?)*

- References to **repeatable actions** that led to or will affect future performance *(What strategies are working, and what new ones can I try?)*

- Context and sufficient detail to **replicate or improve** on strategies/performance *(What specific actions can I take to improve or challenge myself? What's my SMART goal?)*

Teachers can use these success criteria when teaching students how to reflect, setting expectations for student reflective work, providing feedback on reflections, and assessing reflection quality overall. The student-friendly checklist for reflection (see Figure 6.2) is especially handy for these tasks.

Common examples of **ineffective student reflections** when asked what they can do to improve include the following:

- "Try harder"

- "Study more"

- "My goal is to get an 'A'"

Figure 6.2: Student-Friendly Checklist for Reflection

Student-Friendly Checklist for Reflection

> ### My reflection includes:
> - How I did on the task (use the success criteria).
> - How I'm feeling about my learning.
> - Strategies I've tried so far. What's working best?
> - New strategies I can try to improve or challenge myself. Think about the feedback you're received and how you can respond to it.
> - My next steps. Be specific!

I guarantee that you will see these types of responses when you first engage students in reflective practice. This is totally normal! Reflective learning is a skill that students must develop; and, like all new skills, they improve with consistent practice and feedback. In a recent study (Rohanna, 2018), researchers monitored and assessed students' reflections for a cohort of sixth graders over time. Student reflections were scored on a four-point rubric based on the above success criteria. **The median score improved from 1.25 (highly ineffective) to 3.00 (effective) over the course of *one semester.***

One sixth grader in San Jose, California, started the year with weak reflections on her learning, similar to the ineffective examples above. By December, however, she wrote: *"Over the break, I will study more of my vocabulary. This will help me with i-ready because I need more vocabulary. I'll know when I reach this goal by seeing my i-ready report. I will try to achieve this goal by the end of the break."* Her metacognitive growth was powerful and strongly supported academic growth as well.

When students have the opportunity to reflect regularly, they start *paying attention* to the actions and strategies that work best for them, and they shift their academic behavior accordingly. These learners "monitor the process of their learning, ascertain how effectively they are addressing a given learning task, and adjust their efforts accordingly" (Farrington et al., 2012).

Most importantly, students learn to make a habit out of reflective practice when engaging in new or challenging tasks. In addition to mastering content, they build their capacity to **learn how to learn**. The impact on students (in their own voices, Figure 6.3) is inspiring:

Figure 6.3: Student Voices

Access the video in the chapter 6 resources at www.PeerPowerRevolution.com

Xavier (fifth grader): "This [practice] is working good for me because even if I get a lower score, **I know what I can work on next time to get a higher score** and push my limits. So when I'm getting older in school, like college, I can really bring a lot of this."

Shadia (seventh grader): "I feel like before [using this goal-setting and reflection app], I didn't really set my goals well. I would write my essays, but I wouldn't try to improve on them. I would just do it the way I was comfortable and kept going. **But now I know I can get better.**"

How Do I Implement in the Classroom?

There are many ways teachers can use goal setting and reflection in the context of learning. In the **peer review protocol**, goal setting and reflection can and should occur throughout all phases. Let's use Phase 6 as an example, where it is explicitly embedded. After students complete an assessment of their peer's work and confer on the feedback, the student whose work was assessed goes through a reflective process to incorporate the feedback into their next steps. This reflection includes an assessment of their performance so far, as well as specific goals and actions to improve.

Best Practices in Implementing Goal Setting and Reflection

In supporting hundreds of classroom implementations, there are several best practices to consider for your instructional design.

- **Consistent routine:** This concept serves both teachers and students well! With a consistent routine, teachers can plan and embed the practice thoughtfully and regularly. You also elevate the importance of reflection by showing that you are willing to carve out time for it. Students know what to expect and can mentally engage with purpose and regularity. It also ensures ample opportunity to practice the skill and get better at it, as shown in the research above. One rule of thumb in defining your routine: frequency matters more than minutes. It is better to reflect for 10 minutes each week than an hour once a month.

Common routines:

- Weekly (e.g., every Friday for the last 10 minutes of the block)

- Aligned with unit milestones (e.g., after every major task, quiz, or assessment)

- Linked to self-/peer assessment protocols (e.g., every time students engage in peer assessment, there is time built into the protocol to reflect and set goals)

- **Start simple and scaffold:** As shown, students need to build the muscle of metacognition. Start with one familiar item or task that students can track and reflect on, such as a regular homework assignment or weekly quiz. It's most important they learn to reflect on the *how* of learning, not just the content. For example, if a student is struggling with citing relevant evidence, they need to think about specific strategies they can use to improve: use a graphic organizer to help link ideas, self-questioning, get feedback from a peer, and so on.

Common scaffolds:

- Explicitly teach reflection skills using success criteria stated above (e.g., introductory lesson, modeling, examples vs. non-examples)

- Provide example learning strategies that students can reference, and ideally build it together with students (e.g., mnemonics, suggested study steps, checklist of actions)

- Provide sentence frames to support reflection writing (e.g., "The strategies that are working for me are _____. Next time, I will try _____.")

- **Feedback, feedback, feedback:** Timely feedback to your students on their reflections will further build their metacognitive muscles. Feedback is most effective when delivered within 48 hours of the reflection and it is documented so students and teachers can reference it again later. Constructive feedback will often take the form of prompting questions to ensure students are responsive to the success criteria above. For example, if a student says their next step is to try harder (without context or specificity), a teacher might respond with, "Great that you're going to try harder! What specifically will you do?"

Common feedback protocols:

- Brief 1:1 conferences (e.g., during independent learning time, pull individual students to discuss and log their reflections and next steps)

- Peer review (e.g., students can read one another's reflections and next steps, and give feedback based on the success criteria)

- If using an online system, enter feedback in real time or within 24–48 hours of student reflection writing (e.g., using the Sown To Grow online platform, teachers can provide feedback and students will be notified by e-mail or when they log in next)

- **Visualize growth over time:** The power of goal setting and reflection for motivation is palpable, especially when students can visually see their growth on specific skills over time. This is further compounded when they can link specific strategies or actions they are taking to this growth. When building your protocol, it's important for students to not only reflect in the moment on the task at hand but to also be able to see their progress at a higher level. Technology tools can be very helpful in facilitating these types of visualizations.

Common visualization techniques:

- Use a technology tool to help graph and visualize changes in performance (e.g., the Sown To Grow online platform, Google Sheets)

- Have students graphically display their performance (e.g., draw a line chart)

Imagining Success

I was recently in a second-grade classroom where the teacher was diving deep into Reading Informational Text standards. During the week, students had a variety of comprehension quizzes and mini-assessments on these standards. As they got scores back, they jotted them down on a sticky note on their desk.

Every Friday, students spent the first 15 minutes of the day entering the week's scores into their online goal-setting and reflection system. Bar charts would appear, showing them growth or areas where they needed to improve further. They picked an emoji smiley face to illustrate how they were feeling about their work so far and wrote a one- or two-sentence reflection on the strategies that were working best and new ones they could try.

On the wall, the teacher and students had co-created a strategy bank—a list of reading strategies that they came up with together and could continue to add to. It had tactical examples in student-friendly language, such as

- read the headings and subheadings of the article first,
- look at charts/diagrams and connect them back to the text, and
- look back and touch the answer (a visualization exercise).

Students rose to the challenge of this weekly protocol and responded with powerful descriptions of their learning process—despite being only 7 to 8 years old. They named strategies, described new ones, and showed a thirst for improvement that was inspiring. They believed in their ability to improve; more importantly, they knew *how* to improve.

One student said to me, "Did you know, **reading isn't magic?** There are things that I can do to make me a better reader. Isn't that cool?!"

What she calls "cool," we call the epitome of learning! Together, we can transform classrooms and learning environments so all students embody this powerful skill and spirit.

Guiding Questions:

- How does goal setting and reflection enhance student learning? Consider research as well as personal experience as a teacher and learner.

- How might you share the success criteria for quality reflection with students? Describe the lesson you would design.

- What outputs of learning can you have students track and reflect on? Examples include scores on assignments/tasks, mastery of success criteria, or cumulative grades.

- What routine fits into your classroom practice for student reflection? See examples above for ideas.

Connect with Rupa on Twitter @rupa_c_g

Chapter 7

Lifting Language Learning With Peer Power

Rachel Carillo-Fairchild

"Do not go where the path may lead, go instead where there is no path and leave a trail."

–Ralph Waldo Emerson

THE RESEARCH IS CLEAR AND has been for several decades: the answer to the question, "How do we get *all* students to learn?" lies in the power of formative assessment. Highly esteemed intellectuals and practitioners in the field of assessment such as John Hattie, James Popham, and Rick Stiggins have for years attempted to gently guide us to see assessment as not just a separate measurement "of learning" but instead as a process so entwined within the learning that it becomes a part of the learning. They've challenged us to embed assessment within our daily practice and extricate it once and for all as solely a way of grading and rank ordering our students. While the summative assessments that yield that information are a necessary part of our current system, these esteemed assessment giants have presented us with unquestionable evidence that formative assessment and the formative assessment process itself can accelerate the learning of even our most challenging student populations. Rick Stiggins (2014) writes, in his call to action, *Revolutionize Assessment*,

> The mere act of judging student achievement and communicating test results can, if not skillfully and sensitively handled, trigger emotional dynamics within learners that stop them in their tracks, literally driving them from school. On the other hand, when handled well, assessment can launch students into powerful learning trajectories, resulting in major achievement gains for all—but especially those who have struggled to succeed. (p. 37)

For those of us who work with English Language Learners (ELLs), these words have significant meaning. We work with a diverse population of students whose academic performance may at any point in their educational careers be one or more years below grade level. Some of these students have developed the resilience and grit to power through those challenges and be successful. But for countless others, being told year after year that you are not proficient begins to wear away at that spark for learning that once shone brightly inside of them, until they finally decide that their investment in the educational process has not paid off; with that light extinguished, they leave us, becoming a statistic—a reminder to all of us that our system has failed them. In fact, in his article, "5 Million Voices – English Language Learners: How Your State Is Doing," Claudio Sanchez (2017) poignantly reminds us that while the national graduation rate is 82 percent, only 63 percent of ELLs graduate from high school. Building assessment-capable English Language Learners can turn the tide! While we know from the research of John Hattie (2009) that assessment-capable learners have an effect size of 1.44, one of the highest effect sizes found in his renowned meta-analysis, *Visible Learning*, we also know that it has yet to make its way into every classroom in our country. According to the Center for American Progress Report, *Preparing All Teachers to Meet the Needs of English Language Learners* (2012), we also know that English Language Learners are more likely taught in classrooms with teachers who lack the training and support to help them succeed. While many teachers may have the desire to build assessment-capable learners through Peer Review, they often lack the time and support to effectively implement new strategies. Additionally, there are those who believe that ELLs would be unable to participate in Peer Review because they lack the language to do it successfully. In fact, when provided with the access and support, English Language Learners show us time and again that they are not just willing but capable of engaging in Peer Review successfully! On the following pages, you will find not just a call to action but the steps and resources needed to empower your English Language Learners to own their learning through #PeerPower. The verdict is in, and it is time for change—it is time for a #PeerPower Revolution!

Steps to Success

In order to meet the challenges of teaching any population, but particularly English Language Learners, we must begin with clarity. We as educators must know the who, what, why, and how of our content. We cannot expect our students to have clarity about what they are learning if we don't have clarity about what we are teaching. When working with English Language Learners, it is of utmost importance to begin by ensuring that you know the population of students you have been charged with teaching. As a classroom teacher, I create a table or spreadsheet that contains, at a minimum, the following information:

English Proficiency Levels by Language Domain – Having a clear picture of the proficiency levels of your English Language Learners is the first step in teaching them. It is important to distinguish their proficiency in each of the language domains—Listening, Speaking, Reading, and Writing—so that they can be grouped and paired accordingly. For example, if I am partnering my students to provide peer feedback in Writing, then I would want to know the English proficiency levels of my English Language Learners specifically in Writing so that I can partner them effectively and also provide differentiated instruction for those students to meet them at their current level of proficiency.

Primary Language – Knowing the primary language of your English Language Learners as well as knowing their proficiency in that language also helps when grouping or pairing students for the Peer Review process. It's important, for example, to know that you may have English Language Learners born in the United States who do not have proficiency in their primary language. In fact, according to Capps, Bachmeier, Fix, and Hook (2013), over 75 percent of ELLs in elementary schools and more than 50 percent of ELLs in secondary schools were born in the United States and many of those students also had U.S.-born parents. This limits the use of certain strategies for this population of students. Strategies such as primary language supports or scaffolds would not be useful to students who were born in the United States and have no proficiency in their primary language.

Country of Origin – Understanding where our English Language Learners come from is important when grouping students or pairing them for Peer Review. It also helps us to understand cultural differences and distinctions that may have an impact on student learning. For example, an English Language Learner of Mexican descent born in the United States has distinct cultural differences from an English Language Learner born in Mexico, and I as the classroom teacher need to understand those differences. Ensuring that all of our students feel safe and welcome within our classrooms is the cornerstone for establishing an environment where students are willing to take the risks required for learning, and acknowledging their cultures and countries of origin helps establish an environment of acceptance.

Years in U.S. Schools – Knowing the length of time that an English Language Learner has been in our schools is not just enlightening but also establishes the amount of time our students have been formally identified as an ELL and whether they are making progress on their path toward proficiency in English. If, for example, you have a student who arrived in U.S. schools in sixth grade and is now at Intermediate Fluency in Reading in eighth grade, then you can assume that this English Language Learner had a strong foundation in their primary language and that they have made steady and rapid progress in their attainment of proficiency in the domain of Reading. If, on the other hand, you have an English Language Learner in eighth grade who was born in the United States and has been in our schools since kindergarten and is at Intermediate Fluency in Reading, then we potentially have a situation in which this ELL's progress toward English proficiency has stalled. These two students, while at the same exact proficiency level, should receive instruction that differs based on their very different backgrounds. Not knowing this information sets us and our English Language Learners up for failure.

Once we have clarity about the English Language Learners we are teaching, then we can proceed to the next step in the Peer Review process: clarity about the learning itself. Research has confirmed for us that assessment-capable learners can answer three questions about their learning at all points in the instructional cycle:

1. Where am I going? – What is the learning intention that my teacher has set for this lesson/unit?

2. How am I going? – Where am I now in relation to the learning intentions and success criteria that have been established?

3. What do I need to learn next? – What is the exact next step I need to take to advance my learning and get closer to the learning intention?

In order to successfully answer these questions, English Language Learners should be provided with the language structures needed to answer these questions for themselves as well as participate in conversations with a peer. In addition to co-creating success criteria with our English Language Learners, we should also co-create lists of sentence frames/starters that they can use to answer these questions successfully when self-assessing and/or working with a peer. As the year progresses the lists should be revisited and English Language Learners can continue to contribute to the lists as their academic vocabulary grows. Figure 7.1 contains some sample sentence frames/starters to use when teaching our students how to self-assess:

Figure 7.1: Sample Sentence Frames

Where am I going? ¿Qué es lo que voy a aprender?	How am I going? ¿En dónde voy yo en mi aprendizaje?	What do I need to learn next? ¿Qué es lo que me falta aprender?
I'm going to learn . . . Voy a aprender . . . Today, I will learn how to . . . Ahora, yo aprenderé . . . I will learn about . . . Aprenderé sobre . . . At the end of this lesson/ unit, I will . . . Al fín de esta lección, yo sabré . . .	I know how to . . . Yo se como . . . I learned how to . . . Yo aprendí como . . . I am successful at . . . Yo he tenido éxito en . . . I currently know how to . . . En este momento, yo he aprendido . . .	My next step is . . . Lo que me sigue para aprender es . . . I still need to . . . Todavía me falta . . . One thing I need to fix is . . . Una cosa que debo aprender . . . I will be successful when I can . . . Tendré éxito cuando pueda . . .

Self-assessment is a vital step in students taking ownership of their learning. Once students can answer these questions for themselves, then we can co-create success criteria with our students and teach them how to use that criteria in the Peer Review process.

Unpacking the Standards for Linguistic Demands

Unpacking the standards as a grade level is the best way for teachers to deconstruct a standard and help teachers develop clarity around what the standard means and expects of our students. For English Language Learners, it is especially important for teachers to unpack the linguistic demands of the standard they are focusing on. If our ultimate goal is for English Language Learners to acquire the language competencies needed to unlock language proficiency, then understanding the complexity of the language expected of our students should be the starting point. The language objective for a standard also stems from the linguistic demands of a standards-based lesson or task. Therefore, unpacking the linguistic demands of the standard forms the foundation for well-written language objectives. For example, in CCSS RI.4.2, Figure 7.2 has a sample of what unpacking the linguistic demands of the standard would look like:

Figure 7.2: Unpacked Linguistic Demands

Unpacking Linguistic Demands

CCSS: RI.4.2. Determine the main idea of text and explain how it is supported by the key details; summarize the text.

What are the specific ways that academic language will be used by students?

RI.4.2 requires English Learners to use academic language to:
- articulate main idea and details using key vocabulary: main idea, detail
- provide supporting details about the text using adjectives
- priortize details in a text using target adjectives: important, essential, significant.
- ask and answer "how" questions about main events using the past-tense
- develop a supporting detail using complete and varied sentences
- summarize a non-fiction text using general present tense and citation verbs
- introduce essential details in a summary using sequencing transitions

---

Here is an example of how the linguistic demands of the standard, having been identified through the unpacking process, could easily be used by teachers to develop meaningful and well-written language objectives:

Students will . . .

- summarize an informational article using citation verbs: describe, discuss, state, conclude

- introduce essential details in a formal summary using sequencing transitions: first, also, in addition, finally

Success Criteria by Proficiency Level

Let's take a look at an example using a reading progression based upon English Language Development Standards. Below is sample differentiated success criteria developed for English Language Learners. Using a combination of the CCSS fourth-grade standards (Reading Informational Text RI.4.2 Determine the main idea of a text and explain how it is supported by key details; summarize the text) and the fourth-grade English Language Acquisition standards for her state, this teacher has taken the expectations established in the CCSS standards, built a progression for her students, and co-created success criteria that her English Language Learners can use in the Peer Review process. In a state that identifies five levels of language acquisition, what is included in Figure 7.3 is a sampling of three levels: Level 1, Level 3, and Level 5:

Figure 7.3: Reading Progression Using English Language Development Standards

EL Level 1 – Writing a Summary (Informational Text)

Success Criteria	Not Yet ★	Almost There ★★	Got It! ★★★
I can co-construct a bank of words and phrases from a read aloud that align to the main idea and key details.			
I can use words and phrases from a word bank to identify the main idea of a read aloud.			
I can use words and phrases from a word bank to identify the key details that support the main idea of a read aloud.			
I can use a graphic organizer to organize my thinking.			

EL Level 3 – Writing a Summary (Informational Text)

Success Criteria	Not Yet ★	Almost There ★★	Got It! ★★★
I can usea bank of words and graphic organizer to help me determine the main idea in a text that is read aloud to me.			
I can use a word bank and graphic organizer to help me determine the supporting details in a text that is read aloud to me.			
I can use the graphic organizer and word bank to help me surrmarize my thinking including identifying the main idea and explaining how the key details support the main idea.			
I can speak in complete sentences • The main idea is… • One key detail is…			

EL Level 5 – Writing a Summary (Informational Text)

Success Criteria	Not Yet ★	Almost There ★★	Got It! ★★★
I can read a nonfiction text independently.			
I can use knowledge of the text and text structure to annotate the text independently for the main idea.			
I can use knowledge of the text and text structure to annotate the text independently for key details.			

EL Level 5 – Writing a Summary (Informational Text)

Success Criteria	Not Yet ★	Almost There ★★	Got It! ★★★
I can write a short summary of a text I've read independently identifying the main idea and explaining how the key details supprt the main idea.			

English Language Learners armed with clear success criteria for writing a summary that is leveled by language proficiency levels can identify where they are going, where they are now, and what they need to do to improve. This differentiated success criteria gives students the language they need to be able to self and peer assess and provides them with the feedback they need to improve.

Introducing Peer Review to Our English Language Learners

How many of us have tried to learn a second or third language? Any of us who have know all too well the anxiety that comes with having to practice that language out loud, particularly in front of your peers in a classroom. Of the four sources of efficacy—Feedback, Mastery Moments, Models of Success, and Safety—Safety helps to lower the anxiety and fear that English Language Learners experience when faced with learning English. Here are some concrete strategies we can use to introduce Peer Review and help lower the level of anxiety of our English Language Learners when faced with the prospect of providing feedback to a partner.

1. **Model the process** – While it makes perfect sense to provide models of proficient work for our English Language Learners to aim for, we should also provide models of what Peer Review itself looks like by sharing video of students engaged in Peer Review. These models help the students establish a sense for the expectations of Peer Review and also give them an opportunity to hear the language being used in context. Visit our YouTube channel @thecorecollaborative for video of students, including English

Language Learners, engaged in Peer Review! Be clear about your expectations and set your students up for success by giving them an opportunity to see what you expect Peer Review to look like.

2. **Provide visual cues** – Create anchor charts that establish the steps to the Peer Review process along with visual cues that serve as links to the vocabulary they are learning. If they can't remember the exact word(s), the visual cues will help them remember what comes next in the process and prevent them from getting stuck. These anchor charts also build our students' sense of agency as they know exactly where to go and what to do when they are stuck.

3. **Provide sentence frames/starters** – Whether they are newcomers engaging in Peer Review in their primary language or whether they are engaging in Peer Review in English, we need to provide frames and starters for our students that help them navigate the academic language demands of Peer Review. Co-creating lists of sentence frames/starters with your English Language Learners is the best way for them to feel ownership of the criteria and to understand it well enough to be able to turn around and use it in a Peer Review setting. The TAG feedback structure is a basic structure that teachers like to use as an initial step toward implementing Peer Review. TAG is an acronym that stands for the following steps in the process:

T – Tell your partner something they did well. Use the success criteria to help you.

A – Ask your partner a question related to the learning goal/target/intention.

G – Give your partner a suggestion for improvement using the success criteria.

Figure 7.4 is a sample template along with some sentence frames/starters that your English Language Learners can use to help them navigate the language structures associated with Peer Review.

Figure 7.4: Sample TAG Feedback Protocol With Language Supports

T	A	G
Tell your partner something they did well. Use the success criteria to help you. I like how you . . . Me gusta como . . . As a reader, it was enjoyable when you . . . Como lector, fue agradable cuando . . . I was impressed with . . . Me impresionó mucho cuando... _____was a strength. _____ es una verdadera fuerza para ti.	Ask your partner a question related to the learning goal/target/intention. Can you help me understand . . . Puedes ayudarme a entender . . . Can you clarify . . . Puedes aclarar . . . I wonder why . . . Me pregunto porque . . .	Using the success criteria, give your partner a suggestion for improvement. I think focusing on _____ would really help you improve. Creo que centrarse en _____ te ayudaría a mejorar. Being more specific with _____ would really help you improve. Ser más específico con _____ te ayudaría a mejorar.

Peer Review Pitfalls

We all want our students to be successful, but we also recognize that we simultaneously feel the pressure of pacing calendars and testing windows upon us. Sometimes, in our haste to teach as much content as we can within the time allotted, we move a little too quickly or skip steps that may be crucial to our students' overall success. While engaging our English Language Learners in Peer Review will undoubtedly lift their language learning, it will also increase their sense of efficacy and help them become assessment-capable learners. However, the road may not always be smooth. Expect setbacks and be OK with them. Remember that failure is a part of any new learning endeavor, and give yourself permission to not get it perfect the first time! Many of us are perfectionists by nature, but let's not let perfection be the enemy of progress. As Carol Dweck reminds us, "Even in the growth mindset, failure can be a painful experience. But it doesn't define you. It's a problem to be faced, dealt with, and learned from" (Dweck, 2016, p. 33). Accept that trying a new strategy such as Peer Review is going to be challenging; be prepared for setbacks and temporary failures, but also be prepared to learn from those setbacks, make mid-course corrections, and move forward.

With that in mind, there are some pitfalls that the experiences of others who have implemented these practices can help you avoid:

1. **Start small** – When working with English Language Learners, it is important to keep in mind that they are learning content while simultaneously learning the intricacies of the English language. Therefore, it is important to choose a product or task that has been chunked so that your English Language Learners can initially focus on one part of the task. For example, in one classroom, I watched a teacher who was teaching Writing Standard 3.1 (Write opinion pieces on topics or texts, supporting a point of view with reasons) set up her students to focus only on the initial part of the standard, which was to introduce the topic or state an opinion. After sharing several models and co-creating the success criteria with her English Language Learners, she paired them up and had them Peer Review their partners' work focusing only on whether they had introduced their topic and stated their opinion. Armed with models and differentiated sentence frames by level, her English Language Learners, ranging from beginning to intermediate proficiency, were able to successfully Peer Review.

2. **Practice, practice, practice** – English Language Learners require repeated opportunities to practice using language. Keep in mind that the academic language they will be using during Peer Review is typically Tier 2 Academic Vocabulary, which they may not have a lot of experience using. Although we often feel pressured by the time constraints that often rule the classroom, this is not the time to cut back on opportunities for practice. I have been in classrooms with English Language Learners engaged in practicing language structures for Peer Review with the teacher leading the class through a collaborative analysis of student work while using the sentence frames from an anchor chart. This guided practice provided his students an opportunity to familiarize themselves with the success criteria, practice using it, and allowed

them to use the sentence frames under the guidance of their teacher. After several different opportunities to practice, his English Language Learners were prepared for their first experience with Peer Review.

Envisioning Success

Beginning with the groundbreaking Black and Wiliam meta-analysis of 1998 (Black & Wiliam, 1998), researchers and thought leaders have spent the last 20 years working to convince educators of the value of the formative assessment process. The time has come to move past reading the research and considering the value of formative assessment. It is time for all educators to realize the promise of #PeerPower and make it a reality in each and every classroom. Consider for a moment the power of Peer Review for student populations such as English Language Learners, who the research has shown continuously lag behind native English-speaking students in both Math and Language Arts. Imagine the power of English Language Learners engaging in Peer Review conversations successfully using co-created success criteria to provide feedback to a peer using scaffolds such as sentence frames. Imagine English Language Learners armed with differentiated language supports using success criteria and correct academic language to provide each other with feedback. English Language Learners could use this feedback to set goals and to finally understand where they going, where they currently are in the progression, and most importantly, how they can close the gap between where they currently are and where they need to be.

These English Language Learners, armed with a new understanding and ownership of their learning, can finally be the students whose achievement is accelerated because their teacher didn't follow the same path but instead created a new path and was a #PeerPower Revolutionary! It's time for all of us to envision what can be and recognize what is possible and already happening in classrooms across the country. It's time for *all* of us to become #PeerPower Revolutionaries!

Guiding Questions:

- Do teachers have access to the latest language proficiency scores for each of their English Language Learners? Can they easily access overall language proficiency levels? Can they easily access scores in each of the language domains? Listening? Speaking? Reading? Writing?

- Can teachers easily access to basic information about their English Language Learners, such as primary language spoken, level of proficiency in their primary language, or country of origin? If not, how can that information be made more accessible?

- What supports do we need to begin using the formative assessment process with our English Language Learners? What would it look like and sound like in our classrooms if all levels of our English Language Learners were engaged in self- and peer assessment?

- What pitfalls can we anticipate? What supports will we need in place in order to engage our English Language Learners fully in the formative assessment process?

Connect with Rachel on Twitter @rsyrja

Chapter 8

Igniting Goal Setting With Emerging Readers

Isaac Wells

"To learn to read is to light a fire; every syllable that is spelled out is a spark."

–Victor Hugo

Igniting Goal Setting in the Primary Grades

Ask any adult what they believe to be the fundamental learning goal in kindergarten and first grade and you are likely to hear, "Learning to read." Ask any student what they are most excited about learning in kindergarten and first grade and you will hear, "Learning to read." Not surprisingly, educators agree that learning to read is essential. Reading fluently and with comprehension is the foundation for learning and success across all content areas and throughout their school careers. If everyone agrees reading is the focus, why is it we have so many primary students struggling to read?

Reading is a personal undertaking that integrates the prior knowledge and experiences of each individual and elicits unique reactions and reflection. Students at the beginning reading levels need clear, personal, learning goals to focus and motivate their reading efforts. Teachers can help students set, meet, and exceed goals using clear progressions of skills, consistent feedback, and actionable strategies. Through dozens of conversations with you and their peers, children learn to monitor their own learning, set goals, and apply strategies as they navigate increasingly complex and challenging texts.

Igniting Clarity in Reading

Reading is a mysterious process for many children. So much of the work we do as readers is hidden to the outside world, and students of all ages can struggle to understand what happens inside their minds and those of other readers! All children come to school wanting to be readers, but they need you to show them how.

As an instructional coach and consultant, I often go into classrooms and ask students one-on-one what they are currently learning or working on. I have received a variety of responses, but they usually fall into a few categories. Most often the answer is a topic or subject like "Bears!," "Penguins!," or "Science." Sometimes it is a one-size-fits-all answer such as, "To be a better reader." Occasionally I get the classic non-answers, "I don't know" or "Nothing." However, in some of the classrooms I visit, I am answered with *how* each student is working to improve as a reader. What makes the difference is the way teachers partner with children to help them answer the three formative questions—"Where am I going as a reader? Where am I now? and What do I need to learn next?"—which I rephrase as, "How will I accomplish my goal?"

Teacher clarity nearly doubles the rate of learning (Hattie, 2002). Teacher clarity in literacy instruction can be described as the gradual release of responsibility (Pearson & Gallagher, 1983b). The gradual release framework is grounded in clear learning intentions and success criteria, explicit modeling using think aloud, guided practice included guided reading, and then a release to independent practice and application by the reader. Feedback and coaching are necessary to create clarity in the classroom. These components, when combined together, are the key to igniting a student's ability to self-assess and set goals.

Essential Terms

Skills: Something a reader can do when interacting with a text. This can be anything from knowing we read from left to right and top to bottom to making inferences or analyzing a text.

Strategies: A process or series of steps students follow to accomplish a skill

Behaviors: The understanding and skills students demonstrate when they read effectively. Behaviors can range from understanding that a text may be fiction or nonfiction to analyzing and critiquing an author's craft.

Goals: The next steps in learning, both short term and long term. Goals clarify what a student is working on when she reads.

An enduring understanding connected to teacher clarity is that reading happens along a continuum of skills and strategies. The Fountas and Pinnell Literacy Continuum (Fountas & Pinnell, 2017) supports teachers in understanding the reading behaviors required at each level for students to demonstrate thinking within, beyond, and about the text. Each child can grow along this continuum to become the reader they desire. The continuum can be used by teachers to plan instruction, provide feedback, and partner with students to set clear goals during reading conferences. Conferences can prevent and correct ineffective reading habits before they become deeply ingrained. Teaching students "step-by-step" or "how-to" strategies such as "Keep in Mind What Repeats" or "Reread to Get Back in Your Book" supports students' goals (Serravallo, 2015). After goal-setting conferences, student responses to "What do I need to learn next as a reader?" become much more focused and specific. When goals are set to match the reader, and the child has mastered and internalized a few key strategies, every opportunity to read, listen to, or discuss a text becomes an opportunity to strengthen their reading skills.

The way children think of themselves as readers has a powerful effect on how they perform as readers. Students develop a sense of agency, the belief that their actions affect their results, and build self-efficacy when they receive specific feedback on how they are progressing along the continuum and can celebrate milestones related to their goals. Perhaps most importantly, when early readers begin to feel "in charge" of their reading goals they take on more responsibility, know what to think and practice while they read, and are excited to share their learning with anyone who will listen. Spending this time focused on success and good reading habits with students will support the internal narrative, "I am a reader and I can learn to read any book I am interested in." With these mindsets in place, students will be dedicated to improvement and deeply engaged in reading work.

Igniting Learning Throughout the Day

I know what you are thinking: "When am I supposed to address each students' skills, behaviors, strategies?" Across the country, teachers are reaching learners in a personal way through a balanced literacy approach. Personalizing learning is not an add-on, it's a shift in thinking and a way to connect learning and instruction throughout the day.

Shared Reading

Students need examples of *how* to read before they meet these expectations on their own. Some skills can be easily demonstrated, such as pointing to each word on a page for 1:1 correspondence. However, most reading behaviors happen internally. "Think-alouds" draw students' attention to specific details in the print and illustrations as you *think aloud* about how you are monitoring your own reading behavior and why you slowed down, stopped, or reread. To model monitoring and self-correcting, you might say one of the following:

- *I'm going to look back at this page again to see if what I read makes sense.*

- *I used the picture and thought that word would be "bunny" but I noticed it started with an "r" and ended with a "t" so I figured out it was "rabbit."*

- *That didn't sound right. I'm going to reread this part in bear's voice, not rabbit's, because that makes more sense.*

- *Hmmm. I don't remember how this story started. I'm going to look back and make sure I understand before I read on.*

Be very clear and specific when communicating next steps for students. You may even have to model the behavior again while you are explaining the expectations.

For instance, *"For the next few days, I want everyone to pay careful attention to what you do when you come to a word you do not recognize. Slow down and use the first and last sounds of words just like I did. Let's try it together one more time before you practice on your own."*

Guided Reading

Guided reading is a time for children to try out and practice reading behaviors and strategies in texts. To encourage monitoring and self-correction, your prompt may be as simple as, *"Look back at this page (or sentence) again and see if what you read makes sense."*

Each conversation should tie their personal goals to comprehension and to the enjoyment of a text or achievement of a purpose.

> *I know you are working on using the first and last sounds to read new words. Let's look back and see when you used that strategy and it worked. Can you find a place that first and last sounds would have helped you? Noticing when you are not sure about a word and then using first and last sounds is going to help you learn from and enjoy many different books including the Tiny books I know you love!*

Hint: This is new learning to them. When they are unable to recognize errors and strategies in their own reading, refer them to a specific page, illustration, or word and ask them to monitor and correct your reading as you act out errors you know they are making in their own reading.

Primary students often do not realize that they are expected to practice what they learn in interactive read aloud and shared reading during guided and independent reading. Making clear connections to what students are learning in other components of the literacy block focuses and deepens their understanding. I tell Impact Teams (PLCs) I partner with that I would rather they practice one strategy a dozen times than a dozen strategies once.

Making Reading Up-Close and Personal

For our children to be successful in reading they have to know themselves as readers. First, students have to understand exactly what is expected and what is possible. Second, they need many opportunities to practice and receive feedback on their practice so they can set personal goals. Finally, readers have to be taught to monitor, revise, and reflect on their own reading.

Establish Clear Success Criteria

It is imperative that teachers and students have clear criteria for learning how to read. One of the shortcomings of many reading programs is an overabundance of activities that have little or no relation to what people actually do when they read. To define how students should interact with texts, I recommend the *Fountas and Pinnell Literacy Continuum: A Tool for Assessment, Planning, and Teaching*. Fountas and Pinnell use 10 characteristics to describe how readers interact with texts covering twenty-six levels (A–Z) of text complexity (Fountas & Pinnell, 2017). The criteria are organized into 12 systems of strategic action that cover the full range of thinking and behaviors readers use to understand, interact with, and analyze texts. Many of the reading behaviors match the expectations of state standards for reading foundations, but the continuum goes deeper and analyzes exactly what type of thinking students must do to meet those expectations.

Communicate and Connect Criteria to Actions

Reading is as complex as it is important, and no one can teach every skill students' might need; you must have a process to narrow the focus of your instruction. Meet with colleagues to study and discuss the text levels most often read in your grade level, look for trends and identify the key reading behaviors for students to master (see Figure 8.1).

Figure 8.1: Key Reading Behaviors

Selected Reading Behaviors From Level D	Student-Friendly Success Criteria for Level D
• Use two or more sources of information (meaning, language structure, visual information) to self-monitor and self-correct • Make predictions based on understanding a simple sequence of events with a problem and solution • Summarize the problem in a simple story and talk about the solution • Identify a simple story problem and how it is resolved <div align="center">(Fountas & Pinnell, 2017)</div>	• I check to make sure what I am reading makes sense, looks right, and sounds right • I use picture clues and what the story is about to fix words that don't make sense • I use first and last sounds to fix words that don't look right • I reread and try again when the word didn't sound right in the sentence • I stop to think about what I have read • I think about what happened to predict what is next • I can tell how a character solved a problem • I retell the story including the problem and solution

The thinking skills you determine are most important become the success criteria for reading. If you expect students to integrate the reading behaviors into their reading, you have to model and explain exactly what you want them to do and create many opportunities to practice. We have created a Primary Reading Progression Tool (see Figure 8.2) in partnership with Principal Deanna Marco and her teachers from Naples Elementary in Staten Island. This tool lays out key criteria for students to focus on when learning to read. This tool can be used for self and peer assessment, reading conferences, or communicating desired reading behaviors to parents.

Figure 8.2: Primary Reading Progression Tool

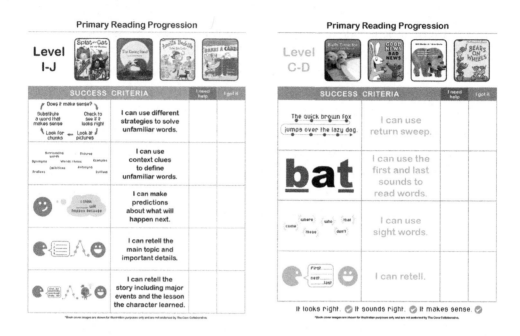

Another way to clarify and connect learning over time is to use what we call mini-progressions. Select an important skill and trace its development to create your own mini-progression. Provide feedback using the criteria to remind children where they were before, highlight where they are now, and suggest where to go next in the progression.

Consider the *Level C Mini-Progression* (see Figure 8.3) for directing attention to the important information on the page and what the dialogue could sound like with a student who is still pointing to each word while reading.

Figure 8.3: Mini-Progression for Level C

Level C Mini-Progression Scanning Text	How It Sounds
Point to the **picture** and tell what you see. Point to the **print** and tell what you think it says (or remember from shared reading). Point distinctly to **each word** in the text as you read. Slide your finger beneath the print to read in **phrases** and then **sentences**. Finally, pull finger away and **read with your eyes**.	*"Do you remember that you used to focus mostly on the picture to try to figure out some of the words when you read?* *You should keep using the pictures, but the books you will be reading will have more and more information in the sentences.* *Right now, you are pointing to and reading every word on the page. You are ready to read even more interesting books, but for them to make sense, you need to read groups of words together like this.* (demonstrate) *Look at how I'm sliding my finger under the words to keep reading until an idea is finished. You try it. See if you can slide your finger and read the words together in phrases.* (student attempts and you support them until they are successful) *Great, when you read like that these books are going to sound better and make more sense.* *Each time you read this way, you are training your eyes to keep moving while you read and soon you are going to be ready to pull your finger away and read in phrases just like when we read big books together."*

Gather Evidence and Provide Feedback

Quality feedback requires quality evidence of student thinking. To gather the information you need, you must observe students reading and discussing books. Taking running records and recording anecdotal notes during these observations provides a clear record of *how* children are reading. Analyze your records to understand how each child is thinking and to identify where they are on the reading continuum. Feedback in reading is most powerful when it is tied to these specific reading behaviors and strategies. The focus of your feedback will vary, but each conversation should connect to the ultimate goal of all reading: comprehension. During a conference or in guided reading, start by highlighting moments the student(s) used reading behaviors successfully, and point out what they did and why it was helpful. Next, draw their attention to a pattern of errors or an opportunity to use a new strategy and share how they can improve (see Figure 8.4). Feedback is only useful if it is implemented immediately, so have students paraphrase the conversation before you send them away to try it out; this way you can clarify and/or summarize what they need to work on next.

Set Personal Goals

Just as quality evidence is necessary for feedback, quality feedback is essential to goal setting. Students must understand how far they are from the expectation to set a personal goal. Setting long-term and short-term goals with readers can bridge the gap between what students are taught and what they do independently. Personalized goals narrow the focus of reading instruction and ensure that the time children spend reading is actually improving *how* they read.

The "why" behind a goal will always be personal. When working with young readers we need to have conversations about their interests and desires and use those to develop long-term goals. For instance, a child might wish to:

"Read a Frog & Toad story all by myself."

"Read a favorite book to my class or group."

"Use books to learn more about snakes."

These long-term goals mean something to the students and are more concrete than being a "J" reader or "doing what good readers do."

Help students develop short-term goals that describe the skills and strategies each student needs to learn and demonstrate in order to close the gap between where they are and where they want to be as readers.

The Primary Reading Progression can be used during conversations with students to clarify expectations, set goals, and guide reflection. At first, goal setting will be teacher directed and will include explaining what the visuals mean and how to use the columns to reflect. The visual support and short list of options ease children's transition into selecting their own goals. At every stage, the conversation should include how to use the goal in their partner and independent reading, monitor whether or not they used the goal, and reflect on how well the goal was used. Refer to Figure 8.4 for examples of teacher-centered and learner-centered goal-setting conversations.

Figure 8.4: Goal-Setting Conversations

Teacher-Centered Conversation Level D	Learner-Centered Conversation Level D
"I noticed that you slowed down or stopped to figure out a lot of words in this book. When you stop so many times it makes it hard to remember what you're reading and really enjoy the book. Many of these words are 'sight' words that you can learn to recognize. *I am going to practice these three words with you until you can recognize them when you read. This is going to make it easier to read and enjoy books like the one we just read."*	*It seems like you're having a hard time talking about what you just read. Was there anything that made it difficult for you to understand and enjoy this book?* (student realizes he had to stop frequently to problem solve words) *Okay, so you say there were a lot of words you needed to slow down to figure out. Can you show me some examples?* *Many of these words are going to be in the books you read. You are using strategies to figure out these words, but if you can read them quickly, it will make it easier to pay attention to what the author is telling you. Do you want to work on learning some of these words so you don't have to stop and figure them out?* (student agrees to this goal) *Great! When you recognize "sight" words, you can read with less work and focus on what the words on the page are telling you. Let's pick three of these words to practice writing and finding in books. We will check back in a week to see if you can read them quickly in a new book. Recognizing words like these is going to help you learn more about your favorite topic: snakes!"* With practice, students can begin to select goals based on your feedback. *We talked about a few goals you could work on: checking for sight words, using first and last sounds, and checking for clues in illustrations. You can work on all of these, but I would like for you to choose one goal to focus on and practice right now.*

Practice the skill or strategy in the book together. They need a reminder of their goal. You might put a star by their goal on a tool like the Primary Reading Progression or have them dictate or write their goal in a journal or on a sticky note.

- *I am going to work on using the first and last sounds to figure out words I don't know yet.*

- *I am describing the characters and setting when I retell the beginning of a story. When I read the beginning of a story, I look for clues in the pictures and words to answer, "Who is this about?" and "When and where is this happening?"*

- *I am working on understanding how characters change and why they do the things they do. I am using the pictures and what I know about people to make inferences about how characters feel.*

Self-Monitor and Reflect

Revision in reading is often simply rereading with a new awareness. Before the end of first grade, students need to be recognizing and correcting their errors smoothly and independently to maintain meaning. Every time a reader slows down, stops, or rereads when they realize something is not right is evidence of self-monitoring. Each time they try again is an example of revision. Identify and celebrate these moments with students and encourage them to recognize how often they check themselves.

Your feedback and coaching are key to students' progress, but eventually they need to be successful without you. Now that they know what to work on, the conversation shifts to how they can monitor their own progress. Most students need a visual reminder, and the Primary Reading Progression is perfect for the job. Develop the routine that each child looks at her goal to establish a purpose before she reads and stops periodically during and after reading to think about how she used the skills and strategies she is practicing. You can model the process with classwide goals in shared reading. However, students really make the connection to independent practice during guided reading and conferences, when you work together to find specific examples of these skills in their reading and discussion.

Igniting an Eternal Flame

You are like the magic mirror from *Snow White and the Seven Dwarfs*: both reflecting the student in front of you and sharing a glimpse of what lies beyond. One year a language learner, relatively new to the country, left me two sticky notes. The first read, "You always see me." And the second, "I love you." Those messages have stayed with me for over a decade and serve as a reminder that relationships are at the heart of all learning. She trusted me because I saw her as a person and she was inspired by what I believed she could do. Students need to know that we "see" them before they are ready to receive our feedback. When we reflect back what we see in students, we help them form ideas about themselves as learners. We extend these ideas of self by showing them what is possible and describing a clear path to success. Each conversation with our primary readers provides an opportunity to build trust and strengthen relationships. Strong relationships position teachers as partners with students, ready to offer support, guidance, and an ear to listen.

Primary teachers spark the foundation for all future learning. #PeerPower lies in goal setting and reflection. When you ensure your students are clear on the criteria of reading and know how to set and monitor goals along a progression, you provide the tools for students to *see* themselves as learners. Their self-reflection leads to success and their success builds confidence. That confidence spreads throughout their lives and impacts everyone around them. They are the spark, but you are the flint. It's time to ignite an assessment revolution!

Guiding Questions:

- How would learning be different in your class, school, or system if all of your primary students were setting and monitoring goals?

- When you ask students what they are learning or working on during literacy, what do they say?

- What is your next step for clarity with reading behaviors?

- What is one thing you can do this week to engage students in setting and monitoring goals?

- Are there barriers to you getting started? Who can help you find a way to success?

Connect with Isaac on Twitter @isaacjwells

Chapter 9

The Anthem of Empowerment in Grades 3–5

Sarah Stevens

"Individual commitment to a group effort-that is what makes a team work, a company work, a society work, a civilization work."

–Vince Lombardi

SPEND 30 MINUTES WITH A preteen and their mobile device and I bet you will endure having to watch a young YouTube star "unboxing" the latest and greatest toy or product, giving a review on a trending topic, or providing real-time gaming commentary. Why have these YouTubers become huge sensations and even millionaires seemingly overnight? Their audience, children ages 8–12, love the unscripted, unrefined, authentic content they are delivering. Why should this matter to us educators, and how does it translate to success in literacy?

This generation of students is shaping up to be pragmatic and intentional with its decisions and interactions. These digital natives have not seen a world without technology to communicate; it is just the way they connect and learn. They crave open-ended conversation, purposeful interaction, and meaningful relationships. They crave to be a part of something, to have a sense of belonging and to have status among their peers. Yet put these same students in the classroom and sometimes they lose interest, tune out, and shut down. You can almost hear the lyrics of the famous Twisted Sister song playing in their head, *"Oh, we're not gonna take it. No, we ain't gonna take it. We're not gonna take it anymore. We've got the right to choose it, there ain't no way we'll lose it. This is our life. This is our song."* #PeerPower Revolutionaries don't have time to rest on their laurels and wait for others to change the system. True revolutionaries have to act now! We have to give students an authentic voice in their learning. We have to give our students the tools to write their own song.

The Core Collaborative Learning Network partners with teams of educators globally to strengthen student peer and self-assessment. The first thing we notice is that most educators start out with a resounding enthusiasm for getting started, but then reality sets in. They hesitate to launch the process, they panic about falling behind in their pacing, they worry about the time it takes to get high-quality peer-to-peer feedback, and they worry about the students not taking it seriously. If we have teachers excited about empowering students *and* we have loads of research to back up the power of this process *and* we have students who are motivated by open-ended conversation, purposeful interaction, and meaningful relationships . . . what exactly is the disconnect?

Current school systems are set up to reward compliance over empowerment. Does our current paradigm give students opportunities to show what they know? Is it possible we have scaffolded the instruction so much that there is no way for students to gain autonomy? Schools and systems nationally have put extensive effort on focused interventions and multitiered systems of support that require drill and kill while failing to take the time to strengthen core reading and writing instruction. This type of "lockstep learning," in which learners are doing the same thing at the same time—in the same way and are all expected to achieve roughly the same results—has stifled our students' ability to become independent (Farquharson, 2011). No wonder students are shutting down! In creating complex tiers of support, we have actually robbed ourselves of the needed time for strong core instruction and inquiry. When we strip away the time for students to collaborate, how are they supposed to get to know themselves as learners? We must empower students to ask and answer these critical questions:

- What am I learning?

- Why am I learning it?

- How do I know I will be successful?

- How will I achieve my goal?

- What's my next step?

Students need time to question, discuss, make mistakes, and try, try again. We have lost sight that learning *can* be unscripted, unrefined, and is most authentic when done *in partnership with* students and not *to* students.

The Power Is in the Partnership

Let's begin with the end in mind. If we want to inspire students in their intermediate years, then one main goal is to help them strengthen their reading identity. These students are at a critical place with literacy where they need to build momentum. They do this by developing skills and gaining strategies to make meaning of complex text and topics that interest them. The focus must shift from learning to read words to reading for deeper meaning and purpose. Making this shift means nurturing a classroom culture marked by strong relational trust and high expectations. Students have to feel safe to make mistakes, take risks, and know that failure is part of learning.

#PeerPower Revolutionaries know this type of learning is cultivated with students through the self- and peer assessment process. "When teachers join forces with their students in the formative assessment process, their partnership generates powerful learning outcomes. Teachers become more effective, students become actively engaged, and they both become intentional learners" (Moss & Brookhart, 2010). Revolutionaries model how to use essential skills and strategies for deeper comprehension that will help them be more fluent critical readers and writers. We emphasize the importance of being strong communicators who have something to say and the skills to back it up! Ultimately, we gradually release students to be responsible for their own meaning making. They are given the power to make strategy choices on their own. They have to make decisions about what to do when meaning breaks down; they must become strategically aware. Engaging students as partners in their learning gives them more authentic experiences with assessment because we are humanizing the learning experience; this will naturally increase a sense of community and collectively engage students in the construction of meaning (Schmidt, 2017). When students can connect socially with their peers and teacher to discuss learning that means something to them, the result will be an unstoppable forward motion of being in harmony for learning.

Clear Pathways for Student Ownership

Ensuring that students stay on a path to mastery with unscripted, authentic learning requires us to establish clarity on what students should be making sense of while reading. Figure 9.1 gives a snapshot of typical learning goals found nationally in literacy standards for students in Grades 3–5.

Figure 9.1: Typical Learning Goals for Literacy in Grades 3–5

Fiction	Nonfiction
Plot & Setting: Retell important events to identify conflict and resolution, rising action and falling action; visualize setting (time and place), synthesize cause and effect relationships	**Main Idea:** Synthesize and infer the main idea(s) from sections, paragraphs and/or the entire text.
Character: Study major and minor characters by inferring or interpreting and analyzing how and why characters change; explore the relationships between characters, understand character motivation and point of view	**Key Details:** Determine important details that support the main idea from sections, paragraphs, or the entire text

Fiction	Nonfiction
Vocabulary and Figurative Language: Monitor for meaning and use context clues to determine unknown words; explore and understand author's use of figurative language	**Vocabulary:** Monitor for meaning and use text features and context clues to determine the meaning of unknown words
Inferencing: Connect ideas from across a text or making meaning without directly reading text	**Text Features/Text Structure:** Synthesize information from text features to support thinking; identify the structure(s) of text to aid in comprehension
Themes & Ideas: Interpret a story by naming life lesson(s) or theme(s), interpret social issues, identify and interpret symbolism	**Researching Across Texts:** Analyze how two or more texts address similar topics in order to build credible knowledge about a topic

Source: Adapted from *The Reading Strategies Book*, Serravallo, 2015.

From these goals or standards, we can look at how learning progresses from one grade level to the next, since most classrooms have students that read below grade level, on grade level, and above grade level. Unpacking standards to discover a learning progression supports teacher teams in making better-informed instructional decisions by creating clear markers of success. However, since standards aren't meant to be taught in isolation, integrating key learning targets from multiple standards is crucial to reveal the relationship between the standards and the complexity of text. For example, standards regarding the story elements and inference must be integrated with a standard that focuses on determining universal theme in text. For this reason, classrooms can use a tool called a continuum. Notice how the statements on the example continuum (Figure 9.2) integrates success criteria from multiple standards to create a K–5 reading focus around universal theme. For example, students may explain how a character's feelings or motivation convey the theme or how the character's point of view affects how he or she responds to a problem or event as another clue to determine universal theme. Continuums break this complex learning into manageable steps and makes the invisible, visible.

Figure 9.2: Theme Continuum

The Core Collaborative

K–1	2	3	4	5
I can talk about what lesson the characters learn by:	I can infer the central message, lesson, or moral by:	I can infer the central message, lesson, or moral (theme) by:	I can infer the theme of the text by:	I can infer the theme of the text by:
Using pictures to understand the main problem in the story	Demonstrating the criteria from the previous step	Demonstrating the criteria from the previous steps	Demonstrating the criteria from the previous steps	Demonstrating the criteria from the previous steps
Describing the main problem and how it helps me talk about the lesson	Tracking details from the story elements that best convey the lesson	Discussing what lessons the story teaches about life	Explaining why themes are universal	Discussing multiple themes in stories and details that support them
Using clues from what the characters say and do to help me explain the lesson	Using evidence from my retelling to support my thinking	Using details from my summary to support my ideas about the theme	Explaining how characters' thoughts support the overall theme	Ranking which themes are more dominant based on the strength of the evidence
Identifying words the author uses to describe characters' feelings throughout the story	Describing and discussing patterns across texts with similar themes (e.g., different versions of the same fairy tale)	Explaining how characters' traits, motivations, and feelings convey the theme	Explaining how the perspective or point of view of the story conveys the theme	Finding details about a character's struggle(s) that convey the theme
Explaining how characters change and how that helps me describe the lesson		Identifying dynamic characters and explaining how they convey the theme	Discussing how the setting conveys the theme	Paying attention to figurative language and what insights it offers into the plot, characters, and theme
		Using textual evidence to discuss how the same author conveys themes in different stories	Tracking evidence from the plot that conveys the theme	Discussing how different perspectives of points of view can influence the theme
			Supporting my ideas about the overall theme by finding a pattern across details (at least three)	Making generalizations about how authors in the same genre illustrate themes
			Discussing how different authors convey themes across stories	

Source: Bloomberg, Stevens, & Mascorro (2017), *The Empowered Learner: Student-Centered Assessment Toolkit.*

Note: Grade-level labels have been added to this figure for emphasis of the progressoin of learning required. Oftentimes, classrooms use colors, icons, or emojis to mark the various levels when working with students.

Teachers can use the continuum to spark a text-based debate; students can place their *"theme"* reading responses on the continuum and engage in rigorous debate; they can give each other feedback using evidence from the text to support their point of view. Using this tool will help students internalize the criteria for success on the continuum. This collaborative learning experience can be done as a class during close reading, in book clubs, during guided reading or with a partner. With this increased clarity around what quality work looks like, students will begin to orchestrate their journey to independence. Continuums can be developed for all major literacy goals in Grades 3–5 to create a clear pathway for students when learning new concepts and skills.

Designing and Co-Constructing Transferable Tasks

Formative tasks in reading can be designed to transfer across texts. In other words, teams can create a general rubric or checklist that can be used with multiple stories and/or novels. Transfer of learning is the influence of prior learning on performance in a new situation. If we did not transfer some of our skills and knowledge from prior learning, then each new learning situation would start from scratch (Clark, 2011). Creating transferable tasks allow students to transfer the learning from one text to another. This transfer helps students to deepen their understanding of the characteristics of text.

The student responses aligned to the rubrics give teacher teams concrete evidence and feedback to ensure that students are making progress. #PeerPower Revolutionaries ask questions like, "Are students getting a chance to practice skills and develop deeper understanding of the concepts across units? Are they strengthening their understanding of the relationship between the standards?" Learning happens by practicing a new skill across different contexts (different stories). Formative, transferable tasks can be used multiple times throughout the year to give students multiple opportunities to practice and multiple opportunities to self- and peer assess to set goals. Repeating the task across units also provides students an opportunity to apply what they know to more complex texts as their reading level increases throughout the year.

When designing transferable tasks in partnership with students, it is vital that students are engaged in the co-construction process because it is a powerful way to give students the autonomy they desire. Co-construction is effective because the language used in the self- and peer assessment process is student friendly and makes it easier for students to give specific, descriptive feedback to each other and to identify concrete next steps to set individual goals. A strategy for co-constructing criteria, suggested by ReadWriteThink.org, is called "Nameless Voice." Nameless Voice asks students to anonymously submit sample work to share with the class. The student work can be projected and used as models to define criteria with students. Partners explore and discuss what elements of the work sample was effective or high quality. Nameless Voice concludes by asking students to write or discuss how the product analyzed is similar or different to their current work.

Asking students to reflect on their work gives us a glimpse of how students are comprehending the criteria for success. For example, if students were making a claim about universal theme in a short story and supporting it with evidence from the text in the form of a quick write, the final co-constructed success criteria might look like what is outlined in the *universal theme success criteria* in Figure 9.3

Figure 9.3: Transferable Task – Universal Theme Quick Write Success Criteria

Remember to:
- Make a claim about the universal theme
  - Theme must be (universal) found in multiple texts
  - Clues for theme:
    » think about the lesson the character learned
    » pay attention to the conflict
    » setting may be integral to theme
    » pay attention to symbols that expose the theme

- Provide evidence from the text to support the claim
  - At least 3 examples from the text
  - Evidence comes from the beginning, middle, and end of the story
    » Evidence must show a pattern that connects to the theme
    » Possible text evidence: character, setting, plot
- Explain how the text evidence selected supports the theme
  - "This evidence illustrates_____."
  - "This evidence reveals_____."

Advanced:
- All the criteria from above *plus* write a brief paragraph making connections to another text with a similar theme

Transferable tasks can be designed to align with the criteria for success for any of the three-five literacy goals outlined in Figure 9.1. For example, a teacher could design a task for understanding perspective and point of view and apply that task to multiple stories. In addition, the teacher could guide students in co-constructing success criteria for a summary that could be used across stories. There are more examples of transferable tasks on www.PeerPowerRevolution. com. Transferable tasks allow kids to practice across units of study for standards that take a lot of time to master. Co-constructing the success criteria for these tasks is crucial if we want students to own and *transfer* their learning.

Going Public With Goal Setting

To make literacy purposeful, students should have the opportunity to go public with their work to receive feedback and make their goals known. Giving students a voice in how they demonstrate their learning to an authentic audience sends the message that feedback and practice are more important than a final grade! Classrooms will create a trifecta for ownership when students can receive feedback through peer assessment, self-reflect to set goals, and determine next steps for mastery.

In order to obtain mastery, students engage in goal-setting rituals daily and/ or weekly. "Students' goals and next steps need to adjust to accommodate the dynamic nature of their lives and development as readers. Therefore, students periodically need to reflect on their performance, celebrate accomplishments, add new goals as new skills develop, and assess the hopes, expectations, and fears for their possible selves" (Gibbs & Reed, 2018). Figure 9.4 illustrates strategies for promoting growth through goal setting.

Figure 9.4: Strategies for Promoting Growth Through Goal Setting

- **Modeling:** Teachers can be vulnerable by discussing situations where they faced a personal challenge. Teachers can describe how they will set their goals using think aloud.

- **Success Stories:** Have veteran students share examples where academic goal setting has enabled them to achieve success.

- **Video:** Observe a student negotiating and setting learning goals in partnership with their teacher. Debrief the video as a group to share best practice.

- **Choice:** Give students a choice on their learning goal. This increases autonomy which increases motivation.

- **Examples:** Use student samples of high-quality goals so students have a clear picture of the target.

- **Mastery Experiences:** Provide students with opportunities for early success through low-stakes targeted goal setting to increase their sense of competence.

There are many factors that influence the effectiveness of students' goals. Oftentimes students get stuck at the goal-setting stage. They could be overwhelmed with the amount of work left to do or simply not know what it sounds like to create a strong goal in a given time frame. Studies (Ferguson & Shelton, 2010) have documented that individuals that write down clearly defined goals are more likely to succeed than those who have vague goals (e.g., "I will work on analyzing how key details help me identify the universal theme by annotating the text vs I need to determine key details"). Since the formative tasks are transferable, students will have ample time to master their goals because tasks can be applied a large variety of texts. Fundamentally, students need to be taught how to set and monitor personal learning goals. When students set ambitious goals, learn how to monitor them, and succeed, they realize that they have the power to learn by themselves.

Going Off Script

#PeerPower Revolutionaries will have students changing their tune when we can give them a purpose for being good readers and writers, the autonomy to learn unscripted, and the skills and strategies for mastery. From the dull, repetitive sounds of students doing work in isolation to the vibrant notes and melodies that come with collaboration, students can write their own song when we give them the opportunity to engage authentically. Let's show them what we can create together! Let's inspire this generation by encouraging them to discover what's possible. #PeerPower Revolutionaries know we can't let them down.

Peer Power Voices From the Field

At PS 20 in Staten Island, New York, fifth-grade co-teachers Nicole Mancusi and Stephanie Poggi use a "theme" rubric that is aligned to a standard based progression so students take ownership of the success criteria through self- and peer assessment. After students self-assess on the rubric, they give it to a peer for a second review of their work against the criteria. To go a step further, students use a cloud-based platform to capture their self-assessment and reflect on the strategy used. Students even have the opportunity to reflect on how they felt during the task.

Figure 9.5: Example of a Universal Theme Rubric

👍	👍👍	👍👍👍
• I can recount a story in sequential order using • transition words such as *first, next, then,* and *finally.* • I can determine the central message, lesson, or moral of a story. • I can locate key details or main events in a story. • I can use key details to explain the lesson, central message, or moral of a story.	• I can determine the theme of a story, drama, or poem. • I can paraphrase or cite three to five key details from a story that best illustrate the theme. • I can provide an accurate summary of a story, drama, or poem that identifies the main characters, the setting, the problem and resolution, and the theme, including three to five key details and/or characters' actions that best support the theme.	• I can determine the theme in a story, drama, or poem. • I can paraphrase or cite three to five key details that best illustrate the theme, including how characters in a text respond to challenges and how the speaker in a poem reflects on a topic. • I can analyze how a character's response to problems affect the theme. • I can analyze how a speaker's attitude or feelings toward a subject are reflected in an author's writing or choice of words. • I can provide a summary of a text that is distinct from personal opinions or judgments and that identifies the main characters, the setting, the problem and resolution, and the theme, including three to five key details that best support the theme.

We interviewed Lindsay, one of the students in Mancusi and Poggi's class, about her experience with self- and peer assessment using her Universal Theme rubric. Lindsay also provided insight into why she likes to receive feedback from a peer and then reflect and set a goal on the cloud platform.

Interviewer: "Tell me what you are working on here."

Lindsay: "We are working on theme. So, we have been reading this book, named *Heart and Soul*. And in the chapter that we read we had to find out what the author was telling us, like the lesson they were trying to teach us, and I did this; I said 'Never give up' because in my chapter they never gave up. They were always strong even though there were rough times and they didn't want them there."

Interviewer: "Cool! So, after you wrote your paper, tell me what this post it is about."

Lindsay: "This sticky note is where I write where I think I fell in the progression and then the partner that you are working with writes on your sticky note and says whether they agree with you or not. They read your writing then go to the progression and see if you did the level that you said you wanted to fall into."

Interviewer: "Awesome. Do you like that process of doing it yourself, then doing it with your partner?"

Lindsay: "Yes, 'cause let's say you fell here, your partner tells you what you need to do to get to the next level and I always want to succeed and move up."

Interviewer: "That's great. Can you tell me what you are putting into the platform?"

Lindsay: "This is where you keep your score. Like over here I wrote what did I get and how I identified theme. I found the lesson that the author wanted to show us, 'never give up.' And I found details that supported the theme I chose."

Interviewer: "Does using this system work well for you?"

Lindsay: "Yes. I like it because you get to pick your own score and explain the strategies and it has emojis where you can say how you feel about it."

Interviewer: "Do you like those?"

Lindsay: "Uh huh. 'Cause when you put it there . . . they [teachers] know how you are feeling about it."

Clearly, the climate of revision and goal setting has enhanced student ownership. Students feel it is safe to be authentic in their responses about their own progress and value feedback from others. They are strategically aware and can take on more responsibility in conducting their next steps.

Guiding Questions:

- Do we have clarity with our focus standards?

- Are we co-constructing formative tools and rubrics in partnership with the students?

- What does unscripted learning look like in our classroom(s)?

- How do students currently share their voice?

- In what ways do we show we trust students to take the reins and make personal choices for their learning?

Connect with Sarah on Twitter @stevens3

Explore more Chapter 9 #PeerPower tools at:

www.PeerPowerRevolution.com

Chapter 10

Learning to Learn With Students for Effective Collaborative Conversations

Lisa Cebelak

"You always have two choices: your commitment versus your fear."

–Sammy Davis, Jr.

HAVE YOU EVER HAD *THAT* class—the class that happens to be your largest class with the chattiest students and somehow manages to be right after lunch? You know, the class that you feel is almost out of your control. The class the principal just happens to suddenly pop in and do an informal observation. *That* class. My first of year of teaching I had *that* class and basically waited out the school year thinking, "Well, that was a fluke. That will never happen again." OK. Stop laughing. I said I was a new teacher! I eventually learned that most secondary teachers have a class like the one I am describing. And when I realized that every semester or year or so I would have *that* class, I think I wept. OK, between you and me, I bawled and panicked. I feared that students in *that* class would revolt and I would never gain back control much less teach them anything. Funny, in the end, the students taught me.

As a newbie, I kept thinking I had a discipline issue with *that* class. My other classes were quiet, worked together in groups, and listened attentively. Or so I thought. It seemed so from afar, but if you looked up close and personal, the students just were compliant. But, back to *that* class. The one I cried about. I tackled *that* class by trying to exert more control. The more rules I created, the more rules the students broke. The more I tried to take charge, the more aggressive my students became. I finally "learned" to keep the class so busy with unnecessary work that they had to hurry to keep up, and I became exhausted working so hard to stay a step ahead of them. I wasn't teaching, I was keeping them quiet and busy. They were not learning, they were just doing enough to stay out of trouble. I had the wrong the goal, and it had no educational value. And I wept.

It was then I decided I had to face my fear. I wish I could say I let go of my fear right away, but it took a few years. Sorry, students. You all deserved so much better. I did get better, and the drive to be a committed teacher for *all* students (even the ones that seemed to be in *that* class) won out. But it was the road less traveled for me.

Eventually I opened up and asked for help within my department. This simple task of asking for help and sharing my story with my colleagues was a monumental deal for me. It meant I had to face my fear of others knowing that I was not a great teacher and had no idea what to do. My anxiety level dropped immediately when my colleagues shared similar stories! I learned that most teachers always had *that* class at some point. And together we worked on how to change the situation so that even *that* class was allowed and even encouraged to have collaborative conversations. I learned my goal should not have been, "I will be in complete charge," but rather, "I will have students talk and engage in conversations that spark their learning!" In other words, I had to trust my students. They wanted to talk! They needed to collaborate! And I was shutting them down like it was going out of style. I realized that I didn't have a classroom management issue at all. Rather, I had a lack of preparation. I didn't know how to lesson plan for student-centered learning. I didn't have teacher clarity, and I certainly didn't know how to teach how to have collaborative conversations. I just expected them to "do." And frankly, I was scared. I was afraid to give up control. What if I let my students collaborate only to lose control of my classroom? Ah, the fear of looking like I didn't know what I was doing—the point here being that I already didn't know what I was doing and that wasn't working either. So, I let go. And, with the help of my English department, we decided to conquer not only my class, but all of our classes. We had never focused deeply on collaborative conversations before. But we knew collectively we needed to start here before we could expect a high level of engaging conversations that had to do with topics and texts we are teaching.

As a team, we decided to go back to the beginning. In other words, what did the standards (if anything) say about collaborative conversations? We found what we needed by researching the Common Core English Language Arts and Literacy Standards for ninth through 10th grades. We focused on Speaking and Listening standard one and unpacked it to learn what skills and concepts needed to be taught when teaching collaborative conversations. Big "a-ha" for me. I realized I had to teach my students *how* to have collaborative conversations—not just expect them to talk on topic or text in sort of orderly fashion with any clarity. Unpacking the standard gave us clarity, and we all felt we had a starting point.

After unpacking our grade band, my team looked at the expectations for middle school (below our grade levels) and what the added complexity for conversations would be in the upper grade levels (11th–12th grade band). Looking at the learning progression within this standard allowed us to move student groups or even classes (yes, like *that* class), according to where they were within the learning progression of collaborative conversations.

Let me pause for a minute here. Not every state has the Common Core, but every state has standards or process standards that reference speaking and listening. For example, in Texas, educators have Texas Essential Knowledge and Skills (TEKS). TEKS addresses speaking and listening and even combine these skills in a teamwork setting. The point being, starting with your standards gives you the baseline needed to jump from.

After we, the English Language Arts Department team, had clarity around speaking and listening in collaborative groups, we knew we had to work to get student clarity. We continued to use the standard(s) to guide us by working to create a rubric for students that not only contained success criteria for collaborative conversations but as a tool for students to use as a checklist for themselves. We were new at this and decided to write "I can" statements because that is what was somewhat familiar in the literature at the time. Our stab at success criteria looked something like this:

- I can come to a discussion prepared with notes on the topic or text assigned.

- I can initiate a conversation effectively by asking an open-ended question.

- I can state my ideas clearly by organizing my points/thoughts ahead of time.

- I can express my ideas persuasively by referring to evidence from texts or research.

- I can propel the conversation by posing questions or responding to questions that relate to broader themes or larger ideas.

- I can actively work to incorporate others into the conversation.

- I can ask for clarity of ideas presented.

- I can verify ideas.

- I can challenge ideas presented.

- I can respond to diverse perspectives and make new connections in light of evidence and reasoning presented.

- I can summarize points of agreement and disagreement.

We used the above points as success criteria for collaborative conversations and used category levels of "met," "progressing," and "not met." We later learned from our students that they struggled with understanding these "levels" and later we clarified the levels as repeated evidence/reoccurring; evidence of attempt, at least once; and no evidence, respectively.

So this was our first round. We all used the rubrics in our classrooms and followed up in our team meetings to check in with each other to discussed how it was going. It was going OK for some of us, not so well with others. It did seem to have some impact with students but not enough. We felt we were on the right track, but something was missing. The students seemed to try to follow the rubric more out of compliance.

One day, in frustration, I shared with *that* class that they weren't taking it seriously. I said something like, "don't you know that these are skills you need? Don't know you know that this is a standard that must be taught?" One student answered me. He said simply, "no." I realized in that moment that the students did not know where the success criteria for collaborative conversations was coming from. They didn't relate to it because we had no conversation around it. I asked for more student feedback that day. And boy, did I get it! I learned that some students didn't understand what some of the statements meant. "What does 'I can validate an idea' even mean?" Huh. "Don't you know that teenagers hate 'I can statements'? It makes us feel like we are in elementary school!" Oh. "Why can't we just talk and do our own thing?" Well. I was starting to finally get the picture. And, in that moment, I let go of my fear of rebellion and started to trust that my students could help me figure this out. I was determined to stay committed. I was ready the next day.

My next class period I abandoned my lesson plan and decided to present a few questions to the class:

- Why should we collaborate with our peers in school?
- How should we collaborate with others in and out of the classroom for effective discussion to occur?
- Does being involved in collaborative conversations help me or hurt me in the long run?

The students walked into class and saw these questions on the board. I asked, "Well, what do you think?" And that is where I started. I didn't give any answers, and I heard all kinds of thoughts. When I heard a student say, "I thought you said you had to teach this . . ." I jumped in. I replied I did. And I showed them the speaking and listening standard. I unpacked it with the class. And I asked for their thoughts. They said they better understood the rubric now, but I could tell they didn't place much value in the standards. I put that rubric aside and instead kept the focus on collaborative conversations. We discussed where we felt we had effective conversations in the past and with whom. I didn't realize it at the time, but my students and I were becoming #PeerPower Revolutionaries and it was exciting!

I shared video examples of effective conversations and non-examples. Although I could have found classroom examples on different educational online sites, I shared cable news examples instead. I could readily find examples of panels of three to six people discussing the politics of the day. I selected a few video clips where everyone on the panel showed respect, listened to each other, and asked good follow-up questions. I then shared non-examples by showing other panels that didn't listen and visibly showed disgust on their faces, where they talked over each other by constant interruption and even yelled. After sharing the examples and non-examples, I asked the class which segments were more effective and why. This gave them so much to pull from! Together, with my students leading the way, we brainstormed a list of what was needed for effective conversations. I probably had listed over 30 items on the board. Next, we grouped items together according to categories. We discussed what was important for this class, crossed some items out, and refined the list. This time, instead of presenting success criteria to the class, we co-constructed it. And, we got rid of the "I can statements" and here is what we ended up with:

Safe Environment:
- Nonjudgmental
- Be vulnerable (willing to take risks)
- Encourage others to join in the conversation
- Thank others for encouraging words

Engaged Body Language:

- Eye contact with who is talking and group

- Face peer or peers and lean in

- Nod, smile, or show you are listening with other kind gestures

Active Listener:

- Echo a question (repeat or paraphrase as needed)

- Ask for clarity when needed

- Do not interrupt

Active Participant:

- Express ideas clearly and persuasively

- Build on someone else's ideas with a question or comment

- Summarize points of agreement and disagreement

Reflection of Learning:

- Respond to diverse perspectives (without arguing)

- Make new connections in light of evidence and reasoning presented and adjust viewpoint accordingly

- Make connections to themes and ideas presented to the real world (outside of the classroom)

As you can see, this list of criteria looks a little different from the original (teacher-created) rubric, and not everything here is part of the standard. But the standard still shines through, with student flavor and relevance, and with items that are needed in real life. So with this co-constructed criteria we moved forward not only was this criteria more meaningful to students, but they better understood the expectations and far exceeded my expectations. I now had teacher clarity and my class had student clarity—exactly what was missing all along. I had finally faced my fear of losing control, only to be surprised with a much better outcome. Without knowing it, we had become #PeerPower Revolutionaries.

That first year was a learning curve. At first the entire rubric was overwhelming and so we focused on certain parts of the rubric, like just "Engaged Listener." I eventually had students self-select what part of the rubric they wanted to work on and set personal learning goals. Toward the end of the year, students were able to use the success criteria to peer assess one another. I would have one student "shadow" another when in a collaborative conversation. That student would focus only on the select student, stand or sit right behind them, and score them on the rubric during the collaborative conversation. Afterward, the student would review the rubric with the student and provide feedback.

The second year, I learned to how to provide feedback on student feedback. This was key! Once I paid more attention to the peer feedback and providing feedback on that, students really understood how to be more specific with their peer feedback and ultimately produced better work because they had internalized the success criteria at a much deeper level. At the secondary level, I found the Ladder of Feedback works best. Students grew in their learning at a rapid pace once this level of feedback was applied. Through this process I learned to focus much more on the self- and peer-assessment process than the actual assessment itself. The time spent on the formative process and honing in on different types of feedback was where I saw students taking charge of their learning as if they didn't even need me anymore! My fear of pushing students to take ownership of their learning faded away, and my commitment only grew stronger as I witnessed student growth at a rapid pace!

I learned a lot during that time. I learned that students needed to understand the *why* before the *what*. And that together, teacher and students, we could work towards the *how*. By co-constructing success criteria, the clarity had by all is what made the biggest difference.

Moving forward, I felt the freedom to try new things. I also ditched a few things and revised along the way. It was fun. I was engaged because my students were engaged. And they were talking and communicating. They were on topic and on task. I wasn't afraid anymore. I was ready to say "Well, that didn't work!" and look stupid at times. I remember thinking *that* class would take over my room and I would lose control. *That* class was the class that I almost gave up on. But it was *that* class that taught *me* what could really happen once I let go and let them lead.

Allowing students to have a voice and make choices allowed them to understand the relevance and real-world application. Student growth was off the charts, but it took me taking that path less traveled. My commitment to do better was stronger than my fear. That path less traveled was a mucky one and I got stuck a few times along the way, but my students were there to pull me up and walk with me on this journey. I learned how to learn with my students, instead of blindly leading the way.

Guiding Questions:

- How do you amplify student voice in your classroom?

- What are some methods to get students to take ownership of the success criteria?

- How are students engaging in collaborative conversations in your classroom? Are they effective conversations? How do you provide feedback?

- How can using examples and non-examples help to define student clarity?

- How can you build collective efficiency with other educators within your discipline?

Connect with Lisa on Twitter @LisaCebelak

Chapter 11

The Case for Problem Solving

Lori Cook

"Many of life's failures are people who did not realize how close they were to success when they gave up."

—Thomas Edison

TRADITIONALLY, MATH EDUCATION HAS FOCUSED on "getting the right answer," and getting it the fastest. Students who took a little longer to work out the problem were viewed as struggling and may not have been given the chance to be successful. I have heard from many teachers that they were encouraged not to take higher levels of mathematics courses because they struggled to grasp math concepts exactly as they were taught, or it took them longer to solve a problem, or they were a girl. Thankfully, the last decade has brought about changes in math education. It is exciting to be part of a "math revolution" (Boaler, 2016) that is making its way across the country.

The Standards for Mathematical Practice (Common Core State Standards [CCSS], 2010) and the Mathematical Process Standards (Texas Education Agency, 2012) have sparked this revolution and are challenging many teachers' and students' approaches to learning math. For students to truly understand math they must be given the opportunity to wrestle with math concepts, connect the new learning to previous learning, and formulate their understanding of the big ideas (National Council of Teachers of Mathematics [NCTM], 2014). In other words, they must use the practice/process standards daily to make sense of the math. These are the behaviors of good problem solvers and how we learn math (CCSS, 2012; Texas Education Agency, 2012).

Standards for Mathematical **Practice**	Mathematical **Process** Standards
1. Make sense of problems and persevere in solving them.	A. Apply mathematics to problems arising in everyday life, society, and the workplace;
2. Reason abstractly and quantitatively.	B. Use a problem-solving model that incorporates analyzing given information, formulating a plan or strategy, determining a solution, justifying the solution, and evaluating the problem-solving process and the reasonableness of the solution;
3. Construct viable arguments and critique the reasoning of others.	
4. Model with mathematics.	
5. Use appropriate tools strategically.	C. Select tools, including real objects, manipulatives, paper and pencil, and technology as appropriate, and techniques, including mental math, estimation, and number sense as appropriate, to solve problems;
6. Attend to precision.	
7. Look for and make use of structure.	
8. Look for and express regularity in repeated reasoning.	D. Communicate mathematical ideas, reasoning, and their implications using multiple representations, including symbols, diagrams, graphs, and language as appropriate;
(CCSS, 2012)	
	E. Create and use representations to organize, record, and communicate mathematical ideas;
	F. Analyze mathematical relationships to connect and communicate mathematical ideas; and
	G. Display, explain, and justify mathematical ideas and arguments using precise mathematical language in written or oral communication.
	(Texas Education Agency, 2012)

The Case for Inquiry

Many of us did not learn math through inquiry (problem solving, exploring, discovering, and conceptualizing math concepts); instead, the teacher did all of the work for us by telling us what and how to think. For many, change is scary and this new way of learning math is pushing everyone to evaluate our practices. Ultimately, math must make sense; we must stop forcing everyone to look at math through the same narrow approach of rules, tricks, and standard algorithms. Inquiry allows students the time to explore and make sense of math. Through inquiry we unlock the mathematics with the goal of building conceptual understanding so *all* students can be successful. Teachers must learn to guide inquiry and facilitate mathematical discourse. However, many teachers and students are not sure how to tackle this new challenge. They are uncomfortable with these new roles and would rather just go back to the "good old days" of direct instruction. The good news is learning through inquiry is possible! We need to focus on structures and protocols that will support students and teachers through this journey.

When students are engaged in inquiry, we should consider providing them tools to regulate their learning. Students don't understand that learning is hard work. They don't understand that being confused actually means you are learning. Countless students do not realize that struggle is normal when they are learning a new concept and they give up. Sometimes they give up just before the concept is realized, just before that "light bulb" moment. To compound the problem, other students do not realize that they should be exploring math independently and collaboratively. They are not aware that they should be looking for patterns, generalizing, discovering, and trying efficient strategies that make sense to them. When teachers integrate the mathematical practices or process standards, they bring inquiry to the forefront. When students are engaged in using the processes/practices during self- and peer assessment, these practices come to life! By integrating the practice or process standards during problem solving, students normalize struggle, create clarity around how to learn through inquiry, and open up a once-closed subject. Math comes to life!

The Power of Success Criteria

Problem Solving Rubric

	When Solving A Problem...	I Can Teach Others	I Got This	A Friend Can Help	I Need Help
UNDERSTAND	I can make sense of the problem • What is the question asking? • What are the important parts of the problem? • What questions do I have of the problem? • What is a reasonable estimate for the problem?				
PLAN	I can choose a strategy to solve the problem • What paths can I take? • What tools can I use? • What operations can I use? • What visual model can I use?				
SOLVE	I can solve with precision • Show your work. • Adjust strategy as needed. • Ask clarifying questions. • **Use at lease 2 strategies.** • Clearly organize, label, and explain your work				
CHECK	I can justify my answer • I can answer the question in a complete sentence. • Using your estimation, is your answer reasonable? How do I know? • Explain and justify both strategies using mathematical language. • What other strategies could you have used?				

I will PERSEVERE!

Sixth-Grade Problem-Solving Rubric • Park Middle School, Kennewick, Washington

Impact Teams across the country are immersing themselves in the mathematical practice/process standards with the purpose of putting students at the center. They collaborate to create success criteria for problem solving to help students regulate their learning through inquiry. At first, teacher teams think they understand the practice/process standards, but when they unpack the standards through the eyes of their students, their collective expectations change and this has a direct effect on their lessons. For example, if we jump in and save students when they are struggling or confused, how will we teach students to persevere when they get a challenging problem? Many teachers share how difficult it is for them to watch students struggle when teaching math through inquiry. However, when they dedicate their lessons to inquiry they also share that the most rewarding moments are when the students experience "Eureka" after that struggle. *Eureka* in Greek actually means "I found it!" (Eureka, 2005). James Nottingham (2015), in *The Learning Pit* video, asks the question, "Do you get that sense of Eureka if you haven't first struggled?" Our job is not to save students from the struggle but to encourage them through the struggle and allow them to make sense of the math. When students use problem-solving success criteria they remind themselves that struggle is normal and they are able to persevere.

To create buy-in with students, teachers typically co-construct problem-solving success criteria *with* their students. They co-construct success criteria after they unpack the standards within their teacher teams. By putting the students in the center of the process and allowing them to have a voice, co-constructed success criteria is more valuable to the students. It becomes something that they meaningfully use because they are the authors and it is in their language. The sixth-grade teachers at Park Middle School in Kennewick, Washington, recently co-constructed a problem-solving rubric with their students by showing a video where other students were engaging in a problem-solving lesson. After watching the video, students brainstormed a list of the characteristics and behaviors that they observed. After all of the sixth-grade classes completed their lists, the teachers met together and compiled the lists, and reconciled them with the teachers' criteria. The teachers were able to create one document that represented the student ideas and the essence of what good problem solvers do. All sixth-grade math students will ultimately use the same problem-solving rubric to monitor their work and actions. To personalize the rubric even more, the teachers asked the students to help choose emojis to represent each section of the rubric.

The Necessity of Clarity

Success Criteria		I Need Help	I Need a Little Help	I Can Do This
Think	I can read the problem 2 times.			
	I can make a movie in my mind.			
	I can act it out.			
	I can circle important information.			
Plan	I can build it.			
	I can draw it.			
	I can write an equation.			

Problem-Solving Success Criteria. Marie Crumbley, Second-Grade Teacher, PS 22, Staten Island, NY

Most students do not naturally know how to use a rubric during self- and peer assessment. This is a skill that must be taught and modeled. The teachers at PS 22 in Staten Island, New York, found that many of the students, especially those in the primary grades, were unable to engage in self-assessment due to their lack of understanding of how to regulate thinking. To help the students, teachers model and think out loud how to use the criteria to monitor their learning. In one second-grade class, students are practicing using their problem-solving criteria, together as a class, to make sense of the problem before they leave the carpet area. The teacher has created a large poster of the success criteria and walks them through each part. When needed, she models and shares how she uses the criteria and then allows the students to engage with the criteria themselves. Together, they use a class set of sticky notes and evaluate each portion of the criteria by placing a sticky note on either the "I need help," "I need a little help," or "I can do this" box. My favorite part is when the class acts out the situation they are about to explore. Students really struggle making sense of contexts, and by acting it out together they have a clearer understanding of the situation. They are able to take this understanding with them to their workstations and use it to tackle the challenge. The students continue to assess themselves and their peers throughout the rest of the lesson using the problem-solving criteria with the help of the teacher if needed.

> *"The co-construction of success criteria is what allows students to truly understand expectations and set goals with purpose and efficacy. Students feel empowered when they have the opportunity to create the plan necessary to raise their level of learning."*
>
> Melissa Brandner, Fifth-Grade Teacher
> PS 22, Staten Island, NY

In a fifth-grade class at PS 22, students use problem-solving success criteria throughout their lessons to regulate themselves as well as their work. They also use co-constructed success criteria for specific math concepts. During a recent visit, the class was exploring multiplication and division of decimals and how the operations are similar to whole numbers. Several students used their whole-number multiplication success criteria to remind themselves of the important steps when multiplying whole numbers and were looking for connections to the new concept of decimal multiplication. The teacher stopped the students in the middle of the inquiry lesson to share what they had discovered and what strategies were useful concerning the new concept. The ideas and strategies that were important to remember for decimal multiplication were added to the class success criteria poster at the front of the room. By stopping the class and sharing criteria, everyone in the class had the opportunity to pause and reflect on their work and journey through the investigation. This powerful practice engaged the students in metacognition, which has a high impact on student learning (Hattie, 2009). Also, students who might have been struggling now had another idea to consider and were engaged again. As new ideas continue to surface throughout the unit, the class will add to their co-constructed success criteria poster. Students also record the success criteria within their math notebooks, allowing them the opportunity to engage with it long after the unit is over.

The Essentials of #PeerPower

Two essential components of #PeerPower that help math come to life are feedback and goal setting (Bloomberg & Pitchford, 2017). Once students have a clear understanding of the success criteria and know where they are in their learning in relation to the criteria, students are able to create a goal to focus their journey. Once the goals are created, students intentionally focus on moving toward attainment of their goal. This is where feedback is essential. Students monitor themselves using the success criteria tied to the concept identified in their goal. The teacher and peers can help the students to regulate their progress by giving specific feedback using the success criteria as a guide. When students are engaged in inquiry, using goals and feedback to focus them, learning comes to life and is purposeful.

The teachers and students at PS 60 in Staten Island, New York, are engaging in goal-setting and with the use of effective feedback. The focus of the math goals this year is how students monitor and use the Standards for Mathematical Practice. By studying the criteria developed from the practices and reflecting on their assessments, students choose which Standard for Mathematical Practice they need to focus on. The teachers meet with the students to discuss and guide the development of the goal as well as plan how each student will accomplish their goal. All students have either a math folder or journal/notebook where their goals and plans are placed so that they can review them when necessary. Once each student has a specific goal, then meaningful feedback is provided from the teacher and peers when appropriate. The feedback, which is given in writing, is timely and specific to the student's work and criteria. This feedback is placed with the student's goals in their notebooks so that they can regularly reference it. Students are given the opportunity to self-assess themselves using the feedback provided and the criteria, allowing them the opportunity to monitor their progress toward their goal.

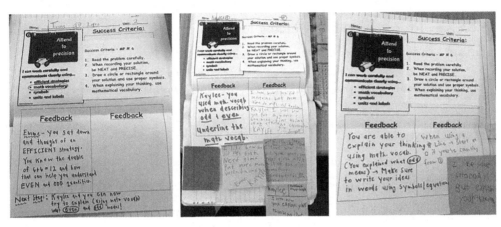

Math journals with success criteria • PS 60, Staten Island, NY

Countless teachers who have watched students give up in frustration and quit math are now watching their students engage in #PeerPower—finding success within this revolution of learning math through inquiry. Self-efficacy is growing within each student. They now realize that struggle is normal and nothing is "wrong" with them. Melissa Donath, principal at PS 22, shares, "Utilizing problem-solving as a schoolwide focus has allowed teachers to take a closer look at how we have students talk, think, and explain their

Tristan, Second-Grade Student
PS 60, Staten Island, NY

thinking about math. Incorporating success criteria with this work has also helped students understand where they need to go to persevere through problems and demonstrate their conceptual understanding. Our students now enjoy talking about math and sharing their ideas with others."

#PeerPower in math allows students the opportunity to regulate themselves and their peers by assessing, setting goals, and providing feedback. The benefits of students engaging in peer and self-assessment within the inquiry math classroom are countless. Students are reminding themselves as well as their peers that struggle is expected, multiple strategies are essential, answers should be reasonable, justification of their work confirms their solution, and that perseverance is necessary for success. All are finding learning through inquiry to be fun and exciting—and most importantly, math makes sense.

We must not give up, we might only be one step away from success!

Guiding Questions:

- Do you intentionally create lesson where students need to use the Standards for Mathematical Practice/Mathematical Process Standards? If yes, how do you do this? If not, what do you need to do to begin?

- Why are inquiry and struggle necessary when learning math? Do inquiry and struggle live within your math learning environment? What are your next steps?

- How are students monitoring their learning in your math environment?

- What tools do students need in your math environment to self and peer assess? What are your next steps?

Connect with Lori on Twitter @_lcook

Chapter 12

Yes! #PeerPower in Chemistry

Eric Bjornstad

"Success is a science; if you have the conditions, you get the result."

–Oscar Wilde

Launching In

Throughout my career as a public high school science educator, whenever I would take a moment to contemplate how to improve upon my instruction (which occurs in that small slice of time between realigning learning targets from Unit 6 and reformatting my assessments for the hundredth time—why can't I ever remember how to *unhighlight* those numbers?), I continuously found myself coming back to one question: How can I enhance the student experience of science class by making the activities and processes that occur in my classroom parallel real science practices that occur in any science-related or technical field? I've always felt that by making *the process of learning* science more relevant and applicable to my students in relation to their everyday life, I'll be able to increase their engagement—which is kind of what every teacher really hopes for by changing anything they do in the first place. After trying a number of different possible solutions (some good, some not so good; I'll leave out the exact percentages to preserve my own self-esteem), at some point a new idea occurred to me: Why not incorporate some sort of Peer Review process into my instruction? It seemed to me that Peer Review is an often-overlooked core formative practice, mainly because of the difficulty involved in implementation—can students actually give feedback in a constructive and meaningful way? Everyone knows that being a "scientist," or technically literate in any field, requires familiarity with the Peer Review process; it is, after all, the process by which most important new ideas in any science or related field come to light! At this point, the direction I would take became apparent: Due to the "real-life" relevance of Peer Review occurring in almost every area of research imaginable, I decided to explore this idea of incorporating Peer Review into my science classroom. I just had to figure out how to get my classroom version of Peer Review to work (at least somewhat) like the real version.

In order for students to have a well-rounded, real-world applicable science education while satisfying state education needs, the first challenge was to address the tricky balancing act of needing to connect real-world science skills (mainly the Peer Review process) to state standards. Many of us have discovered that there are a number of science skills reflected in practices defined by common standards, such as the Next Generation Science Standards (NGSS). Upon a careful review of the existing NGSS science practices, I decided that I would make a concerted effort to focus on several of these practices within my curriculum. There were four practices that appeared (at least in my mind) to directly mirror the current laboratory practices that I already had in place and could also serve as the backbone for the process of incorporating Peer Review into my instruction. The science practices (as defined by NGSS) that I chose to focus on were:

- **Asking Questions and Defining Problems**
- **Planning and Carrying Out Investigations**
- **Analyzing and Interpreting Data**
- **Constructing Explanations and Designing Solutions**

As I worked out exactly how I was going to incorporate core formative practices in a collaborative manner within my instruction, I also wanted to implement those that I felt would best assist students in developing the recurring skills related to learning outcomes that I had previously developed for my courses. I found firsthand that this can be a daunting task; there currently do not exist a plethora of "best practices" that teachers can rely on when creating new activities related to their content area. I was able, however, to incorporate several additional core practices within the Peer Review process, which I will expand upon as I describe the implementation further.

Particularly in terms of real-world science application, Peer Review became a perfect fit in my classroom. It expands not only the amount of feedback students receive but also the depth. I wanted my students to be more reflective, careful, and precise in creating high-quality work; incorporating Peer Review became an effective way to provide extensive feedback to each student while effectively managing the time constraints under which an educator perpetually operates. Integrating Peer Review within the context of a science course provides many benefits in terms of overall student learning: (1) a task-oriented approach to an increased focus on quality of work, (2) a method of providing students with authentic tasks on which to give and receive feedback with opportunities for revision, and (3) an increased social responsibility to peers that could ultimately assist in building the classroom community while further establishing a culture of learning. In the following paragraphs I will outline exactly how I developed a Peer Review system that is able to bring these benefits of Peer Review together with the aforementioned NGSS practices I chose to focus on.

Step 1: Clarity

The first task in my process would be to assist students with clarity of the learning outcomes that I had mapped to the NGSS Science Practices. The avenue that I chose to accomplish this task was to co-create success criteria with students that relate to those learning outcomes. I decided to launch the school year by asking students a driving question. I wanted my students to really think about the role of a scientist. This would be a question that I could return to throughout the year.

What Exactly Does a Scientist Do?

I like to start the whole process by involving my students in some precursory conversation as a class, centered around what does a researcher (scientific or otherwise) do, exactly? And why do we (or why does anyone) investigate anything? I like to put this question through the lens of something of which students have some background knowledge: maybe finding an unmarked substance in some container in the fridge and no one is around to identify what the substance is—what would you [the student] do in this situation? Responses vary (and some give you some *really* interesting insight into various dietary habits), but ultimately what the students end up doing is outlining the science practice of asking questions and defining problems. From that conversation, I try to move the discussion into consideration of a slightly more detailed question: What is data? More importantly, how does a "scientist" analyze and/or interpret data? I ask students to give some simple definitions and also use the conversation as a method of comparing data to calculations—which becomes important as the school year progresses, as the distinction between the two is usually fairly new to students. Finally, in the last part of our conversation, I bring about the final question: How does a scientist communicate his/her ideas? This discussion is where students are introduced to the process of Peer Review as well as its importance in ensuring scientific integrity within a community.

As a class, we formally began the process (in terms of actions) by completing a fairly simple lab activity, where I have students collect data in groups but submit their own lab report detailing their results. We then spent time looking at each other's work (which, unbeknownst to them, was the start of our Peer Review process) and coming up with aspects of each other's work that we, as a class, think are important and that would reflect how a scientist would communicate their results. I then use this conversation and resulting list of criteria to co-create success criteria for any lab as a class. Figure 12.1 contains an example of co-created success criteria as each role relates to a specific science practice from the NGSS, in an attempt to divide the investigation process into fairly equal roles (in terms of responsibility and work) for each student in a group. Since I intended for students to use these roles for each investigation we would complete throughout the school year, I needed to help students create roles that could vary based on group size (2–4 students) as well as the final product—which could be more quantitative or qualitative depending on the investigation.

Figure 12.1: Co-Created Success Criteria Aligned to NGSS

NGSS Science Practice	Role	Student-Created Success Criteria
Planning and Carrying Out Investigations • Ask questions that arise from careful observation of phenomena, or unexpected results, to clarify and/or seek additional information. • Analyze complex real-world problems by specifying criteria and constraints for successful solutions.	Procedurist	• Create and share Google Doc with group members. • Include given procedure and data table, or if none exist, design your own with the group. • Make sure proper procedure is followed during lab. • Submit final lab document before due date.
Analyzing and Interpreting Data • Plan and conduct an investigation individually and collaboratively to produce data to serve as the basis for evidence. • Select appropriate tools to collect, record, analyze, and evaluate data.	Data Analyst	• Measure and record all data accurately, with units, in a data table. • Complete all necessary calculations. • Calculations will include all units, labels, and are formatted correctly. • Any necessary graphs are included and formatted correctly.
Constructing Explanations and Designing Solutions • Construct and revise an explanation based on valid and reliable evidence obtained from a variety of sources • Apply scientific ideas, principles, and/or evidence to provide an explanation of phenomena and solve design problems, taking into account possible unanticipated effects.	Summarizer	• Compose a brief but in-depth summary of results. • Use data or calculations as evidence to back up results. • Make connections to class content. • Ensure summary is accurate and logical according to results.

NGSS Science Practice	Role	Student-Created Success Criteria
Asking Questions and Defining Problems • Ask questions that arise from careful observation of phenomena, or unexpected results, to clarify and/or seek additional information. • Ask questions to determine relationships, including quantitative relationships, between independent and dependent variables.	Error Analyst	• Identify error that is not human or mechanical in nature. • Explain which piece of data was affected and how it was affected. • Explain how this effect will affect the overall results.

Step 2: Designing Rubrics

To be able to implement the Peer Review process with fidelity amongst all students in multiple classes, having a well-defined rubric or rating scale is a cornerstone of the process. As a result, the next step was to develop detailed rubrics for each investigation in which students will be practicing the skills related to the learning outcomes from which their success criteria was created. Additionally, I found that creating detailed rubrics for each lab activity or investigation allowed for consistency in student expectations as well as in my evaluation of their work. I've included a sample procedure in Figure 12.2 as well as sample rating scale in Figure 12.3 to show how the previously created lab roles would be defined within a lab activity.

Figure 12.2: Sample Lab Investigation

THE ATOMIC MASS OF BEANIUM

FRONT OF WORKSHEET

A new element has been discovered and has been named Beanium. It has been found to have 3 isotopes: redium, whitium, and greenium. Your mission is to determine the average atomic mass of Beanium.

The cool thing about the atoms of Beanium is that they are large enough to see and weigh. However, if you weigh just one atom on our balances, you will have only one known digit and one uncertain digit. We want more significant figures, so we will measure the mass of a pile of atoms and calculate the average mass of one atom.

Pre-Lab Question #1: If you have a pile of 47 red isotopes, and that pile has a mass of 3.08 grams, what is the mass of each red isotope?

Pre-Lab Question #2: If you have 47 red isotopes and 202 total Beanium atoms, then what is your percent abundance of red isotopes?

Pre-Lab Question #3: What two pieces of information do you need to have about each isotope to calculate the average atomic mass? (Hint: Why do questions #1 and #2 exist?)

BACK OF WORKSHEET

DATA: Use your answer to the pre-lab questions to determine what data you need to collect about each isotope. Create a data table below to organize this data, and then collect the data you need to fill it in:

CALCULATIONS:

Use appropriate units in your work and in your answers.

1. Calculate the total number of atoms in your sample of Beanium.

2. Calculate the mass of one atom of each isotope.

   Greenium:

   Whitium:

   Redium:

3. Calculate the percent abundance of each isotope:

   Greenium:

   Whitium:

   Redium:

4. Calculate the atomic mass of Beanium:

Figure 12.3: Sample Rating Scale for Peer Review,
to Accompany Example Lab Investigation

THE ATOMIC MASS OF BEANIUM RATING SCALE						
Procedure	Numbered list with complete sentences	List not numbered or sentences incomplete	Section Missing			
Data Table	Complete with units for every measurement	Missing units and/ or values needed for calculations	Section Missing			
Calculation #1	Correct value with units, labels included	Missing units and/ or incorrectly calculated	Section Missing			
Calculation #2	Correct with units, labels included	Missing units and/ or incorrectly calculated	Section Missing			
Calculation #3	Correct with units, labels included	Missing units and/ or incorrectly calculated	Section Missing			
Calculation #4	Correct with units, labels included	Missing units and/ or incorrectly calculated	Section Missing			
Conclusion	Addresses purpose, uses results as evidence, makes connections to class content	Missing 1 criteria	Missing 2 criteria	Missing 3 criteria	Section Missing	
Error Analysis	Error is identified correctly piece of data is identified, effects of error on data identified effects of error on final results identified	Missing 1 criteria	Missing 2 criteria	Missing 3 criteria	Section Missing	

Step 3: Launching Peer Review

My next task was to institute a Peer Review process that utilized the rubric/rating scales that I created, while also allowing for revisions of the tasks. I felt it was extremely important for students to be able to revise their previous work to address specific feedback they received from their peers. I have the advantage of being able to utilize *Canvas* as a learning management system, which really helps facilitate this process since the rubrics are built into each assignment and anonymous peer reviews are an option for all assignments created in the system. Having access to a Learning Management System (LMS) no doubt makes this process streamlined, but I also believe that creative (and paper-based) solutions can be found that can be just as effective. Additionally, I believe student anonymity is important in whatever Peer Review system is created; students tend to be more critical of their peers' work when they know their constructive comments won't be traced back to the reviewer. Overall, how this process is implemented within the allotted class time may vary, but for me the main goal during Peer Review is being able to get students to identify the existence (or lack thereof) of specific criteria within their peers' work, as well as be able to communicate possible areas for improvement to their peers. Figure 12.4 contains an example of a sample task that has students use the accompanying rating scale that I developed for this assignment to give specific feedback to their peers. At first, at least in my experience, students struggle with the Peer Review process—mainly, developing their feedback. However, in my mind, that's just further evidence for why there needs to be a focus on peer feedback. In the beginning, students will need a considerable amount of critique on their feedback to help move them in the right direction.

This is where introducing students to the "Ladder of Feedback" (Figure 12.5) and frontloading the possible avenues that they could use to communicate their observations during Peer Review comes in handy. I've found that one of the most important features of combining rubrics with the "Ladder of Feedback" is their ability to bring students' understanding of Peer Review full circle.

Figure 12.5 Ladder of Feedback

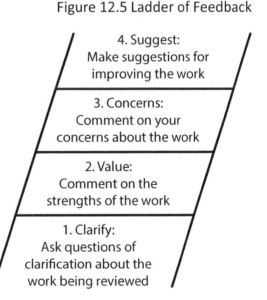

4. Suggest:
Make suggestions for improving the work

3. Concerns:
Comment on your concerns about the work

2. Value:
Comment on the strengths of the work

1. Clarify:
Ask questions of clarification about the work being reviewed

Figure 12.4: Peer Review Task

Directions: Provide one of your job-alike peers with peer reviews of their work using the correct section of this handout (see labels below). Circle the amount of points for the criteria of which you are evaluating your peers. Then leave feedback for your peer with the prompts below, if the amount of points you circled would not be full credit for that criteria.

Procedurist Rubric		
Procedure	Numbered list with complete sentences	List not numbered or sentences incomplete	Section Missing
Data Table	Complete with units for every measurement	Missing units and/or values needed for calculations	Section Missing

Things I noticed were missing/incorrect:

Things you might want to add/remove:

Data Analyst Rubric		
Calculation #1	Correct value with units, labels included	Missing units and/or incorrectly calculated	Section Missing
Calculation #2	Correct with units, labels included	Missing units and/or incorrectly calculated	Section Missing
Calculation #3	Correct with units, labels included	Missing units and/or incorrectly calculated	Section Missing
Calculation #4	Correct with units, labels included	Missing units and/or incorrectly calculated	Section Missing

Things I noticed were missing/incorrect:

Things you might want to add/remove:

Summarizer Rubric					
Conclusion	Addresses purpose, uses results as evidence, makes connections to class content	Missing 1 criteria	Missing 2 criteria	Missing 3 criteria	Section Missing

Things I noticed were missing/incorrect:

Things you might want to add/remove:

Error Analyst Rubric					
Error Analysis	Error is identified correctly piece of data is identified, effects of error on data identified effects of error on final results identified	Missing 1 criteria	Missing 2 criteria	Missing 3 criteria	Section Missing

Things I noticed were missing/incorrect:

Things you might want to add/remove:

Step 4: Expanding Reflection

Once I had set up a system for students to track scores of the various roles that they performed within their lab groups, I realized that I had also created another opportunity to incorporate further formative tasks within the process. I decided that I would have students reflect on their growth in relation to the defined skill/science practice that they were performing at key points throughout the year. At first, I decided that this should be done with physical artifacts that I created and had students utilize at the semester; eventually, I was able to enhance this practice through a digital goal-setting and reflection platform: Sown To Grow. A student sample from that platform, which has students track their score for each role as well as set goals for future tasks, can be found in Figure 12.6.

Figure 12.6 Student view of to-do list on Sown To Grow platform

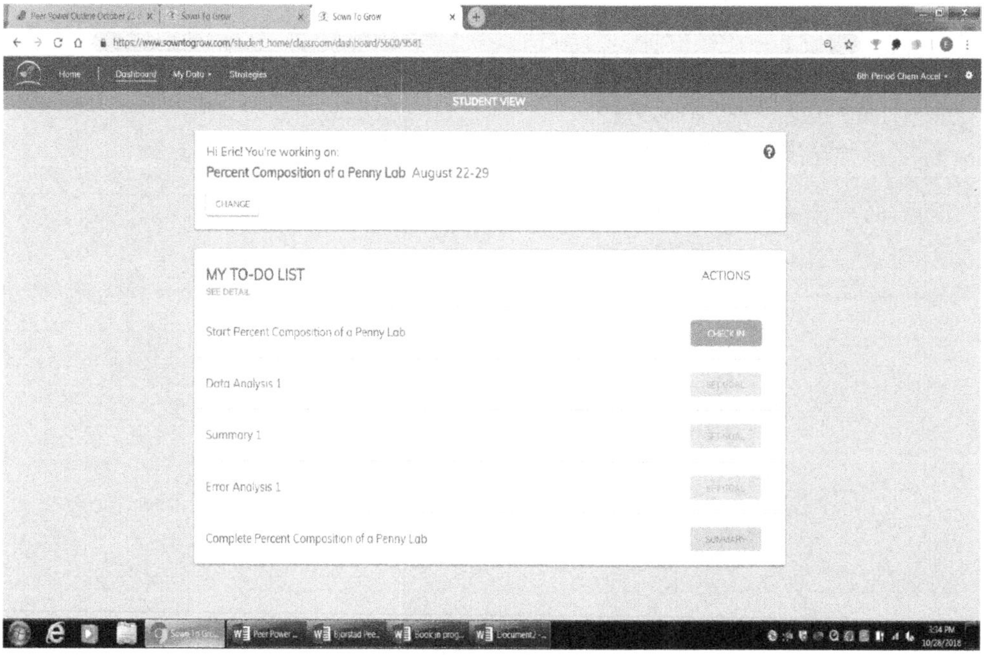

A sample video of two students using Sown To Grow to reflect on and create goals aligned to a task can be found on www.PeerPowerRevolution.com.

Step 5: Leverage Goal Setting

The last step that I added to the process was to have students set SMART (or similar) goals in relation to the learning outcomes that were identified in their success criteria, and then track their individual progress toward that goal. This can also be done through the use of teacher-created artifacts, various learning management systems, or online digital platforms, as shown in Figure 12.7.

Figure 12.7: Sample Student Goal Using Sown To Grow

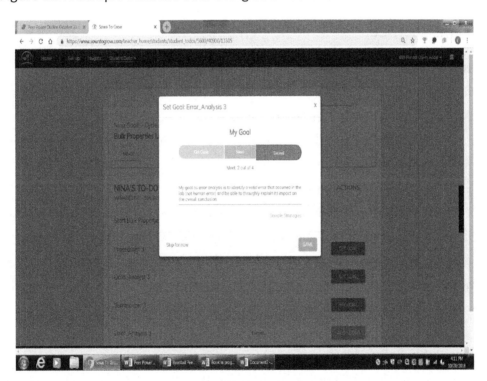

Here are some samples of high-quality goals that some of my students have written, after which many have expressed the helpfulness of writing those goals.

> "I plan to correctly analyze my data by double checking my work and make sure it correlates with explanations by the summarizer."

> "My goal as error analyst is to focus on identifying a valid error that occurred in the lab (not human error) and be able to thoroughly explain its impact on the overall conclusion."

"I plan to not only write a more thorough but concise summary, but I also want to make sure that I connect our results to what we are learning in class by referencing my in class notes."

One key aspect of goals that students will often need help with is identifying specific actions that they can take to improve. I highly recommend giving students feedback as often as possible as to how to improve the specificity of their goals—the more specific the action, the better the result will be.

Lessons Learned

Lesson 1: Relationships Matter

Throughout this process, I've learned several important lessons. First and foremost, creating and maintaining an atmosphere of mutual respect between the teacher and students as well as student-to-student interactions is key in establishing the Peer Review process in instruction. Students need to feel comfortable with the instructor and with their peers in order to express their ideas and receive feedback about them in a constructive, low-stakes manner. Often times facilitating this atmosphere will result in some interesting (and occasionally irreverent) feedback—take it in stride. I found firsthand that it's hard to build an atmosphere of trust unless you're open to change yourself, and sometimes the best suggestions come from the places we least expect.

Lesson 2: My Beliefs Matter!

I've also found that teacher buy-in into the Peer Review process (as perceived by the students) is also very important, as modeling the tasks you want them to perform is important not just for the work but for the attitude surrounding the work as well. If you, as an instructor, don't fully embrace the Peer Review process—and most importantly, believe that students can and will benefit from the work—students will not believe it either, thus compromising the integrity of the process. Many students will need a lot of encouragement along the way; be positive even if the results don't always trend that way.

This whole process is about creating space for students to focus on improvement in relation to specific tasks or skills, which eventually leads to better end results and student growth. Taking the time (which can be hard to find within the curricular schedule for some of us) to provide students with feedback on the various skills they're practicing, within a larger concept or task, creates better versions of those tasks.

Lesson 3: Take Baby Steps

One final lesson I learned along the way is that when altering your instruction, one small step at a time is far more effective than a general overhaul. It's surprising how implementing just one improvement to your instruction, one task or one formative practice at a time, can have positive benefits that will become more apparent over time. Create some space for yourself to be innovative; in the end, even if they don't say so (and they probably won't), they will appreciate it.

Needless to say, I did not perfect this process the first time around. Far from it, actually. It probably took me somewhere between five and six semesters to get from concept to implementation with fidelity for every student on every lab—and it's still far from a perfect system. Take your time and enjoy the journey.

Measuring Success

There are several measures of success that I have been able to administer or observe at the end of the process, along with some evidence that I've collected from various student reflections:

- A dramatic increase in student collaboration and meaningful discussions within the classroom.

  "I asked [my group] questions during peer reviews and looked over the rubric not only when I was working and revising it, but during peer reviews too."

- An increase in student ownership of the course material and process by which it is obtained. Student engagement is at an all-time high.

"I looked at the data table carefully and really analyzed the properties of the different substances to know which were metals, nonmetals, or metalloids. I also did the pre-lab reading and filled out the chart thoroughly, so I'd have more background information to properly sort the substances."

- More opportunities for students to demonstrate, as well as appreciate, leadership qualities created by completing tasks in a group setting.

"I want to fulfill my capabilities as a Procedurist by accurately applying all steps and properly checking the data table during labs."

- A dramatic increase in overall quality of student work. The depth and detail of thought processes (as well as students' ability to articulate them) was far more evident than it ever had been in previous iterations of the lab assignments that my classes have completed in past years.

"In my summary, I made sure to reference my results for the lab using specific data as well as a reference to class content that supported my conclusion."

"I felt happy that I achieved more than 3 of 4. In the next upcoming labs and projects, I will follow the example that is set by this lab by looking at what I wrote before and then mirror it with what my current lab is."

Guiding Questions:

Here is a short list of some important questions for you to consider before beginning this process:

- What set of science practices or skills is our curriculum aligned to?

- What science practices or skills should lab reports focus on?

- What are the components of a good lab report?

- What methods will you use to measure the success of Peer Review tasks?

- What recurring skills are present in the curriculum that can be an avenue for peer assessment?

- How do you create tasks that allow for implementation of Peer Review in a laboratory-based classroom setting?

Connect with Eric on Twitter @E_D_Bjornstad

Chapter 13

Learning for Democracy With #PeerPower

Gary P. Giordano

"The progress of one member has worth for the experience of other members."

–John Dewey, Democracy and Education (1916)

IN OUR RAPIDLY SHIFTING WORLD, it is impossible to predict just what society will look like 50 years from now. Technologies will continue to evolve, societal conditions will change, and career paths will transform before our eyes. Thankfully for us #PeerPower Revolutionaries, the need to create an engaged citizenry with command of their voice will always be valued. It is the cornerstone to the success of our American democracy, and as educators we play an integral role in preparing our students. We want our students to grow into compassionate and empathetic citizens who can dialogue across differences, overcome conflict through compromising, reach consensuses with others, and exhibit trust and respect. However, achieving this ambitious democratic goal is no easy task. It requires

- teaching and **modeling** the importance of sacrificing our self-interests,

- exhibiting vulnerability,

- engaging in active **listening**,

- **sharing** that is nurtured through practice and **reflection**, and

- providing opportunities for giving **feedback** to one another.

These dialogic teaching practices uplift and improve our community as a whole: modeling, listening, sharing, reflection, and feedback. Sounds oddly familiar, right? This unwavering need for an engaged citizenry is essentially Peer Review in its purest, most authentic and democratic form.

In our classrooms, Peer Review between students mirrors the same democratic purpose that it serves in our society. In fact, the purpose of teaching students how to "do peer review" is to prepare them for participation in our democracy. We strive to teach students how to share ideas and creativity, provide feedback, and push one another to improve their habits of mind, acknowledge and praise individual strengths, suggest routes for improvement, reflect on and track their goals and progress, and learn from one another, not just for the immediate task or activity at hand, but in preparation for future engagement and participation in our democracy. It's the work we do every day as empowered citizens!

However, this meaningful work cannot be done overnight. It requires crafting a classroom environment and culture that values, models, and fosters the respect and trust needed for constructive feedback, authentic reflection, and social-emotional growth. Relationships that are built on mutual understanding and a desire to learn side-by-side must be fostered between students and teachers. Opportunities for students to apply their Peer Review skills from classroom learning to the context of their everyday lives is crucial for their own transition into engaged democratic citizens. In his manifesto, "My Pedagogical Creed," John Dewey (1897) said it best: "The progress is not in the succession of studies but in the development of new attitudes, and new interests in experience" (p. 82). The "experience" in which Dewey is referring to are the conditions that we create in our classrooms that reflect existing social life, but in a reduced form; where our youth are exposed to opportunities to dialogue across differences, Peer Review, and formulate new habits of mind as they take command of themselves through building their own voices. In pragmatic Dewey-like character, below are the conditions or strategies that I like to use to create this "learner-centered experience."

Eight Steps to Success

Step 1: Building Trust in the Classroom

We know that establishing a classroom culture of respect, trust, collaboration, and high expectations will lend itself to students' willingness and commitment to using #PeerPower. When students feel safe in their learning and know that their voices are valued, they are more willing to share their work with their peers and provide, as well as receive, critical feedback on their progress.

At the beginning of the school year, we team up as a class to create our Essential Question of the Year. This question is aligned to the values inherent to students' social-emotional learning and habits of mind, such as exhibiting respect, building trust, persevering through adversity, and listening with empathy. Some examples include:

- How do we respect ourselves while respecting others?

- As a class, how can we improve behaviors that build and nurture trust?

- What does it look and feel like to listen with empathy? How can we practice this?

We also define habits of mind, identify synonyms, brainstorm examples of what these terms looks like in action, and continuously return to and discuss these ideas, especially during moments of conflict. It is vital to point out when we see these values in our readings of historical people or events. A Peer Review pitfall would be failing to incorporate habits of mind across content lessons or continuing to nurture them throughout the year. For my class, some key habits of mind that are vital to student learning include actively listening with empathy, perseverance and patience, remaining open to new learning and ideas, taking responsible risks, working interdependently, and thinking about thinking (reflection).

For example, my classes take a Team Trust Survey, share out results, and engage in a discussion leading to improvement goals that can help us improve working relationships and trust-building behaviors. These goals may include

- identifying and build on each other's strengths,

- reducing gossip by addressing any problems directly with the person or seeking an adult for assistance,

- accepting that making mistakes and failing is a part of learning—keep on going!, and

- displaying empathy and practice uplifting others instead of placing unfair criticism on or judging others.

Step 2: Activate Socratic Seminar to Set Personal Goals

In my classroom, Socratic Seminars are the perfect opportunity for students to bring all their learning tools to the table and shine: speaking and listening skills, habits of mind, historical knowledge, and voice. It is also lends itself perfectly to the Peer Review that will engage students in our democratic society. Students set and track their own personal speaking and listening goals during the many Socratic Seminars that we conduct throughout the school year. Before setting a goal, it is vital to set the expectations for a Socratic Seminar, review the ground rules and golden rule ("Learn from one another!"), dissect the success criteria, and model effective Socratic Seminar practices using videos (my go-to resource is the Teaching Channel). Next, consider the thought-provoking question or controversial topic that you'd like to create to engage students in a Socratic Seminar. This can be a major pitfall for this work. If the prompt or question is, for lack of better words, boring, the discussion will be too and the student engagement will fall flat (trust me, I've been there). The topic must be aligned with the content being studied and allow students to dig into and question the materials, readings, or research. They should walk away from the discussion better informed with further questions, wonderings, and bursting with new ideas. The topic should be specific enough to allow for a focused discussion but also general enough for real-life experiences and other relevant examples to be incorporated into the historical content allowing for direct application to the students' own lives. Furthermore, it should lend itself to critical thinking, problem solving, the sharing of multiple viewpoints, the use of evidence, and listening with empathy to others.

Socratic Seminar topics, prompts, and guiding questions in Social Studies class have included:

- *Alexander the Great:* Was Alexander the Great all that great? Hero, villain, or in between?

- *Neolithic Revolution:* Why was the Neolithic Revolution a significant turning point in world history?

- *Human Rights, Technology and Education:* What are human rights, and how do we protect them? Is Internet access a human right? How and why is access to a quality education a human right? How does technology affect our world, education, and human rights?

- *Exploring Theories of the Death of King Tut:* How did King Tut die? Murder, illness, accident, or sabotage?

- *World Religions and "I Am Malala" text:* How do the challenges faced by Malala relate to issues of human rights or women's rights? How does religion impact Malala's life? Why do societies have religions? Is it important to understand cultures different than our own? What impact does education have on Malala? Is education a human right? Are there any cultural differences between the people of Swat Valley and the people in New York?

- *Digital Citizenship:* Is social media helping or hindering us and our society? Is it somewhere in between? Why is it important to be mindful of your digital footprints?

- *Colonial Development:* What role did African Americans and women play in the development of the American colonies and New York specifically? How did issues of power, wealth, and morality influence colonization in North America?

- *Columbus and the Encounter:* Who, and/or what, was responsible for the slaughter of the Taino Indians in the years following 1492? Columbus? His men? King Ferdinand and Queen Isabella of Spain? The Tainos themselves? The System of Empire?

- *Constitution/Government:* Why do people create, structure, and change governments?

- *American Revolution:* Did the American Revolution accomplish its goals? How did the political, economic, and social outcomes of the Revolution affect different groups of people?

- *Hamilton:* How does "Hamilton: An American Musical" examine people, events, and ideas during the Revolution and the building of a new nation? What does it reveal about this time period? How does it corroborate with primary sources from that time?

- *Mexican American War:* Was the Mexican American War a justifiable war?

- *Civil War:* Was the Civil War inevitable?

Next, students can set goals for themselves. Some possible goal examples may include:

a. listen more carefully to the ideas of others

b. ask for or provide clarification when needed

c. add to and elaborate on a friend's comments by asking questions to the group that deepens the conversation

d. use evidence on the topic, text, or issue that is being investigating to support answers and explanations.

A Peer Review pitfall to look out for is ignoring the success criteria prior to setting goals. We need to ensure that #PeerPower students recognize what they need to do to be successful during discussion to set the most appropriate and meaningful goal possible. Goal setting requires collaborative discussion and brainstorming where students are reflecting on their own skill sets, sharing thoughts or stories of past experiences with peers, and reviewing the related success criteria. Some sample speaking and listening success criteria taken directly from the *Grade 7 CCSS Speaking and Listening Standards* and translated into student-friendly language include the following:

- I can **prepare** for a class discussion by having **read or researched** the material we are currently studying. [SL.7.1a]

- I can **track my progress** toward specific **goals** and carry out **my role** as participant in the discussion. [SL.7.1b]

- I can **ask questions** during a discussion to elaborate on the remarks of others and **connect the ideas** of several speakers. [SL.7.1c]

- I can **respond to others' questions** and comments with relevant **evidence**, observations, and ideas. [SL.7.1c]

- I can **review new ideas** or information expressed by others and demonstrate an understanding of **multiple perspectives** presented during the discussion. [SL.7.1d]

- I can **identify claims** that are **supported by reasons/evidence and** those that are not. [SL.7.3]

- I can **present my ideas** and findings by sequencing my ideas **logically** and using important facts and descriptions. [SL.7.4]

Some of my favorite sample Socratic Seminar goals set by my students include "act like a boss (have confidence) and really make sure my opinion is heard and understood," "ask more questions about the reading and try to get into the conversation more," "listen to others extremely carefully and try not to take over the conversation," and "use more evidence to back up my ideas and say if someone else's ideas are not supported by evidence."

Students also address *how* they plan on reaching their goal by identifying three specific action steps or strategies that they can engage in before, during, or after our group discussion. A Peer Review pitfall would be failing to introduce and define strategies for students to reach their goals. It is important to model effective and ineffective uses of the strategies, provide process-based feedback, and highlight moments of strategies being used meaningfully by other students. Some possible strategies or actions for *how* students will reach their goals include the following:

- Prepare open-ended questions ahead of our discussion based on the reading/research.

- Sticky-note key pages and quotes from the text prior to our group discussion.

- Use boxes or bullets to outline key points for our discussion.

- Have a friend invite me into the discussion by using my Purple Card to signal to the class that I'd like a chance to speak and share.

- Prepare a list of five content-specific or academic words that I'd like to use in the discussion. Check off each time you use one.

- Practice reading and interpreting others' body language in everyday scenarios to help prepare me for the discussion. Keep a log of your findings.

- Practice using a strong, clear voice and giving eye contact in your everyday interactions leading up to our discussion.

Following our Socratic Seminars, students reflect on the discussion by asking themselves if they reached their overall personal goal. They identify a "glow" or source of self-value based on their participation in our discussion by internally asking themselves, "What do I think was a particularly impressive moment or strength I had?" They also note any moments of clarification that they may need by asking themselves, "Are there any specific parts of our discussion or aspects of this work that I don't believe I have understood as well I could have?" Students also note any suggestions for next time by reviewing their moments of clarification and asking themselves, "Do I have a specific suggestion on how to address the concerns I identified above?" Students also ponder any other concerns or issues they may have had based on our seminar by asking themselves, "Did I detect any potential problems or challenging moments during our discussion? How did I handle or respond to it? What are some ideas or suggestions I have for the whole group when facing difficult moments in a discussion?" After engaging in this deep reflection of their learning progress, students are ready to set an improvement goal by asking themselves, "Based on our success criteria and my participation in this discussion, what is one specific aspect of our work that I want to improve on?" This improvement goal may be the same goal that they initially set if they feel they have not met it or an entirely new goal. Students also jot down one strategy for how they will specifically achieve their goal, which they will revisit during the next seminar. This series of self-reflective questioning can also be adapted into a peer assessment or review using the TAG protocol, where a partner answers these questions for a peer who has finished participating in the Socratic Seminar.

Step 3: Amplify Student Voice With Student Peer Coaches

During our Socratic Seminars, students listen carefully to their #PeerPower coaches during our coaching moments and review the peer coach's notes on the claims they shared during the seminar and any moments of conflict or difficulty. Students on the outside circle act as the peer coaches to their assigned partner on the inside. Students are paired based on personality quizzes they take online (check out the 16 personalities.com free personality test) or by their own choice. During our coaching moment, #PeerPower coaches provide feedback to their partners, just like good sporting coaches would do for their players. This includes a suggestion for what their partners can do to improve their performance for the second round of their participation. Peer coaches also uses a tally mark system to note the number of times their partners speak in the discussion, look at the person who is speaking, refer to the text, ask a question, respond to another speaker, interrupt another speaker, and engage in side conversation. #PeerPower Coaches complete their "peer coaching playbook" for their partners and review a peer assessment-learning continuum for various reading, speaking, and listening standards aligned to key learning indicators, such as preparation, accountable talk, questioning, use of evidence from the text, and historical accuracy. Peer coaches mark off the level that they believe their partners performed at, which includes advanced (above the grade level), proficient (on the grade level), close to proficient (one grade level below), and working toward proficient (two grade levels below). Finally, they identify the overall grade that they would give their partners and record a "glow" (compliment) and "grow" (area needing further work). This process is repeated once the inner and outer circle partnerships switch to allow all students in the room the opportunity to serve as both a Socratic Seminar participant and peer coach.

Step 4: Discussion Mapping and Reflection

Discussion mapping is a strategy that allows for students to immediately review the patterns of speaking and flow of dialogue following a Socratic Seminar. During the seminar, the teacher writes the names of all participating students on the perimeter of a circle on a piece of paper then draws lines to connect participants as the discussion takes place. At times, the teacher can jot down ideas being discussed or key questions being asked. After the seminar, the whole class reviews this document on a classroom document reader (ELMO) and reflects on the trends, such as how the discussion flowed around the circle, if speaking time was equally distributed allowing for all voices to be heard, or the number of times each participant spoke to determine how the discussion was facilitated and who can pull back on their speaking time to allow others to engage in dialogue. We also discuss the number of ideas or questions asked to determine if there should have been more shifting to new ideas or more time spent on a particular topic before switching to a new one. My seminars typically consist of one round of discussion, a coaching moment, and then a second round of continued discussion, where the most improvement takes place. The discussion mapping strategy can also be employed between the first and second round of seminar participation to allow for more equitable sharing of voice and inclusion in the second round of dialoging.

Step 5: Leverage Google Docs to Expand Peer Review

Students often utilized Google Docs associated with their Google Classroom accounts to share and peer review one another's writing during classwork activities or essay writing performance-based assessments by commenting in the margins and providing suggestions for improvement. This process is especially useful during our Socratic Seminar, where we have utilized a full classroom set of Chromebooks to allow peer coaches to talk directly to their partners inside the circle while the seminar was happening. This was in lieu of waiting until the coaching moment occurred for discussion participants to receive their feedback. Within their Google Docs, students had developed their questions for the seminar and added their speaking and listening goal to the predesignated templates provided, including the specific success criteria, reflection protocols, and peer coaching forms. Partners shared their respective Google Docs with their peer coaches so they could directly type into each other's documents during the Socratic Seminar. At the top of the Google Doc, a space was provided for this "In the Moment" coaching. This type of activity took skilled multitasking and maturity that required practice and deep trust within the classroom. A common peer review pitfall would be trying this out during the first Socratic Seminar with a new class, or even the second or third. First, let students focus on the protocols of the Socratic Seminars using paper to find their flow with it. Once students have mastered this, incorporate the 21st-century technology tools to elevate the peer review and feedback. Trust must be present to ensure students are not online or doing other things during the seminar but rather are fully engaged in what's happening in the circles. Having the Chromebooks does lend itself to more depth in the discussion because participants can quickly search for answers to a historical-based question posed in the discussion or look up more information on a related topic to share with others. However, it takes extreme practice, trust, and multitasking to get to this point and may only occur in a Socratic Seminar in the latter half of the school year.

Step 6: Explore Peer Review Scavenger Hunts

A fun twist for conducting a Peer Review is having students work in collaborative teams to develop graphic organizers for informational- or argumentative-based writing tasks. Students complete graphic organizers using collaborative Google Docs with one another then utilize a Scavenger Hunt app called Goose Chase to review other groups' graphic organizers while having to answer specific questions in the scavenger hunt. They are asked to identify and share the strengths and weaknesses of each group's graphic organizers using video and picture evidence that are worth points. Some prompts include the following:

- Identify this group's claim in their graphic organizer and snap a picture of it.

- What were the three major pieces of evidence or historical examples they referred to in their graphic organizer? Record a video of a group member explaining this.

- Snap a photo of this group's counterclaim and rebuttal.

- Record a video assessing the strength of their counterclaim and rebuttal. Did it weaken the opposing side's argument enough to help them win their case?

- Record a video assessing the reasoning of one piece of evidence for this group. Did their reasoning link back to and support their overall claim? Did it introduce new ideas in the writing?

- Record a video of discussing your overall "glow and grow" for this group.

This learning activity allowed for deep peer review to occur during our brainstorming session that was documented using pictures and videos. It motivated students to use pictures and videos as evidence to support their findings and remain engaged to earn the most points and win the overall scavenger hunt.

Step 7: Peer Review the Teacher

Every year in January, students complete a peer review or teacher evaluation of my performance as a teacher. It is their opportunity to voice how they believe the class is progressing and what we can improve together to extend our learning. Students provide me with a "glow and grow," similar to what they do in their own peer review. This exercise strengthens the importance of peer review in our classroom and helps to build trust between myself and the students to allow for more meaningful critical feedback to be given and drawn on to improve our learning environment and classroom rapport. Some examples of feedback provided to me as the teacher included, "I like when you use PearDeck for our class lessons. It's hard to copy class notes and listen to you at the same time," and "Do more class courts and Socratic Seminars. I like activities where we can rotate around the room and work in stations."

Step 8: Analyze Exemplars With Student-Led Impact Teams

The goal of our Student-Led Impact Teams is for students to take ownership in and make an impact on their own learning while contributing to the learning of others. In Student Impact Teams, students rotated around the class to various stations where they peer reviewed sample papers for a performance-based assessment that they were working on. The exemplars were separated into four categories: novice, approaching, proficient, and mastery. All exemplars were written and saved by students from years past. The rubric and final grade for each paper was removed so students did not know what score the student had earned on the task.

Students had to refer to their current task rubric, success criteria, and learning continuum to decide what score the student should receive. They had to write out the major reasons why each paper deserved the grade they assigned them based on the rubric and defend it with evidence. Often participants debated with one another and had to reach a group consensus on which score the paper should receive. This exercise allowed students to grow as peer reviewers because they had to reason and dialogue across different opinions, while referring to the rubric and success criteria to score each paper objectively. They often naturally identified the missing components of each paper and the areas of weakness that did not align with the proficient and mastery levels of the continuum. They would also note specific action steps that the students could take to improve the work and bump up their score. Finally, student groups also identified strengths and moments of success where it was clear that the paper fell short of the mastery level. This work modeled the EAA protocol that we as educators use in our Impact Teams to review student work aligned to success criteria, analyze the students thinking through the task and where they excelled or struggled, and develop action steps to help them reach success.

Envision Success

Success in Socratic Seminars would include all students in a discussion with real democratic dialoguing occurring—something that is needed now more than ever in our polarized society. Students would exhibit increased mastery of key critical thinking and problem-solving life skills essential to operating in society today. These habits of mind would include perseverance; managing impulsivity; listening and understanding with empathy; thinking with flexibility; questioning and posing problems; applying past knowledge to new situations; responding with wonder and awe; gathering data through all senses; communicating with clarity and precision; thinking interdependently; creating, imagining, and innovating; remaining open to new learning; taking responsible risks; finding humor; and thinking about thinking (metacognition). As students practice and master these habits of mind during Socratic Seminars and Peer Review, they will grow into empathetic and empowered learners with a command of their voices and the skill set to work and communicate through real-life situations. They will possess the mindfulness, creativity, and strategic reasoning skills to display their vulnerabilities, trust in others, and respond to situations with awareness, purpose, and intentionality to achieve progressive outcomes that benefit the collective whole, not just their individual self-interests. They'll be ready, and prepared, for democracy!

Guiding Questions:

- What are some strategies you use to nurture student-to-student trust as well as teacher-to-student trust in your classroom?

- How are students engaging in speaking and listening activities in your classroom? How can you incorporate Peer Review into these activities?

- How can you create a thought-provoking question or controversial topic to engage students with in a Socratic Seminar? Will this question lend itself to critical thinking, problem solving, the sharing of multiple viewpoints, the use of evidence, and listening with empathy to others?

- How can students set speaking and listening goals in your classroom as well as reflect on their own progress? How many times a year would you like to reassess their progress?

- What type of EdTech tools can you incorporate into your activities to help your students achieve their learning goals and elevate the Peer Review and reflection processes that are already occurring?

Connect with Gary on Twitter @MrGiordanoNYC

Chapter 14

History Class: A Microcosm of Society

Katherine Smith

"You can't learn in school what the world is going to do next year."

–Henry Ford

History Teachers Love Content!

History teachers love their content. We are the people who pull over when we see a brown historic sign on the highway and drag our families through a self-guided tour. We are the people who visit historical graveyards, get geeked out by re-enactments, criticize movies for their lack of historical accuracy, and rant endlessly about politics and past events. We are the people you want on your trivia team because we love our content.

And yet, all the history content won't teach our students "in school what the world is going to do next year" (Henry Ford Quotes, n.d.). That is not to say that history teachers or history content are not vital; rather, it is to say that teaching students transferable skills in conjunction with historical content is what is needed to prepare them for the future. When the unknown presents itself to our students, they will need to be able to act collaboratively, react responsibly, and evolve as productive members of a larger society.

As #PeerPower Revolutionaries, we have the power to transform our discipline. Our classrooms can truly be structured as a microcosm of society, in which our students apply critical 21st-century skills to a different historical context daily. We can teach our students the positive impact of civic participation by allowing them, through the co-creation of success criteria, to be part of the vision of classroom success. We can teach our #PeerPower students that being a productive member of the classroom (or society) means working together through peer assessment and peer planning to actualize the larger vision of success. Through goal setting and revision opportunities, we can demonstrate that improvement occurs only after individuals take responsible, informed action.

Activating Self- and Peer Assessment

Think Curriculum

In order to revolutionize our discipline, we have to think intentionally about the curriculum. Learning takes place as a result of focused instruction, deliberate practice, feedback, and revision. If we want learning to occur, our curriculum has to provide students opportunities to receive instruction regarding a skill (or particular set of skills), as well as opportunities to practice the skill(s) multiple times both within and across our units of instruction.

This means that we have to identify the transferrable, reoccurring skills in our discipline. To assist with this identification, consult the relevant standards in your state, the C3 Framework, or applicable course frameworks. Since all historians form and write arguments about the past and support them with analysis of primary and secondary sources, we will use argumentative writing and source analysis as examples of transferrable, reoccurring skills that can be practiced in every unit of instruction. Figure 14.1 identifies standards and AP practices associated with these two skills.

Figure 14.1: Standards Chart: Source Analysis & Argumentative Writing

Standards related to *analysis of sources*:

- **CCSS.ELA-LITERACY.RH.9-10.1:** Cite specific textual evidence to support analysis of primary and secondary sources, attending to such features as the date and origin of the information (Common Core State Standards Initiative, 2010).
- **CCSS.ELA-LITERACY.RH.9-10.2:** Determine the central ideas or information of a primary or secondary source..." (Common Core State Standards Initiative, 2010).
- AP Practice 1: Analyze historical evidence
  - Primary Sources: "Explain the relative historical significance of a source's point of view, purpose, historical situation, and/or audience" (College Board, 2018).

Standards related to *argumentative writing:*

- **CCSS.ELA-LITERACY.WHST.9-10.1:** "Write arguments focused on *discipline-specific content.*" (Common Core State Standards Initiative, 2010). See also CCSS.ELA-LITERACY.WHST.9-10.1:B and C.
- AP Practice 2- Argument development
  - "Support an argument using specific and relevant evidence" (College Board, 2018).
  - "Use historical reasoning to explain relationships among pieces of historical evidence" (College Board, 2018).

In order to assess student growth and proficiency with the targeted recurring skills and corresponding standards, select an aligned task or performance to administer multiple times in a unit and in your course. Continuing with the aforementioned example, a document-based question (DBQ) is a task that assesses argumentative writing and source analysis, and can easily be incorporated into any history unit. Since an entire DBQ is very comprehensive and time-consuming, a team could assess these skills by focusing on a body paragraph of a DBQ.

Once the repetitive task has been identified, collaborate with your team to determine the success criteria. Make a list of exactly what students need to include in their product to demonstrate proficiency with the targeted skills. Figure 14.2 articulates one team's success criteria for a body paragraph of a DBQ.

Figure 14.2: Learning Targets & Success Criteria

Learning Targets	Assessment Product	Success Criteria

• I can analyze a series of historical sources.
• I can explain a claim or topic sentence using evidence and reasoning.
	Body paragraph of a DBQ	• A minimum of 3 sources are used as evidence to support the claim/topic sentence.
		  • It is clear why the sources were grouped together.
		  • The content from each source is described (not just quoted).
		  • An additional piece of evidence, not in the documents, is provided to further support the claim.
		• For each source, explain how or why *one* of the following aspects about the source is relevant to the claim/topic sentence:
		  • Point of view
		  • Purpose
		  • Historical situation
		  • Audience
		• The paragraph uses evidence "to demonstrate complex understanding of the historical development that is the focus of the prompt" through one of the following means:
		  • "Explain nuance of an issue by analyzing multiple variables"
		  • "Explain relevant and insightful connections within and across periods"
		  • "Confirm the validity of an argument by corroborating multiple pieces of evidence across themes"
		  • "Qualify or modify an argument by considering diverse or alternate views or evidence"

Source: Adapted from College Board, *Rubrics for AP Histories + History Disciplinary Practices and Reasoning Skills,* 2017b.

With skill-based standards, an aligned task, and criteria for success identified, it is time to provide opportunity for practice within and across units. Further channel your inner Wiggins and McTighe (2005) by confirming your units of study and your essential unit questions. Then, identify content standards to add to the skill standards and create student-friendly learning intentions (that address both skill and content). Finally, make your tasks relevant to each unit by incorporating unit-based prompts, questions, and sources.

With each successive unit in this course, the skills of *source analysis* and *argumentative writing* would continue to be a focus (amongst others). This reoccurring focus would allow the product and success criteria to remain constant, which would allow students the time and practice needed to improve with source analysis and argumentative writing. Basically, the content from unit to unit would shift, but the skills regarding source analysis and argumentative writing would remain constant. Figure 14.3 illustrates how to incorporate the previously mentioned skill-based standards and the aligned task of a DBQ body paragraph into a unit of study in an AP European History course. The learning intentions would change slightly to incorporate unit content goals.

Figure 14.3: Developing Standards-Based Formative Tasks

Essential Unit Question	What forms have European governments taken, and how have these changed over time?

Skills Standards	**Standards related to Analysis of Sources:**
	• **CCSS.ELA-LITERACY.RH.9-10.1:** Cite specific textual evidence to support analysis of primary and secondary sources, attending to such features as the date and origin of the information (Common Core State Standards Initiative, 2010).
	• **CCSS.ELA-LITERACY.RH.9-10.2:** Determine the central ideas or information of a primary or secondary source... (Common Core State Standards Initiative, 2010).
	• AP® Practice 1- Analyze historical evidence
	  • Primary Sources: Explain the relative historical significance of a source's point of view, purpose, historical situation, and/or audience (College Board, 2018).
	Standards related to Argumentative Writing:
	• **CCSS.ELA-LITERACY.WHST.9-10.1:** Write arguments focused on *discipline-specific content."* (Common Core State Standards Initiative, 2010). See also CCSS.ELA-LITERACY.WHST.9-10.1. B and C.
	• AP® Practice 2: Argument Development
	  • Support an argument using specific and relevant evidence
	  • "Use historical reasoning to explain relationships among pieces of historical evidence"

Relevant Content Standards	• **Perspectives SS.H.5.9-12:** Analyze the factors and historical context that influenced the perspectives of people during different historical eras (Illinois State Board of Education, 2017). • **Perspectives SS.H.8.9-12:** Analyze key historical events and contributions of individuals through a variety of perspectives, including those of historically underrepresented groups (Illinois State Board of Education, 2017). • IS-5: Explain how identities such as ethnicity, race, gender, religious affiliation, and class have affected the individual's relationship to society from 1450 to the present (College Board, 2017a).
Learning Intentions	• I can analyze a series of primary sources concerning Elizabeth I. • I can explain the impact of gender on female rule by providing primary source evidence and reasoning.

Essential Unit Question	What forms have European governments taken, and how have these changed over time?

Assessment
 	
Product
	Product: Analyze the provided primary source documents. Write a body DBQ paragraph addressing the prompt below. Make sure your paragraph includes analysis of 3 sources and meets the outlined success criteria.
	
	Prompt: How did attitudes toward gender affect the ways in which female rulers exercised power? Use the reign of Elizabeth I as your case study (College Board, 2011).
	
	Success Criteria
	A minimum of 3 sources are used as evidence to support the claim/topic sentence.
	
	• It is clear why the sources were grouped together.
	
	• The content from each source is described (not just quoted).
	
	• An additional piece of evidence, not in the documents, is provided to further support the claim.
	
	• For each source, explain how or why *one* of the following aspects about the source is relevant to the claim /topic sentence:
	
	   • Point of view
	   • Purpose
	   • Historical situation
	   • Audience
	
	• The paragraph uses evidence "to demonstrate complex understanding of the historical development that is the focus of the prompt" through one of the following means:
	
	• "Explaining nuance of an issue by analyzing multiple variables"
	
	• "Explaining relevant and insightful connections within and across periods"
	
	• "Confirming the validity of an argument by corroborating multiple pieces of evidence across themes"
	
	• "Qualifying or modifying an argument by considering diverse or alternate views or evidence"

Source: Adapted from College Board, *Rubrics for AP Histories + History Disciplinary Practices and Reasoning Skills*, 2017b.

Defining Criteria With Students

Success criteria must be defined *with* students not *for* students! After the teacher has achieved a clear vision of what the success criteria looks like when integrating content with skills, the students have to arrive at the vision of success on their own. One way to help students understand where they are headed in their learning is to engage them in the co-construction of success criteria using models of strong and weak work. In Figure 14.4, students read two models of a body paragraph in a DBQ. In small groups, they compare and contrast these two models to determine which one is the strong model. Then, they analyze the strong model to determine its characteristics.

Figure 14.4: Group Activity – Identifying & Analyzing the Strong Model

Directions: Read the two examples (Sample A and Sample B) that have been provided. One of these examples is a strong model, meeting all of the success criteria. The other model is missing several of the success criteria.

1. As a group, determine which model is the strong model.
2. Raise your hand, so I can confirm your choice.
3. After I affirm your choice, work together to answer the question, "what makes this a strong model?" Generate a list of characteristics of the strong model.

Sample A

Finally, female rulers like Elizabeth I maintained control by continuing to carry out the ceremonial roles of the monarchy. William Tooking, Elizabeth's personal chaplain, described a ceremony of healing that he saw. Elizabeth knelt and prayed over a sick person and placed her hands on them in order to heal them (doc 6). This ceremony reflects a monarchial duty outside of making and executing law. Elizabeth and all female monarchs carried these out in order to keep control of their position and to remind the people that they had power. Another example of this is leading the troops into battle. Elizabeth spoke to troops in 1588 before the attempted invasion of the Spanish Armada. She asserted that although she is weak due to her womanly status, she is willing to die for her country just like the troops. She says she will join in the fight as its leader and the ruler of the nation (doc 7). The Armada was successfully beaten by the English in that very battle, and this meant Spain had to give up its fight to reunify Europe under Catholicism as England was aiding the Protestant Netherlands in the Dutch civil war. The purpose of this speech was to give the troops spirit and instill confidence in the country, and based on the results of the battle, Elizabeth I succeeded despite leading troops into war being a male role. Thus, she and other female rulers remained true to royal ceremonial duties even if they were meant for men. Lastly, a painting by Marcus Gheeraerts the Younger, the court painter, portrays Elizabeth I in large gowns, standing over a map of England (doc 5). As the court painter, Gheeraerts was hired by Elizabeth I, so his positive portrayal of her may have been due to bias created by his occupation's contingency on his ability to please the queen, the subject of the painting. Nevertheless, the purpose was to portray her as an all- powerful and glorious ruler, just like the art style that would develop later, the baroque. The portrayal of Elizabeth I as an all-powerful queen is a part of her ceremonial duties and the belief in the divine right that fueled her absolutist rule. Because she was given her position by god, it was her duty to exercise her power by showing the world that she was powerful through lavish paintings.

Sample B

Throughout Europe, beliefs of women as evil and deceitful were incredibly widespread, leaving many to be outraged at Elizabeth I's reign in England. For example, Scottish religious reformer John Knox wrote a piece outlining his anger to Elizabeth I. John Knox's profession of a religious reformer most likely impacted his point of view that women were evil and weak, and a woman in rule was against nature and ungodly. Since he was a reformed in this time, in Scotland, he most likely was a Protestant leaning towards Calvinism and therefore interpreted scripture as a fact and accepted many of the anti-women themes in the Bible at the time (doc 1). Similarly, Jacques Bochetel de La Foret reported on a speech Elizabeth I gave to Parliament. Parliament proposed a petition in hopes to rule her succession invalid. In the document, it can be seen that these attitudes toward women were taken into consideration by Elizabeth I. As when speaking to Parliament, Elizabeth I cautiously, yet with much authority, asserted her power by stating that Parliament was meant to be in service to her and without her there was no government (doc 4). Although, Elizabeth did rule very strongly and made sure to assert her power, many people did speak out against her rule. For example, a portrait made by Marcus Gheeraerts the Younger shows Elizabeth I standing on top of England (signifying her control grip over England) and behind her a blue skinny sky is seen to her left and a stormy sky illustrated to her right; representing his belief that Elizabeth I was leading England into darkness (doc. 5).

Which model is the strong model? (circle)
Sample A or Sample B

What makes this a strong model? List the characteristics below:

To ensure the students are seeing the characteristics of success that you intend, ask the small groups to share out. Create a class list of co-created success criteria that can be viewed by all students. For any criterion that is suggested that is invalid or unclear, ask strategic questions to guide the revision of this criterion. Provide students an opportunity to argue to remove a criterion that they may not agree should be on the class list. Figure 14.5 showcases a completed class list of co-constructed success criteria.

Figure 14.5: Co-Construction of Success Criteria

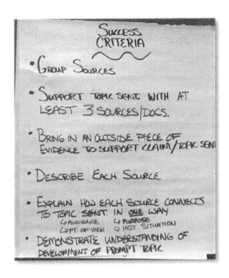

Success Criteria

- Group sources
- Support topic with at leas 3 sources/docs
- Bring in outside piece of evidence to support claim
- Describe each source
- Explain how each source connects to the claim in one way (audience, point of view, purpose, historical situation)
- Demonstrate understanding of development of prompt topic

While the process of co-constructing success criteria gives students a voice in articulating the performance expectations, it is the act of annotating a model for the success criteria that allows students to internalize the vision of success. Another way of defining criteria with students is through color coding and annotating. In Figure 14.6, students highlighted each criterion with a specific color that is indicated in the column titled, "designation • key." By simply scanning student papers for the correct highlighter colors, the teacher can determine whether or not the students can identify where each criterion lives within the body paragraph of a DBQ.

Figure 14.6: Annotating Samples of Student Work

Directions:

Part I

1. Look at the class list of criteria. Each criterion has been assigned a different designation (highlighter color or underline).
2. Using the appropriate designation, individually indicate where each criterion lives in the strong model.

Part II

1. After 10 minutes, we will project an annotated version of Sample A onto the screen. Compare your highlights and underlines to the projected version.

2. Ask questions regarding the highlights or underlines you may have missed.

DESIGNATION • KEY	SUCCESS CRITERIA
Highlight grouping in *orange*	• It is clear why the sources were grouped together.
Underline each source and its content description	• A minimum of 3 sources are used as evidence to support the claim/topic sentence. • The content from each source is described (not just quoted).
Highlight outside information in pink	• An additional piece of evidence, not in the documents, is provided to further support the claim.
Highlight which aspect of each source is explained • Point of view = *Red* • Purpose = *Green* • Historical situation = *Aqua* • Audience = *Yellow*	• For each source, explain how or why *one* of the following aspects about the source is relevant to the claim/topic sentence: • Point of view • Purpose • Historical situation • Audience
NOTE: Typically, complex understanding is conveyed throughout the entire paragraph. This paragraph does not demonstrate complex understanding. Be prepared to discuss which means (listed on the right) could be incorporated to historically develop the focus of the prompt.	• The paragraph uses evidence "to demonstrate complex understanding of the historical development that is the focus of the prompt" through one of the following means: • "Explaining nuance of an issue by analyzing multiple variables" • "Explaining relevant and insightful connections within and across periods" • "Confirming the validity of an argument by corroborating multiple pieces of evidence across themes" • "Qualifying or modifying an argument by considering diverse or alternate views or evidence"

Source: Adapted from College Board, *Rubrics for AP Histories + History Disciplinary Practices and Reasoning Skills,* 2017b.

Identifying the success criteria in a strong piece of work will help the students understand the performance expectations, but this activity will not necessarily help the students understand how to make a weak product stronger. After students interact with the strong model, ask the students to work in groups to analyze the weaker piece of work. Student groups should identify the missing success criteria and articulate a plan for revision. Figure 14.7 reflects a group's effort to annotate the success criteria that is present, communicate the success criteria that is missing, and outline a plan for revising Sample B. By committing a plan for revision to writing, the students provide each other with the "how-to" steps for making a weak product stronger. At this point, the students have a vision of success and a roadmap of how to get there in the forefront of their mind, so they are ready to engage in creating their own product.

Figure 14.7: Strategic Revision

Group Names: Jane, John, Joe, Sarah

Analyzing and Revising Sample 2 Directions:

1. *Look at the class list of criteria. Each criterion has been assigned a different designation (highlighter color or underline).*

2. *Using the appropriate designation and colors, indicate where each criterion lives in the weak model.*

3. *Then, check off the criteria that are present in the weak model.*

4. *Together, write a plan for revision.*

Sample 2

Throughout Europe, [*ORANGE*: beliefs of women as evil and deceitful] were incredibly widespread, leaving many to be outraged at Elizabeth I's reign in England. For example, Scottish religious reformer John Knox wrote a piece outlining his anger to Elizabeth I. [*RED*: John Knox's profession of a religious reformer most likely impacted his point of view that women were evil and weak, and a woman in rule was against nature and ungodly. Since he was a reformed in this time, in Scotland,] [*PINK*: he most likely was a Protestant leaning toward Calvinism] [*RED*: and therefore interpreted scripture as a fact and accepted many of the anti-women themes in the Bible at the time (doc 1)]. Similarly, Jacques Bochetel de La Foret reported on a speech Elizabeth I gave to Parliament. **Parliament proposed a petition in hopes to rule her succession invalid.** In the document, it can be seen that these attitudes toward women were taken into consideration by Elizabeth I. As when speaking to Parliament, Elizabeth I cautiously, yet with much authority, asserted her power by stating that Parliament was meant to be in service to her and without her there was no government (doc 4). Although, Elizabeth did rule very strongly and made sure to assert her power, many people did speak out against her rule. For example, a portrait made by Marcus Gheeraerts the Younger shows Elizabeth I standing on top of England (signifying her control grip over England) and behind her a blue skinny sky is seen to her left and a stormy sky illustrated to her right; representing his belief that Elizabeth I was leading England into darkness (doc. 5).

After students annotate Sample 2, they return to the checklist to organize their thinking based on the evidence gathered while annotating. Then, they check off the success criteria that they have evidence for. The checklist becomes a tool for strategic revision. The student group then uses the completed checklist to create a plan for revision.

Our Plan for Revision:

What exactly will you do next to ensure each of the missing success criteria is met?

We will:

- add a clear statement to the beginning of the paragraph that states the documents reveal a culture of misogyny.

- remove document 5 from the body paragraph because it is misinterpreted and does not support the focus of misogyny.

- add document 3 to the body paragraph as the third source supporting the claim/topic sentence focused on misogyny.

- add a clear description of each document. There is currently a brief description of document 4, but documents 1 and 3 are lacking a description.

- revise the explanation of document 1 so it more clearly ties to the focus of misogyny.

- revise the explanation of document 4. Currently, the explanation suggests purpose connects this piece of evidence to the topic sentence, but this needs to be stated more directly.

- add an explanation to document 3 that unites this document to the topic sentence through the intended audience.

- ensure that the paragraph, in its entirety, confirms the validity of the DBQ's claim statement by looking at multiple pieces of evidence across course themes.

Model and Teach a Peer Review Structure

After students create their own product, it is crucial that you provide an opportunity for them to receive effective feedback. It is not practical to assume a high school teacher (with five sections of classes) can provide the amount of feedback students need to improve (especially when writing lengthy essays or DBQs), so we must look for ways to involve the students in giving feedback. While this seems like an easy solution, it is often balked at by educators because as one teacher put it, "students are horrible at giving feedback." If you have found yourself saying this, you are not wrong. Research shows that feedback provided by students to one another is typically inaccurate (Nuthall, 2007). Yet, it doesn't have to be. It has been inaccurate because students are rarely taught how to craft or share feedback using success criteria. In order to ensure feedback from peers is effective, it is essential to teach students a Peer Review structure and it is impera-tive to emphasize that the feedback they provide should be rooted in the success criteria. PQP (Praise, Question, Polish) is a Peer Review strategy originally de-signed for writing tasks (Neubert & McNelis, 1986). Students begin by reading a peer's work, then (1) they give praise to the work around the success criteria, (2) ask a question to get to the reason for the missing criteria, and (3) provide one action-oriented suggestion.

Before the students attempt the strategy, model how to complete a PQP Form and how to engage in a PQP conversation. Figure 14.8 is a completed PQP Form reflecting peer feedback that could be given to the student author of Sample 2 (shown in Figures 14.4 and 14.7, above). The peer feedback written here utilizes some of the feedback sentence stems and continuously refers to the success criteria that were included or missing from the work. Using this example, I would set the expectations for student discourse by selecting a student to act as the author of Sample 2. I would then hold a mock PQP conversation in front of the class with this student using the feedback written in Figure H. After clearly setting the expectations for peer feedback, send students an electronic PQP tem-plate and let them begin the Peer Review process.

Figure 14.8: Sample of a Completed PQP Feedback Form

Directions:
1. Read your classmate's work.
2. Review the success criteria.
3. Using the success criteria, determine the strength of the work and write 1 or 2 praise statements.
4. Using the success criteria, ask and record 1 or 2 questions (either for clarification, wonderment, or enhancement) concerning your partner's work.
5. Using the success criteria, make one suggestion to improve or enhance the work. The suggestion must be accompanied by a concrete action. Record this suggestion and action as a statement.

Praise, Question, Polish Peer Feedback Structure

PRAISE	
• What are the strengths of the work? • Which success criteria have been exceeded? How is this beneficial to the work?	• The strongest part of your work is ___ because ___ • You exceeded ___ criterion by ___ • Your use of ___ benefits your overall piece by ___
QUESTION	
• As a reader, what questions do you have about the work? • What do you not understand? • What do you wonder?	• What did you mean by ___? • Would more relevant evidence ___? • If you combined ___, would ___? • Is it necessary to include ___? • Does ___ support ___?
POLISH	
• Which success criteria could the author meet or enhance? • What action should the author take to propel him/her toward improvement?	• In order to ___, add content concerning___. • In order to ___, combine ___. • In an effort to ___, cite ___.

Sources: Adapted from Neubert & McNelis, 1986; Neubert & McNelis, 1990.

Peer Reviewer: Jane D.

Author of the Work: Clifford F.

P (Praise): You start your body paragraph off strong with a claim/topic sentence that unites the documents through "beliefs of women as evil and deceitful." Additionally, you meet one of the success criteria by explaining how point of view of document 4 relates to the topic/sentence.

Q (Question): Do you think your word choice of "beliefs of women as evil and deceitful" can be described as a culture of misogyny? Do you think document 5 supports the same focus as documents 1 and 4, or would there be a stronger piece of evidence to pull into the paragraph?

P (Polish): In an effort to make the strongest argument possible, I suggest removing document 5 and replacing it with document 3. Additionally, I suggest adding a sentence about each document that clearly explains how each document shows that there was a culture of misogyny present during the time of Elizabeth I's reign.

Feedback on Feedback

After providing initial instruction on how to write and share accurate and meaningful feedback, the teacher must hold the students accountable for applying this instruction by evaluating the feedback. After students submit their first PQP, provide electronic feedback to every student that wrote praise, asked a question, and made a polish statement concerning their classmate's work. Figure 14.9 demonstrates how the comment feature in Google Docs can be utilized to link teacher feedback to the relevant portion of a peer reviewer's PQP Feedback Form. Provide affirmation to students who wrote praise statements that are related to the success criteria and ask an interventionist question to those who did not tie their praise statement to the success criteria (Chappuis, 2009). Compliment students who asked questions that guided the author to look at the root-cause of their deficient criteria. To those who were off-base with their question, provide a sample question. When reviewing a student's suggestion for polishing the work, write a comment that points out how the suggestion is action-oriented or write a question that would guide the student towards an action-oriented suggestion.

While this seems time consuming, you will only need to evaluate student feedback two to three times before your students are giving each other quality feedback. Imagine how much better the DBQs you receive will be if the students become the first line of defense by accurately editing each other's initial drafts.

Figure 14.9: Google Docs Feedback on Feedback

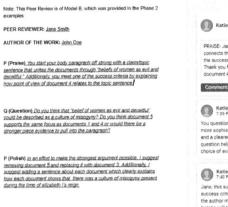

In this example you can see the feedback that the teacher gave to the student's Peer Review feedback.

Notice how the teacher gives positive specfic feedack to the students because they used the success criteria to give feedback to one another.

Leveraging Goal Setting and Revision

Not only do #PeerPower students need to be held accountable for the quality of feedback they give to their peers, but they also need to be held accountable for applying the feedback they receive from their peers. Both measures of accountability add value to the formative assessment process. If the students understand that they will be expected to use the feedback they receive, they will give better feedback in the first place.

Unfortunately, students often enter high school having learned through their prior school experience that feedback is irrelevant. It has often been given to them without the expectation of revision or application. It is usually given to them in conjunction with a grade. As a result, students hunt for the grade and ignore the feedback. They simply have not been expected to read, process, or value the feedback.

If we want to cause a paradigm shift, then we have to build a structure that requires application of the feedback. One way to achieve this is through goal setting and revision. After receiving peer feedback, ask the students to read the feedback and use it to identify a goal for revision. When initially applying this process in the first two or three units, consider providing an extra scaffold by asking the students to take an additional step of articulating an action plan for achieving their goal. By creating an action plan, they will be creating the "how-to" steps for their own personal revision. Figure 14.10 shows a completed goal-setting and action plan template. To clarify your expectations, share a completed goal-setting and action plan template with the students before giving them a blank template to complete on their own.

Figure 14.10: Goal-Setting and Action Plan Template

Directions:
- After you have engaged in the PQP conversation with your peer reviewer, take the PQP Feedback Form they completed and read it again.
- Then, look at the sample goal below.
- Write a revision goal that will incorporate the feedback from your partner. This goal must be SMART.
- Develop an action plan to guide your revision.
- Submit your goal and action plan with your revision on Friday, October 20.

My SMART Goal: *By this Friday, October 20, I will revise my body paragraph to demonstrate, through the analysis of three primary sources, that a culture of misogyny existed and influenced the reign of Elizabeth I.*

S	Specific	• Revision of body paragraph to show how a culture of culture of misogyny influenced the reign of Elizabeth I
M	Measurable	• One body paragraph • Analysis of 3 primary sources • Goal reflects the paragraph success criteria
A	Attainable	• The proposed revision of one paragraph is manageable and achievable.
R	Relevant	• The proposed revision will result in the paragraph meeting more (potentially all) of the success criteria.
T	Timebound	• This Friday, October 20

After the students submit their goal and action plan electronically, give them time to revise their work before submitting their final product. To truly shift the paradigm for students and add value to the peer-assessment process, the teacher should tie the quality of the final product to the student's goal and action plan, which was influenced by the PQP feedback. Figure 14.11 reflects the teacher's initial and final review of the DBQ paragraph. Prior to this point, the paragraph was reviewed by a peer. The teacher utilized the same list of success criteria that the peer used to evaluate the student's work. Then, the teacher wrote feedback to the student that intentionally connected the quality of the final paragraph to the peer's PQP comments, the student's goal, and the informed actions the student took.

My Action Plan:
- Add a clear statement to the beginning of the paragraph that states the documents reveal a culture of misogyny.
- Remove document 5 from the body paragraph because it is misinterpreted and does not support the focus of misogyny.
- Add document 3 to the body paragraph as the third source supporting the claim/ topic sentence focused on misogyny.
- Add a clear description of each document. There is currently a brief description of document 4, but documents 1 and 3 are lacking a description.
- Revise the explanation of document 1 so it more clearly ties to the focus of misogyny.
- Revise the explanation of document 4. Currently, the explanation suggests purpose connects this piece of evidence to the topic sentence, but this needs to be stated more directly.
- Add an explanation to document 3 that unites this document to the topic sentence through the intended audience.
- Ensure that the paragraph, in its entirety, confirms the validity of the DBQs claim statement by looking at multiple pieces of evidence across course themes.

Figure 14.11: Teacher Feedback

John, applying your partner's suggestions regarding the sources to include and exclude, committing to your action plan, and achieving your SMART goal led to an impressive improvement in your work. All of the success criteria have been met. The three sources you ultimately analyzed were well-grouped. Your explanations illuminated how each source connected to the topic sentence concerning a culture of misogyny through point of view, purpose, and intended audience.

Lessons Learned and Worth Sharing

Lesson 1: The Social Studies Advantage

When it comes to implementing this process, history and social studies teachers have a huge advantage. There is a direct connection between each step in the peer-assessment process and essential concepts in our discipline. For example, co-constructing success criteria can become a metaphor for democracy and imposing grading criteria upon students without their voice can become a metaphor for a dictatorship. Another example is the process of revision. We can connect revision to the steps a bill goes through before becoming a law. The committee aspect of creating a bill can be related to peer feedback. While there are numerous relevant connections, we can draw between engaging students in the peer-assessment process and our content, we can easily miss this advantage if (1) we do not take the time to think about, identify, and explain the metaphors to ourselves, and (2) we do not take the time to explain these larger connections to the students. See Figure 14.12 below for additional ways to connect the steps of the peer-assessment process to our content.

Figure 14.12: The Social Studies Advantage – Additional Examples of Disciplinary Metaphors

Defining Criteria: Co-Creating Success Criteria	**Yalta Conference** The 3 major powers had a vision of what a post-world war should look like. They knew they had to keep Germany industrial; therefore, they outlined steps (similar to criteria) that they would need to take to avoid the mistakes of Versailles.
Peer Review	**Creation of the Steam Engine** Newcomen designed the steam engine, but it was inefficient because it could not pump enough water out. Watt took Newcomen's design, sought financing from Matthew Boulton, and made improvements. As a result of the peer power and financial support, Watt perfected the steam engine.
Feedback on Feedback	**Formation of the Temperance Movement With Women** In the 1820s, women learned how to work at night in their sewing circles to develop a process for becoming socially active, which led to creating a voice for women. For example, Harriet Beecher Stowe took to the pen to convey her anti-slavery stance. Her work became fundamental to illuminating the contentious relations between the North and South. Additionally, her work demonstrated how women could move into the political realm. Women continued to write in pro-suffrage publications and unite to form the American Woman Suffrage Association.
Goal Setting	**Otto von Bismarck** Otto von Bismarck gave the "Blood and Iron" speech in 1862. This speech clearly conveyed his goals of making Germany great through war and industrialization. **Articles of Confederation** The Founding Fathers knew that the goal was to unify the states with a strong central authority so they had to improve the Articles of Confederation. Eventually, they realized they had to start over with the Constitutional Convention; yet, the goal remained the same, which was to create a strong central authority, but not a dictatorship.
Revision	**Ratification With the Constitution and the Addition of the Bill of Rights** When the initial constitution was proposed, the Anti-Federalists were not willing to ratify because they believed states needed more rights. As a result, the Constitution was revised to include the Bill of Rights. Amendment 10 met the Anti-Federalists' desires.

Sources: Ayers, 2009; McKay, Hill, Buckler, Crowston, & Wiesner-Hanks, 2013.

227

Lesson 2: Don't Make Assumptions

Another lesson learned concerns making assumptions. It is easy and logical to assume that teenagers know their classroom peers, or what constitutes a quality conversation, or how to write quality feedback. Yet, having witnessed teenagers stumble to use their classmate's name after half a year of being seated 12 feet apart, shift in their seat during uncomfortable and unnecessary conversation lulls, and write text-like feedback (LOL), we can no longer assume. Now, we need to ask the students to paint a picture of what they should see and hear before we release them to engage in the peer-assessment process. For example, "What constitutes good feedback? What does 'interventionist feedback' mean (Chappuis, 2009)? How does it sound? What does it look like in writing?" Potential student responses include:

- "Feedback that points out what is missing and gives you a suggestion for adding the missing parts are really helpful."

- "Feedback that asks you questions about what needs to be improved or what direction you need to go in is very helpful."

- "Good feedback is productive and clear. It does not include a vague comment of 'Nice Job,' 'I like this,' or 'add more.'"

- "Interventionist feedback tries to help you by asking a question, pointing out a problem, or addressing what you partially understood and misunderstood" (Chappuis, 2009).

- "It sounds like, 'You have identified the most well-known cause of the war, but what are some secondary causes?'"

After soliciting their responses, we can then provide clarification (orally and in writing) of the expectations.

Lesson 3: "Time" Is Our "Thing"

While we have an advantage as history teachers with the peer-assessment process, we also have a disadvantage. Time is justifiably our thing. We do teach what happened in the past; so, if anyone has claim to the excuse of "not enough time and too much to cover," it is us. Nevertheless, we have to refrain from falling in the time trap. We can do this by trusting in the process and committing fully to implementation. Invest the time at the onset of your course to thoroughly engage students in the five-step process around reoccurring skills, and then create additional opportunities for students to peer assess around these same skills in successive units. These efforts will yield the production of higher-quality work at a faster rate than what has been previously witnessed. If implemented with relentless persistence and patience, the peer-assessment process becomes routine and time will be returned twofold in the latter half of the school year.

Revolutionize Our Discipline

How will you know your discipline has been revolutionized? Observe and listen.

Has the classroom power structure shifted to reflect democratic ideals? Are students proudly heard exercising their voices in the classroom around history content? Is collaboration seen as a cornerstone of your classroom? Are students collecting and analyzing evidence in one another's work? Are students asking meaningful questions to challenge their peer's thinking and guide improvement? Are students making informed changes to their work? Revolutionizing our discipline means creating a classroom that is "for the people by the people." There is no way to make this shift without handing the reins over to the students. Please note: This is not supposed to be a smooth shift. When in history has there been a smooth transition as a result of a dramatic change in governance?

Mea Culpa

As a control freak, a lover of details, and a fan of the typically unknown stories of the past, I was very skeptical of the idea of incorporating peer assessment and student ownership of learning into history classrooms. I thought the content would suffer. But in this unprecedented moment of my personal history, I am admitting I was wrong. We can use the past to teach students the skills that will prepare them for the future.

Guiding Questions:

- **Disciplinary Relevance:** What are the disciplinary metaphors you can draw to the four steps of the peer-assessment process? When teaching students each step, how will you explain these metaphors and demonstrate that this process is relevant to your content area?

- **Transferable Skills and Success Criteria:** What are the transferable skills in your course? Where do these skills appear in each unit? What are the success criteria that your team has established for these transferable skills? Do you have strong and weak models associated with each skill that will illuminate what the success criteria looks like and when it is missing? How will you engage students in the five-step process around these skills at the onset of the year? How will you continue to engage students with peer assessment around these skills in each successive unit?

- **Implementing Peer Assessment:** Which peer-assessment method will you use? What will you be listening for in student conversations? What will you be looking for in written feedback and goal setting? What are the success criteria tied to your method of peer assessment?

Connect with Katie on Twitter @KatieSmith2007

Part III:
Empower Teams to
Empower Learners

Chapters 15–17

"We must empower teacher teams if we want to empower students!"

–Paul Bloomberg & Barb Pitchford

WE TALK ABOUT REVOLUTIONIZING ASSESSMENT by empowering students to take ownership of their learning, to be at the very center of the assessment process. However, we cannot empower students without first empowering teachers around their own professional learning. Teaching is complicated, and with ever-increasing challenges it becomes even more so every year. To activate and engage in relevant, impactful professional learning, teachers must learn to collaborate effectively and efficiently around those things that matter. The greatest resource for strengthening expertise in a school is the teachers themselves. What teacher teams need, quite simply, is the time, structures, and shared focus and purpose to strengthen collaborative expertise in service to *all* students—to learn together how to build #PeerPower! The following three chapters explore the importance of empowering teacher teams to expand student ownership and agency.

Chapter 15

Five Keys to Developing High Impact Teams

Paul J. Bloomberg & Barb Pitchford

"Remember that the revolution is what is important, and each one of us, alone, is worth nothing."

–Che Guevara

Question 1: What is the purpose of your team? Why do you meet?

- Unit planning?

- Developing common assessments?

- Curricular calibration and alignment?

- Data analysis?

- Initiative implementation—to understand and implement the latest initiative?

- Grouping students for intervention?

- All of the above?

Question 2: How many hours have you spent in "team meetings"?

Seriously, take a minute and estimate the amount of time you've spent with your team:

- Analyzing data
- Planning your next unit
- Writing assessments
- Talking about strategies to meet the needs of *all* students
- Listening to a colleague go on (and on?) about a teaching moment or "adventure"
- Trying to figure out how to engage students
- Managing behavioral problems

Make it easy on yourself. About how much time have you spent in teams this year?

Question 3: Given the time you've spent, how valuable has it been in improving your practice? In engaging you in learning?

Keeping It Real

Here's the reality. Most teachers spend *less than 1 hour per week* formally (scheduled time) collaborating with colleagues. Given the 40 hours a week we work in school (not counting the many hours *outside* of school we prepare, worry, plan, etc.), that's about 2.5 percent. Most teacher teams have an uneven understanding of *why* they meet.

So what can teams do to make the time spent with colleagues so purposeful and so valuable that they can't wait to get to their team meeting to share, to learn, to debate, to celebrate? What can teams do to make their time together not just productive but a powerful tool to improve teaching that actually has an impact on student learning?

Before we go there, let's briefly identify why collaboration has become an essential part of how we do business, and not just in education. Google recently conducted a three-year study on teaming called Project Aristotle. Not surprisingly, they found that working effectively together can reap powerful results. Quite simply, effective teams

- innovate faster,

- see mistakes more quickly,

- find better solutions to problems,

- get better results, and

- have higher job satisfaction (Duhigg, 2016).

Teams Are a Very Big Deal

Time spent in professional collaboration has ballooned by 50 percent in the past few decades. Organizations in all professions know that "*we* is smarter than *me*." Now teams are the fundamental unit of organizations and the unit of change in a school.

However, what Google (and every principal in the world) knows is that not all teams are created equal. So how do we ensure dynamic collaboration across the school? Quite simply, it is not about *who* is on the team (finding the perfect mix of skills and traits), rather it's about *how* the team interacts, structures their work, and views their contributions.

What Makes Successful Teams

We actually know exactly what makes teams productive (and what does not). Gallimore, Ermeling, Saunders, and Goldenberg (2009) cite five components:

1. Job-alike teams (common relevant focus)

2. Clear goals

3. Trained peer facilitator

4. Inquiry-based protocols

5. Stable settings (protected time, principal commits to the process over time)

Recently, a paper out of Harvard Graduate School of Education by Johnson, Reinhorn, and Simon (2015) examines how collaboration works best, listing five factors that contribute to a team's success:

1. Clear worthwhile purpose

2. Sufficient regular time

3. Administrative support and attention

4. Trained teacher facilitators

5. Integrated approach to teacher support

Beginning to see some consistencies?

Five Critical Components

First, Impact Teams have a singular purpose and that is to learn together to strengthen student efficacy and ownership. In our work with hundreds of school teams and based on a ton of research on effective teaming, we have identified five critical components of "Rockstar Teams" that ensure engagement, innovation, and results that build teacher, student, and collective efficacy.

1. **Trust** – Psychological safety is the number one ingredient in developing effective collaboration. It is the underpinning of the next four components. It is not just feeling safe to take risks (and learning is risky); it is about dependability, that is, trusting one another to do their part, to get the work done and done well.

2. **Purpose** – All team members share a clear understanding that the purpose of their collaboration is to learn together to build student ownership and efficacy. Their commitment is to share expertise on how to create the conditions for students to learn what learning is, what it takes to learn, and to

believe in themselves as learners. All team members share an unshakeable belief that this is meaningful work.

3. **Support** – Administrators actively promote and participate in team learning (walk the talk). Collaboration time is scheduled and protected (not hijacked for other "business"), roles are identified, and goals are aligned.

4. **Trained facilitator** – Intentional training and practice are a constant around inquiry-based protocols. Feedback is studied and applied with the focus on equal voice and responsive facilitation. Building teacher ownership and leadership is woven into the collaborative process.

5. **Collective action** – It's not just talk. Collaboration *always* results in thoughtful action specific to students' learning, social emotional needs, and is always aligned to the four sources of efficacy. Instructional improvement is constant and expected based on focused analysis of students' responses.

At the core of the work, these teams are learners—they are constantly and relentlessly reflecting on their practice, their strategies, their actions and asking, "What is our impact on student learning?" They are constantly learning in service to their students. And in the process, they are building efficacy, that is, the belief that they can and will make a difference in building student ownership and engagement in learning. These teams make a difference.

As longtime educators who believe in the power of good teaching and even more, good teachers, our belief was validated when John Hattie (2014) identified collective teacher efficacy (CTE) as the highest educational influence found in the research literature to date, 1.57 effect size! This translates to more than quadrupling the rate of learning (.40 effect equals about a year's growth in one year's time). In fact, CTE is one of the few influences in education that has the potential to mitigate the effects of poverty (Hoy, Sweetland, & Smith, 2002).

Growing From Within

Schools don't get better from the top down. They get better from learning and growing from within. And the core of the "within" is teachers learning from one another, to engage in collaborative inquiry to strengthen their practices and create the conditions for students to be partners in their own learning. We know how outrageously complicated teaching and learning is in today's world. It's simply not possible to teach consistently well alone—we need our peers to succeed! We must work together purposefully, efficiently, and effectively to have a significant impact on all students, to ensure they not only understand what learning is, but more importantly, that they believe in themselves as learners.

Guiding Questions:

- What is the purpose of your current PLCs? How do they take collective action to expand student ownership and agency?

- How do you support teacher leaders to strengthen peer facilitation?

- What processes or protocols does your PLC have in place to strengthen student ownership?

Connect with Paul and Barb on Twitter
@Bloomberg_Paul and @BarbPitchford

Learn more about the Impact Team Model
at www.LeadingImpactTeams.com

Chapter 16

Relational Trust: The Glue That Holds Teams Together

David Horton

"Remember Revolution is not something fixed in ideology, nor is it something fashioned to a particular decade. It is a perpetual process embedded in the human spirit."

–Abbie Hoffman

CONSIDER THE IDEAS YOU'VE READ about in this book. If you take a moment and think of the implications of these ideas on the function of a classroom, the impact is profound. The more time and effort spent reflectively working on not just *what* kids are doing but *why* and *how* they are doing it carries tremendous potential. Indeed, when teachers assist students in becoming "true monitors" of their own learning the ripple effect is dramatic. Students find ability and confidence to know they are learning and making progress. Students with more confidence raise the collective tide in the entire classroom. This new "tide line" creates a collateral effect into other subject areas and disciplines. And the ripple continues—a rather exciting sequence of events to be sure.

But, somewhere inside each of us we recognize that there is a certain limit if only one classroom dives into our #PeerPower Revolution. It is truly fantastic to have one classroom and one teacher "catch the fire" of #PeerPower, but in our minds we can't help but think of the magnified power if a partner teacher or a whole team engaged in the same focused work. Wouldn't that be the next logical step? Wouldn't that be a true force when a grade level or subject area team collectively builds, thinks about, gathers evidence, analyzes, and takes collective action to further improve the work done with and by students? The research is sound: When teachers work together to understand their impact on student learning, they build a common belief that they can make a difference for all students. This is collective teacher efficacy. When collective efficacy is realized, schools and systems can quadruple the rate of learning in their classrooms (Hattie, 2015). This is collective teacher efficacy. When collective teacher efficacy is present, teachers can quadruple the rate of learning in their classrooms (Hattie, 2015).

So, how can we expand our #PeerPower Revolution beyond one teacher to two? Or from a partnership to a whole team or department? Or to a whole school? Are there some basic steps to keep in mind to create the right foundation for this work to expand? The short answer is yes. And, perhaps, as important as any idea is this: The ideas in this book have everything to do with giving quality feedback to self, to peers, and to students. If you don't have trust, you *can't* receive critical, honest, and actionable feedback from your peers (Bloomberg, 2018).

It's About Dialogue, Dialogue, Dialogue

When you are ready become a #PeerPower Revolutionary with a partner teacher or team, there are some practical ideas to get you started. First, consider the discussion in *Leading Impact Teams* by Bloomberg and Pitchford (2017) related to "Rock Star Teams" and the components of Impact Team architecture. The guidance they give is that there are basic fundamentals that successful and consistent teams do and how they organize themselves. Teams have to have three fundamental components: (1) a learning network, (2) structures, and (3) processes (Bloomberg & Pitchford, 2017). The learning network focuses on how a team learns together—for instance, relational trust, communication, and norms. The structures focus on the organizational architectures that teams use to physically do their work, such as agendas, roles, a designated facilitator, and others. And finally, the processes teams use are the things that impact student learning; the process recommended by this author is the Leading Impact Teams, where crucial Visible Learning (Hattie, 2012) strategies become operationalized in classrooms and team rooms. (Note: Team development is a journey, not a destination—do not think that it is right or wrong to spend a certain amount of time working through one particular area. Some teams need more time in one area compared to another. This is neither right nor wrong. It's just the personality of that team. The only thing that matters is doing the work, not how long it takes.) Teams are organisms unto themselves. They require a certain organization, care, and maintenance. Putting in time and effort toward the well-being of the team is a required and crucial to-do item. It keeps the team running well. It is the act of a team thinking and working on *how* they do their work. One particular area to be mindful of is the connection between members—the learning network. In particular, relational trust is the glue that holds a learning network together. So, how can we care for, maintain, and build relational trust?

Building and Maintaining Trust Through Dialogue

The building and maintenance of relational trust is done via communication (dialogue). A critical aspect of the dialogue is the importance of *how* we dialogue not just *what* we dialogue about. Indeed, Daly (2018) notes that vulnerability is a crucial precursor of building trust through dialogue. The ability for teams to have sustained, escalating, reciprocal, and personal self-disclosing discussions allows for bonding through vulnerability, and this vulnerability is the incubator of trust (Daly, 2018). Indeed, relational trust is built on, anchored by, and fed by purposeful dialogue (Horton, 2017). Teams become teams with deep trust when they talk, share, and build common dialogue around professional concepts that matter (Horton, 2017).

Vulnerability and trust are interesting companions. Common sense says that we stand on solid ground, build trust, and then leap into the unknown (Coyle, cited in Daly, 2018). Research seems to show that we may have it backwards. Leaping into the unknown when done alongside others causes the solid ground of trust to materialize under our feet (Coyle, cited in Daly, 2018). This means that if we dare to take on worthy processes and get started even if we have a less than perfect path for execution but, and most importantly, we do it as a team that is together, we build more trust and a stronger team. Not to mention, as efficacy improves, so too will the process initiative the team is focused on.

Consider the implications of this thought for teams. Having a bond and relationship, even if in its infancy, provides the needed ingredients for a team to engage in challenging work if done together. They leap together into the unknown and uncertainty of their road ahead knowing that by maintaining a network and bond they will get stronger together and weather any storm that comes. This, when done consistently, builds both the relational trust and the learning network simultaneously.

Building Relational Trust

This chapter brings a deeper dive into a particular component of a strong learning network (meaning the connections between members and how they learn with and from each other), which is building relational trust. The format of this work (directed conversations) is built on the structures of the book *Leading School Teams* (Horton, 2017).

Trust between teammates is the glue that holds teams together. When trust is not present between team members, the function of the team is greatly compromised and the potential for deep collaborative work suffers. Indeed, the goal of collective teacher efficacy will not be fully realized if relational trust is low or nonexistent. A simple and powerful method to maintain and build trust is to hold periodic dialogues about professional topics.

Below are a couple of framed discussions to get teams started with some dialogues about their work. These dialogue discussions are adapted from *Leading School Teams* (Horton, 2017).

Dialogue 1

Directions:

Step 1: Read this discussion prompt and have each team member share for 30–45 seconds. Discussion Prompt: *How do ideas that can impact learning come about in your team and your school?*

Step 2: After all members have shared, ask this question: "Is there anything in common from the sharing that we could focus on or work on that might propel us even further in this area?" A recorder should be recording ideas shared.

Step 3: After all members have shared, ask this question: "What are two or three action steps we could take to get this work into action?" A recorder should be recording ideas shared.

Step 4: After all members have shared, ask this question: "How will we calendar some to-do items from our Action Steps to get our ideas into concrete action?" Ideas should be charted or recorded.

Step 5: If time allows, or in a future meeting, use these Follow-Up Prompts to continue the discussion. Follow the same Steps 1–4 for each prompt. Additional Follow-Up Prompts: Are all stakeholders "allowed" to have ideas? Are these ideas given equal weight? How are less-than-good ideas handled?

Dialogue 2

Directions:

Step 1: Read this discussion prompt and have each team member share for 30–45 seconds. Discussion Prompt: *What challenges has your team or school had in the past with generating ideas or solving problems?*

Step 2: After all members have shared, ask this question: "Is there anything in common from the sharing that we could focus on or work on that might propel us even further in this area?" Chart or record the ideas shared.

Step 3: After all members have shared, ask this question: "What are two or three action steps we could take to get this work into action?" Chart or record the ideas shared.

Step 4: After all members have shared, ask this question: "How will we calendar some to-do items from our Action Steps to get our ideas into concrete action?" Chart or record the ideas shared.

Step 5: If time allows, or in a future meeting, use these Follow-Up Prompts to continue the discussion. Follow the same Steps 1–4 for each prompt. Additional Follow-Up Prompts: What processes have been evident previously in your team or school to support problem solving? How does your team or school currently involve a cross-section of people to be part of an idea or problem-solving session?

Dialogue 3

Directions:

Step 1: Read this discussion prompt and have each team member share for 30–45 seconds. Discussion Prompt: *Does your team support self-reflection on a regular basis to examine* how *things are getting done?*

Step 2: After all members have shared, ask this question: "Is there anything in common from the sharing that we could focus on or work on that might propel us even further in this area?" Chart or record the ideas shared.

Step 3: After all members have shared, ask this question: "What are two or three action steps we could take to get this work into action?" Chart or record the ideas shared.

Step 4: After all members have shared, ask this question: "How will we calendar some to-do items from our Action Steps to get our ideas into concrete action?" Chart or record the ideas shared.

Step 5: If time allows, or in a future meeting, use these Follow-Up Prompts to continue the discussion. Follow the same Steps 1–4 for each prompt. Additional Follow-Up Prompts: Handling ideas is not a "throw-away" activity. Ideas require a culture of not just having them but knowing how to examine them and talk them through for viability. Does your team and school have this culture? If not, what things can be done to improve or correct it? Does your organization treat all ideas, on their inception, equally? Do all ideas get equal treatment? How do people react if their idea is rejected? Does your team have a mechanism to sift, channel, and funnel ideas to vet them for viability?

Continued Work: Where You Can Go Next

Once you get some practice with the dialogues above, you will likely find that building relational trust via dialogue opens some wonderful conversations. These conversations build trust, expand thinking, and support team direction by sharing and understanding each other's professional thoughts. Visit www. PeerPowerRevolution.com for more tips and tools.

The Wrap-Up

Empowering students to take ownership of their learning is our quest. The tools in this book are designed precisely for this purpose. Students should have multiple opportunities to deeply think and work in their grade level and subject area to learn not just where they are but how they know where they are going next. The tools in this book help teachers build experiences for students to "flex their intellectual muscles" to grow and make progress in high-quality ways. As this unfolds it becomes a powerful part of the journey to do this work collaboratively. This chapter has some beginning steps to get teams off on a strong foot. Take these suggestions one at a time to get better together in the work you undertake, build relational trust, and set the stage for the giving of quality feedback that improves everyone. Happy Teaming!

Guiding Questions:

- How do you strengthen relational trust with your PLC or Impact Team?

- How do members of your team model vulnerability? Why is this important?

- How might you use dialogue discussions with your PLC or Impact Team?

Connect with Dave on Twitter at @Horton_David_DH

Chapter 17

Empowering Teacher Teams to Drive Their Learning: Transforming Professional Learning with Impact Team Inquiry

Paul Bloomberg & Barb Pitchford

"Passion is needed for any great work, and for the revolution, passion and audacity are required in big doses."

–Che Guevara

Impact Team Inquiry

If our goal is for students to take ownership of their learning, then we must empower teachers to take ownership of their learning. This notion of empowerment is the core of collaborative inquiry, and inquiry is the heart of a robust learning environment. Creating the conditions for a learning culture in which all members of the school community are actively engaged in inquiry, investigation, and innovation requires teachers to take the lead both formally and informally, to advocate for teacher voice and to model key learning dispositions. The best way to cultivate these academic mindsets is for teacher teams to drive their own learning through collaborative inquiry that puts learning at the center. Growth, community, a sense of personal and collective agency, and creating meaningful work are the goals of the Impact Team System Innovation Model.

Schools don't change and innovate one teacher at a time or one leader at a time. Teams are the unit of change in a school, and all teams are not created equal. Like any relationship, teaming requires attention, relational trust, and commitment. To accelerate effective collaboration school-wide, systems began piloting the Impact Team Model nationally in 2013. Supported by John Hattie's Visible Learning research (2009), the core belief of the Impact Team Model is that all schools have what it takes to be extraordinary. Teachers are a school's greatest resource for innovation. What is needed, quite simply, is for teachers to be given the time to share best practice, to experiment with high-impact strategies, to investigate and innovate—to learn together. "As teachers in a school feel empowered to do great things, great things happen" (Eells, 2011).

Protocols for Inquiry and Innovation

Impact Teams focus their inquiry on expanding student ownership and agency with the aim of strengthening student and collective teacher efficacy. Embedded in this approach are 10 purposeful protocols that teams use to investigate and strengthen their practices around creating learner-centered classrooms—students know where they're going, how they're going, and what they need to do next to reach their learning goals. This approach requires teacher teams to determine their focus of inquiry and to design their own job-embedded professional learning. The Impact Team Model provides the processes and structures to share and build teacher leadership across the school community through strengthening peer facilitation.

To do this, Impact Teams collaboratively determine what core, formative practices (feedback, self- and peer assessment, goal setting, reflection, etc.) they want to strengthen so they can participate in and contribute to systemic innovation to gain a deeper understanding of what works best. The development and design of the Impact Team Model is based on extensive evidence-based research that identifies those practices that maximize student learning. Impact Teams operationalize multiple Visible Learning (Hattie, 2009) influences that are proven to have the highest effect on student learning.

- Help seeking: .72 ES (effect size)

- Teacher–student relationships: .72 ES

- Reciprocal teaching: .74 ES

- Feedback: .74 ES

- Teacher clarity: .75 ES

- Evaluation and reflection: .75 ES

- Classroom discussion: .82 ES

- Teacher estimates of achievement: 1.29 ES

- Assessment-capable learners: 1.33 ES

- Collective teacher efficacy: 1.39 ES

Growing From Within

What has become clear is that top-down, all-school, or all-district initiatives don't work. It is expensive, exhausting, and in no way empowers teachers or students to be engaged, curious, or motivated. Top-down approaches don't create optimal conditions for collaboration, collective inquiry, and innovation. Nor do these approaches attend to strengthening student or teacher efficacy. Empowerment is not part of this familiar formula. Impact Teams find innovative ways to partner with students in the inquiry process, which opens up endless possibilities for student involvement. Researchers have learned from educators that "inquiry is not a 'project', an 'initiative' or an 'innovation' but a professional way of being" (Timperley, Kaser, & Halbert, 2014). Collaborative inquiry propels the collective to learn together with a goal of strengthening student ownership, motivation, and agency.

Impact Team Innovation

Our belief and our experience is that every school and system has what it takes to innovate and improve every school. We don't believe that teachers or schools are broken. In fact, every school has the resources under the roof of a building to be extraordinary. Schools and systems need leadership that believes in the capacity of all teachers and all students to learn and lead together by creating formal and informal structures for teachers and students to access one another's expertise (Bloomberg & Pitchford, 2017).

Every school has strengths, and we must optimize those strengths to ensure that both teachers and students take ownership of their learning. When teacher teams are encouraged to innovate to expand student ownership, they

- take risks,
- embrace challenge,
- learn together,
- create new ideas,
- problem-solve,
- teach to their passions, and
- most important, make an impact.

Driving Questions

The Impact Team Inquiry cycle begins with a curiosity or an educational innovation that teams wish to explore. Impact Teams develop informed questions and/or theories of action about pedagogy and use the following driving questions:

- **What will we learn together?**
  How will our inquiry allow us to learn new skills and understanding to put students in the driver's seat?

- What is the moral purpose that propels our inquiry?

  How can we make a difference for all learners?

- What formative practices do we want to strengthen as a team?

  Are these practices proven to accelerate learning?

- What will we solve together?

  How will our inquiry allow us to identify problems and design improved solutions?

- What will we create together?

  How will our inquiry allow our team to invent and create new teaching tools or improve existing ideas?

  What practices can we let go of to make space for student ownership?

- What are our passions?

  How will our inquiry allow our team to follow our passions, dreams, and ambitions?

- How can we share our impact?

  How will our inquiry benefit others?

  How will we share our innovations and discoveries with others in our school and community?

Ideate, Design, and Envision

Ideate: Impact Teams ideate. They invest collaborative time to determine their learning focus. Teams define why their focus is important, and they validate their inquiry with the Visible Learning synthesis to ensure that their cycle is evidence-based. They determine what expertise resides in their team and school with a vision of bringing research to life in their classrooms in service of student ownership. The Impact Team's ultimate objective is to *empower* students to

- find and pursue their passions with purpose;

- enjoy designing and showcasing products and performances;

- articulate the processes they use to increase their own learning;

- expand intrinsic motivation to own and drive their learning;

- increase control and responsibility for their learning;

- strengthen content knowledge, metacognition, self-regulation, and executive function; and

- cultivate student agency.

Impact Teams have autonomy over the focus of their research-based inquiry cycle. Their inquiry focus may be grounded in solving a problem of practice or goals they wish to explore with their students. Keep in mind, their inquiry should be aligned to the overarching school goals. Therefore, it is important that overarching school goals offer flexibility to teams. For example, The Public School 13 in Staten Island, New York, had an overarching goal of strengthening student engagement and involvement. Teams had choices in what formative practices they would strengthen based on what their learners needed and what they wanted to explore. This broad goal gave teams autonomy when making decisions about their learning focus or inquiry. When schools offer this kind of flexibility for teams, it creates optimal conditions for team creativity, increased motivation and innovation. For example, some teams may focus on leveraging reflection, some teams may explore self and peer assessment with their students, some teams may focus on expanding goal setting with students; team's inquiries may vary. Conversely, in some schools the instructional leadership team, with support from all stakeholders, collaboratively decides to do a full school inquiry. As long as shared-decision making is used, the inquiry will prove effective because of teacher buy in. Especially, since all team's inquiries serve to strengthen dispositional learning and expand student ownership and agency.

Voices From the Field

Norris School District | Bakersfield, CA

Kelly Miller, Superintendent, and Chantel Mebane, Director of Instruction
"To begin the Impact Team process, we had to get full investment from our principals to lead the way for their school sites. They embraced the chance to try something new and change collaboration as we knew it. They were immersed in the professional development process with their teachers and learned right alongside them. Throughout this journey, our teams have developed a common language of learning and have gained a deeper understanding of the standards while being able to differentiate for all learners. The Evidence, Analysis, Action Protocol (EAA), a foundational protocol from the Impact Team Model, has become a regular routine that keeps teams engaged in constantly making instructional adjustments to meet the needs of all learners. Impact Teams (PLCs) analyze a variety of evidence (student work, student voice, observations, etc) and take collective action in the service of strengthening student efficacy and ownership.
 As a result of the powerful collaborative practices with a focus on teacher clarity, students are now taking more ownership of their learning. They can self-assess and provide constructive feedback to their peers. With the use of success criteria, our students are able to identify where they are at in the learning process at any given point and what they need to do to progress and achieve mastery."

Design: Impact Teams design their cycle by specifying what evidence they will analyze to understand impact. A variety of evidence is key for teams to have a clear understanding of their impact. The evidence can be qualitative, quantitative, or both. Using multiple sources of data strengthens the trustworthiness and reliability of the *Impact Team Inquiry*, because different forms of evidence can be compared or "triangulated." For instance, in exploring student ownership, one evidence source might be student interviews and another might be student work. A third evidence source might be to participate in an *Impact Team Evidence Walk* as a way to observe teacher and student experiences in the peer and self-review process. These three sources of data, drawn from interviews, observations, and student work products, are triangulated to provide a multidimensional perspective on the inquiry being explored. The following evidence can be used as sources of evidence for *Impact Team Inquiry:*

- **Student Work:** Analyzing student work is foundational to Impact Team Inquiry. The analysis of work provides teacher teams with valuable insight into their students' understanding of concepts and skills relating to the focus standards. Teams focus on transferable tasks to ensure that transfer takes place under a variety of conditions and environments.

- **Student Voice:** Student voice or student perception are terms commonly used to describe students' expression of their learning process and their overall perceptions about learning. Student voice data can be collected with surveys, focus groups, interviews, reflections, and self- and peer assessments. For example, if problem solving is the focus of a team's inquiry, asking an identified group of students what it means to be a problem solver is a great way to gather student voice data throughout an inquiry cycle.

- **Video:** Impact Teams create and analyze video-based evidence of students and their peers to strengthen their inquiry. This evidence is a form of observation data and allows teams to use video to stop and rewind while analyzing the evidence to enhance pedagogy around deeper learning outcomes.

- **Observation:** Effective teams may choose to collect observation data while students are collaborating, during a 1:1 conference, during small-group instruction, and during classroom discussions. Teacher teams may also choose to observe one another during inter-visitations, lesson study, and during evidence walks. Observation data are often overlooked as a data source. This qualitative data provide critical insight to strengthen next steps.

- **Teacher Voice:** Teacher voice or teacher perception data supports teams in understanding teachers' perceptions of the Impact Team's learning focus. Perceptions are usually the attitudes and beliefs held about a school by the people with a vested interest in seeing the school succeed. Teachers can be asked about their ideas and feelings about their team's inquiry. Teachers may discuss where expertise resides in their team or across their school. Teachers check in with one another during the inquiry process to ensure that all voices are heard. Understanding each teacher's attitudes and beliefs of the learning community is important—because perception does shape reality.

Once the evidence is determined, Impact Teams decide what protocols they will use to guide their inquiry; these protocols ensure that the team stays focused on deeper learning outcomes for students. Trained peer facilitators guide teams to choose from 10 purposeful protocols to drive their inquiry. The peer facilitator ensures that norms, guidelines and/or rules of engagement, and structures are used to make the meetings efficient and effective. The protocols teams use are purposeful and generated from what effective teams choose to learn about:

- Getting to know standards and/or creating student-friendly, criteria-based rubrics

- Calibrating student work samples

- Analyzing impact through analysis of student work

- Aligning the curriculum

- Analyzing student voice data

- Sharing and trying out innovative teaching strategies

- Engaging in lesson study through peer-to-peer observation

Impact Teams use classroom protocols to provide routines and processes to ensure that students remain at the center. Efficient routines and learner-centered protocols have been developed to guide students in

- personalizing learning intentions,

- defining the criteria of success,

- giving and receiving evidence-based feedback,

- effective self- and peer assessment,

- reflection and goal setting, and

- strengthening self- and social awareness.

Envision Success: Impact Teams envision success before they begin their inquiry. They build a shared vision of the future. They dream big and imagine what success will look like, sound like, and feel like if they are successful with their inquiry. They imagine what students will be thinking, feeling, saying, and doing if their team worked at optimal levels to realize their inquiry becomes a reality. When teams envision success, they co-construct the success criteria for their Impact Team Inquiry Cycle. By envisioning success (see Figure 17.1), they share their dreams and visions that move them from where they are today to where they want to be in the future.

Figure 17.1: The Envisioning Process – Impact Team Inquiry Design

If we engage students in the self- and peer review process, then they will be:

Thinking	Feeling
• *What feedback will I give my friend?*	• *I am nervous to show my mistakes.*
• *How can I be very specific and use the success criteria to guide my feedback?*	• *I feel like the teacher trusts me to lead my learning.*
• *I need to make sure I communicate respectfully.*	• *I am worried that my feedback might not help my partner.*
• *I need to make sure I give my partner a strategy to close the gap.*	• *I feel confident because I know this is just practice and the feedback will help me.*
• *What if I give the wrong feedback?*	• *I feel safe because I can make mistakes, and mistakes are a part of learning.*
• *I love taking ownership of my learning!*	
• *I need to be honest with my feedback.*	

Saying	Doing
• One strength that you have is ___ and one next step could be ___.	• Giving feedback using academic vocabulary
• What was the hardest part?	• Receiving feedback through active listening
• This may help you achieve your goal.	• Revising work using feedback
• Have you ever tried thinking about this?	• Setting goals using the feedback from our partners and teacher
• You may have forgot this step.	• Talking through the steps of a strategy
• This would make your work even better.	• Reflecting on the feedback given

Building a Culture of Efficacy

Effective professional learning must be job-embedded, differentiated and focused on both content and pedagogical expertise. It must be sustainable over time and aligned to what increases learning the most, that is, student ownership. When students know where they are going, know where they are at, and can articulate why the learning is relevant to them, teams know that their inquiry is getting results, changing behavior, and accelerating the learning process. Sharing knowledge and collaboratively developing pedagogical expertise reaps significant gains (Bloomberg & Pitchford, 2017). Goddard, Hoy, and Hoy (2000) suggest that to improve student learning system-wide it is crucial to raise collective efficacy beliefs of the staff. Eells (2011) states that collective teacher efficacy is the pervasive belief that directly affects the school's ability to raise achievement. Believing in the combined intellect, sharing the commitment, and focusing the energy of the group on student ownership moves a school to even greater learning and higher impact (Bloomberg & Pitchford, 2017). The shared mastery experiences that occur over time develop an unshakeable optimism, collective confidence, and a profound belief that no matter the challenge, together, we can and will make an impact. When teachers believe they can make a difference for all students, they do.

Guiding Questions:

- How does your school empower teacher teams to drive their own professional learning?

- Do your PLCs engage in the collaborative inquiry process? How and why do you decide on your team's inquiry focus?

- What is the goal of your current PLCs? How do they expand student ownership?

- What could your school do to expand teacher agency? Why is teacher agency important?

Connect with Paul and Barb on Twitter
@Bloomberg_Paul and @BarbPitchford

Learn more about Leading Impact Teams at
www.LeadingImpactTeams.com

Part IV:
A Call to Action

Chapter 18

"The revolution is not an apple that falls when it is ripe. You have to make it fall."

—Pawan Kalyan

Chapter 18

Unite, Learn, and Prosper . . .
Become a #PeerPower Activist!

"The only way to support a revolution is to make your own"

–Abbie Hoffman

NOW THAT YOU HAVE JOINED our #PeerPower Revolution, it is time to turn beliefs and ideas into collective action. It is time for *you* to become a #PeerPower Activist. You don't have to cover yourself in paint, throw yourself on the ground, or stand in a picket line to become an activist. An activist is a person who campaigns for change. As humans, we have the power to change things that we don't agree with. When you take collective action to bring awareness to our cause, you become an activist in the process. All that it takes to become an activist are passion, knowledge, skill, and a true desire to bring about change. Here are six ways that you can get involved in putting learners at the center of the formative assessment process.

1. **Lead by Example:** One of the simplest and most important forms of activism is practicing what you preach. You can make a powerful statement through leading by example or *conscious activism*. Conscious activism is activism by *doing*. Practicing conscious activism means infusing activism into

your everyday life by making sure that you are living and working toward the ideals you believe in. If you lead by example, you will be well on your way to inspiring innovation and change.

2. **Educate:** You have to be informed and educated if you want to make change: listen to podcasts, engage in Twitter chats, join a Facebook group, and/or start a book club at school. An informed #PeerPower Activist is able to point out credible and reliable resources that are trusted by other people. If you can't articulate your vision clearly based on solid evidence, read, research, and study until you can. Check out the bibliography of this book for research to back up our cause. Whatever you can do to learn more about our cause will only make you a better activist by giving you the knowledge you need to educate others and ignite change.

3. **Give It a Go!** By trying some of the practices and strategies in this book, you can not only practice but also determine the impact of the changes you made. That impact will validate not only what you are doing and what your students are doing but also what others might try because of your impact.

4. **Raise Awareness:** Social media has revolutionized the way we communicate, and it is a powerful tool for activists. Whatever platform you choose, there are tons of connections to be made with individuals and networks that share the same values and goals as our network. Activism can take on many forms: write a book or article, blog, develop a YouTube channel, post videos on social media, develop a wiki, and/or create *sketchnotes* of your favorite articles, keynotes, or books. Be sure to share each other's posts on your personal social media platforms as well.

   • **Tweet:** Use the hashtag #PeerPower to celebrate your impact. @TheSocialCore @MimiToddPress

   • **YouTube:** Develop videos of self- and peer assessment in action and post them on our YouTube channel. www.youtube.com/corecollaborative

- **Facebook:** Join a Facebook group with like-minded people to get ideas and strategies.

  facebook.com/groups/LeadingImpactTeams

- **Instagram:** Post a video or picture of your ideas in action.

  @corecollab

5. **Find Like-Minded Partners:** When you network with like-minded people, our cause takes on a stronger purpose. You will benefit from the support, knowledge, and camaraderie of learning with people with similar values. Bring up your #PeerPower Activism in everyday conversation—you never know who will also share the same passion. It shouldn't be hard to find teachers, coaches, and principals who believe in empowering students to take ownership of their learning; you may inadvertently recruit another person for our cause. When it comes to activism, there is strength in numbers.

6. **Don't Stop Engaging:** Never pass up the opportunity to share what you know and the impact self- and peer assessment has on learning. Talk to as many people as you can, share our vision, and ask them to join our cause. Apply to present at conferences locally and/or nationally. Present in front of teachers in your school and invite them to your classroom to experience your impact. Send emails to the school board and local government officials. Be relentless in your pursuit of student ownership, and be clear with everyone about the benefits.

The #PeerPower Manifesto

The #PeerPower Manifesto functions as both a statement of principles and a bold call to action. We wrote this manifesto to inspire you when you don't feel like your efforts are valued. Our greatest hope is that reading this manifesto will inspire you to recommit to our worthy cause of strengthening learner-centered schools and systems.

- If you want to change the educational landscape around you, you have to change yourself first.

- Be able to articulate who and why you are doing this.

- Remember to trust the students; they are your legacy.

- There is strength in numbers. The greater the unity of the movement, the better chances of bringing our vision to life.

- Keep your eye on the big picture. Don't get swallowed up by the details.

- Don't get caught up on getting everyone on board. Get a critical mass and move forward. Others will learn from your success.

- Always speak the truth; this work is messy and hard to manage at first. Just be real about the *failures, fits,* and *starts* and celebrate success.

- To be successful, you need to be totally committed to the process and not give up.

- Take feedback and input from others. Revolution can't happen just because of one person; don't be a vigilante. It takes a village to make sustainable change.

- The revolution is not about you, it is about everyone collectively—most importantly our students. We *are* stronger together.

- Envision success. What would your school be like if students were taking ownership of their learning? What would students be thinking, feeling, saying, and doing if our revolution was successful?

A Call to Action

We began this book with a call to action, and now it is time to *unite, learn,* and *prosper together.* Let's activate an assessment revolution.

> Never doubt that a small group of thoughtful, committed citizens can change the world; indeed, it's the only thing that ever has.
>
> —Margaret Mead

References

Almarode, J., & Vandas, K. (2018). *Clarity for learning: 5 essentials practices that empower students and teachers.* Thousand Oaks, CA: Corwin.

Ambrose, S. A., Bridges, M. W., DiPietro, M., Lovett, M. C., & Norman, M. K. (2010). *How learning works: Seven research-based principles for smart teaching.* San Francisco, CA: Jossey-Bass.

Ayers, B. (2009). *American anthem* (1st ed.). New York, NY: Holt, Rinehart, & Winston.

Baker, L., & Brown, A. L. (1984). Metacognitive skills and reading. In P. D. Pearson, M. L. Kamil, R. Barr, & P. Mosenthal (Eds.), *Handbook of research in reading: Volume III* (pp. 353–395). New York, NY: Longman.

Bandura. A. (1994). Self-efficacy. In V. S. Ramachaudran (Ed.), *Encyclopedia of human behavior* (Vol. 4., pp. 71–81). New York, NY: Academic Press.

Black, P., & Wiliam, D. (1998). Inside the black box: Raising standards through classroom assessment. *Phi Delta Kappan, 80*(2), 139–148. http://www.pdkintl.org/kappan/kbla9810.htm

Bloomberg, P. (2018). *Keynote address.* MindFuelED Conference. Coronado, CA. June 2018.

Bloomberg, P., & Pitchford, B. (2017). *Leading impact teams: Building a culture of efficacy.* Thousand Oaks, CA: Corwin.

Bloomberg, P., Stevens, S., & Mascorro, L. (2017). *The empowered learner: Student-centered assessment toolkit.* New York, NY: Schoolwide Publishing.

Boaler, J. (2016). *Mathematical mindsets: Unleashing students' potential through creative math, inspiring messages and innovative teaching.* San Francisco, CA: Jossey-Bass.

Bray, B. (2018). *Levels of engagement: Balancing challenges and skills.* Retrieved from https://barbarabray.net/2018/07/14/levels-of-engagement-balancing-challenges-and-skills/

Brookhart, S. M., Andolina, M., Zuza, M., & Furman, R. (2004). Minute math: An action research study of student self-assessment. *Educational Studies in Mathematics, 57*(2), 213–227.

Capps, R., Bachmeier, J. D., Fix, M., & Van Hook, J. (2013). *A demographic, socioeconomic, and health coverage profile of unauthorized immigrants in the United States.* Migration Policy Institute, Washington, D.C. Retrieved from www.migrationpolicy.org/pubs/CIRbrief-Profile-Unauthorized.pdf.

Chappuis, J. (2009). *Seven strategies of assessment for learning.* Boston, MA: Pearson.

Chappuis, S., & Stiggins, R. J. (2002). Classroom assessment for learning. *Educational Leadership, 60*(1), 40–43.

Clark, D. (2011, October 22). Transfer of learning. Retrieved from http://www.nwlink.com/~donclark/hrd/learning/transfer.html

Clarke, S. (2008). *Active learning through formative assessment.* London, England: Hodder Education.

Claxton, G. (2006). *Expanding the capacity to learn: A new end for education?* University of Bristol Graduate School of Education. Opening Keynote Address, British Educational Research Association Annual Conference. September 6, 2006. Warwick University.

Claxton, G. (2008). *Cultivating positive learning dispositions.* Draft chapter for Harry Daniels et al., London, England: Routledge Companion to Education.

Claxton, G. (2018). *The learning power approach: Teaching learners to teach themselves.* Thousand Oaks, CA: Corwin.

College Board. (2011). *AP® European history free response questions.* Retrieved from https://secure-media.collegeboard.org/apc/ap11_frq_european_history.pdf

College Board. (2017a). *AP® European history course and exam description.* Retrieved from https://apcentral.collegeboard.org/pdf/ap-european-history-course-and-exam-description.pdf?course=ap-european-history

College Board. (2017b). *Rubrics for AP® histories + history disciplinary practices and reasoning skills.* Retrieved from https://apcentral.collegeboard.org/pdf/rubrics-ap-histories.pdf

College Board. (2018). *AP® history disciplinary practices and reasoning skills.* Retrieved from https://apcentral.collegeboard.org/courses/resources/ap-history-disciplinary-practices-and-reasoning-skills

Common Core State Standards Initiative. (2010). *Common core state standards for English language arts & literacy in history, social studies, and technical subjects.* Retrieved from https://ccsso.org/sites/default/files/2017-12/ADA%20Compliant%20ELA%20Standards.pdf

Common Core State Standards (CCSS). (2012). Retrieved from www.corestandards.org/Math

Cooper, D. (2006). Collaborating with students in the assessment process. *Orbit, 36*(2), 20–23.

Costa, A. (n.d.). *What is habits of mind.* Singapore: Art Costa Centre for Thinking. Retrieved from https://artcostacentre.com/html/habits.htm

Costa, A., & Kallick, B. (2014). *Dispositions: Reframing teaching and learning.* Thousand Oaks, CA: Corwin.

Coyle, D. (2018). *The talent code: Greatness isn't born. It's grown. Here's how.* New York, NY: Bantam Books.

Csikszentmihalyi, M. (1990). *Flow: The psychology of optimal experience.* New York, NY: Harper & Row.

Csikszentmihalyi, M. (2016). *Mihaly Csikszentmihalyi: All about flow & positive psychology.* Retrieved from https://positivepsychologyprogram.com/mihaly-csikszentmihalyi-father-of-flow/

Cyboran, V. (2006). Self-assessment: Grading or knowing? *Academic Exchange Quarterly, 10*(3), 183–186.

Daly, A. (2018). *Keynote address.* MindFuelED Conference. Coronado, CA. June 2018.

Dewey, J. (1897). My pedagogical creed. *School Journal, 54*(3), 77–80.

Dewey, J. (1916). Democracy and education: An introduction to the philosophy of education. New York, NY: Macmillan.

Duhigg, C. (2016). What Google learned from its quest to build the perfect team. *New York Times Magazine.* Retrieved from https://www.nytimes.com/2016/02/28/magazine/what-google-learned-from-its-quest-to-build-the-perfect-team.html?smid=pl-share

Dunning, D. (2007). *Self-insight: Roadblocks and detours on the path to knowing thyself.* New York, NY: Taylor and Francis.

Dweck, C. (2006). *Mindset: The new psychology of success.* New York, NY: Random House.

Dweck, C. (2016). *Mindset: The new psychology for success.* New York, NY: Random House.

Economy, P. (2015, January 3). Forget SMART goals—try CLEAR goals instead. *Inc.* https://www.inc.com/peter-economy/forget-smart-goals-try-clear-goals-instead.html

Eells, R. (2011). *Meta-analysis of the relationship between collective teacher efficacy and student achievement.* Ann Arbor, MI: UMI.

Eureka. (2005). In *New dictionary of cultural literacy* (3rd ed.). Retrieved from https://www.dictionary.com/browse/eureka

Farquharson, B. (2011, February 20). Developing learning autonomy. Retrieved from http://www.witslanguageschool.com/NewsRoom/ArticleView/tabid/180/ArticleId/45/Teaching-Tips-Developing-Learner-Autonomy.aspx

Farrington, C. A., Roderick, M., Allensworth, E., Nagaoka, J., Keyes, T. S., Johnson, D. W., & Beechum, N. O. (2012). *Teaching adolescents to become learners. The role of noncognitive factors in shaping school performance: A critical literature review.* Chicago, IL: University of Chicago Consortium on Chicago School Research. Available at https://ccsr.uchicago.edu/publications/teaching-adolescents-become-learners-role-noncognitive-factors-shapingschool

Ferguson, Y., & Sheldon, K. M. (2010). Should goal-strivers think about "why" or "how" to strive? It depends on their skill level. *Motivation and Emotion, 34,* 253–265. doi:10.1007/s11031-010-9174-9

Flavell, J. H. (1985). *Cognitive development.* Englewood Cliffs, NJ: Prentice Hall.

Fountas, I. C., & Pinnell, G. S. (2017). *The Fountas & Pinnell literacy continuum: A tool for assessment, planning, and teaching.* Portsmouth, NH: Heinemann.

Gallimore, R., Ermeling, B. A., Saunders, W. M., & Goldenberg, C. (2009). Moving the learning of teaching closer to practice: Teacher education implications of school-based inquiry teams. *Elementary School Journal, Chicago Press Journals, 109*(5), 537–553.

Gibbs, A., & Reed, D. K. (2018, February 20). *Using possible selves to facilitate student literacy achievement.* Retrieved from https://iowareadingresearch.org/blog/possible-selves-literacy-achievement

Goddard, R. D., Hoy, W. K., & Hoy, A. W. (2000). Collective teacher efficacy: Its meaning, measure, and effect on student achievement. *American Education Research Journal, 37*(2), 479–507.

Gregory, K., Cameron, C., & Davies, A. (1997). *Setting and using criteria.* Courtenay, BC: Classroom Connections International Inc.

Hansell, S. (2008, May 12). Why Yelp works. *Bits.* https://bits.blogs.nytimes.com/2008/05/12/why-yelp-works/

Hatano, G., & Inagaki, K. (1986). Two courses of expertise. In H. Azuma & K. Hakuta (Eds.), *Child development and education in Japan* (pp. 262–272). New York, NY: Freeman.

Hattie, J. A. (2002). Classroom composition and peer effects. *International Journal of Educational Research, 37*(5), 449–481.

Hattie, J. (2009). *Visible learning: A synthesis of over 800 meta-analyses relating to achievement.* London: Routledge.

Hattie, J. A. (2012). *Visible learning for teachers: Maximizing impact on teachers.* New York, NY: Routledge.

Hattie, J. A. (2014, July). *Keynote address.* American Visible Learning Conference. Palos Verde, CA: Corwin.

Hattie, J. (2015). *Keynote address.* California Visible Learning Institute. Universal City, CA. October 2015.

Hattie, J. A., & Clarke, S. (2019). *Visible learning feedback.* New York, NY: Routledge.

Hattie, J. A., & Donoghue, G. M. (2016). *Learning strategies: A synthesis and conceptual model.* Nature Publishing Group, www.nature.com/articles/npjscilearn201613

Henry Ford Quotes. (n.d.). BrainyQuote.com. Retrieved from https://www.brainyquote.com/quotes/henry_ford_383552

Horton, D. (2017). *Leading school teams: Building trust to promote student learning.* Thousand Oaks, CA: Corwin.

Hoy, W. K., Sweetland, S. R., & Smith, P. (2002). Toward an organizational model of achievement in high schools: The significance of collective efficacy [Electronic version]. *Educational Administration Quarterly, 38*(1), 77–93.

Illinois State Board of Education. (2017). *Illinois learning standards for social science 9–12.* Retrieved from https://www.isbe.net/Documents/SS-Standards-9-12.pdf

Johnson, S. M., Reinhorn, S. K., & Simon, N. S. (2015). *Ending isolation: The payoff of teacher teams in successful high-poverty urban schools.* Working paper. The Project on the Next Generation of Teachers. Retrieved from http://projectngt.gse.harvard.edu/files/gse-projectngt/files/ending_isolation.teams_._october_2015.pdf?m=1465278593

King, M. L. Jr. (1947). The purpose of education. *Maroon tiger.* Morehouse College. https://kinginstitute.stanford.edu/king-papers/documents/purpose-education

Knight, J. (2013). *High-impact instruction: A framework for great teaching.* Thousand Oaks, CA: Corwin.

Lamb, M. (2014, March 27). Self and peer assessment Dylan Wiliam [Video file]. https://www.youtube.com/watch?v=5P7VQxPqqTQ

Martin-Kniep, G. (2012). *Neuroscience of engagement and SCARF: Why they matter to schools.* Retrieved from https://neuroleadership.com/portfolio-items/neuroscience-of-engagement-and-scarf-why-they-matter-to-schools-vol-3/

McKay, J. P., Hill, B. D., Buckler, J., Crowston, C. H., & Wiesner-Hanks, M. E. (2013). *A history of western society since 1300 for the AP® course* (11th ed.). Boston, MA: Bedford/St. Martin's.

Mitchell, A., Holcomb, J., & Barthel, M. (2016, December 15). Many Americans believe fake news is sowing confusion. *Pew Research Center.* http://www.journalism.org/2016/12/15/many-americans-believe-fake-news-is-sowing-confusion/

Moss, C. M., & Brookhart, S. M. (2010). *Advancing formative assessment in every classroom: A guide for instructional leaders.* Alexandria, VA: Association for Supervision and Curriculum Development.

Muncaster, K., & Clarke, S. (2018). *Thinking classrooms: Metacognition lessons for primary schools.* London: Rising Stars UK Ltd.

National Council of Teachers of Mathematics (NCTM). (2014). *Principles to action: Ensuring mathematical success for all.* Reston, VA: NCTM.

Neubert, G. A., & McNelis, S. J. (1986). Improving writing in the disciplines. *Educational Leadership, 43*(7), 54–58.

Neubert, G. A., & McNelis, S. J. (1990). Peer response: Teaching specific revision suggestions. *English Journal, 79*(5), 52–56.

Nottingham, J. (2015). The learning challenge with James Nottingham. Retrieved from https://www.jamesnottingham.co.uk/learning-pit/

Nuthall, G. (2007). *The hidden lives of learners.* Wellington, New Zealand: NZCER Press.

O'Connell, M. J., & Vandas, K. (2015a). *Partnering with students: Building ownership of learning.* Thousand Oaks, CA: Corwin.

O'Connell, M. J., & Vandas, K. (2015b). *Parent teacher conferences: Something's got to give.* Peter DeWitt's: Finding Common Ground, *Education Week,* April 26, 2015.

Paulson, F. L., Paulson, P. R., & Meyer, C. A. (1991). What makes a portfolio? *Educational Leadership, 48*(5), 60–63.

Pearson, P. D., & Gallagher, G. (1983a). The gradual release of responsibility model of instruction. *Contemporary Educational Psychology, 8,* 112–123.

Pearson, P. D., & Gallagher, M. C. (1983b). The instruction of reading comprehension. *Contemporary Educational Psychology, 8,* 317–344.

Reivich, K. (2010, November). Promoting self-efficacy in youth. *Communique, 39*(3), 16–17.

Ritchhart, R. (2002). *Intellectual character: What it is, why it matters, and how to get it.* San Francisco, CA: Jossey-Bass.

Rohanna, K. (2018). *Evaluation brief: Impact of Sown To Grow on academic achievement.* Retrieved from https://s3-us-west-1.amazonaws.com/sown-to-grow/sown-to-grow-evaluation-summary-april-2018.pdf

Rolheiser, C., & Ross, J. A. (2001). Student self-evaluation: What research says and what practice shows. In R. D. Small & A. Thomas (Eds.), *Plain talk about kids* (pp. 43–57). Covington, LA: Center for Development and Learning.

Ross, J. A. (2006). The reliability, validity, and utility of self-assessment. *Practical Assessment Research & Evaluation, 11*(10), 1–13.

Samson, J., & Collins, B. (2012). *Preparing all teachers to meet the needs of English Language Learners.* Center for American Progress, Washington, D.C. Retrieved from https://files.eric.ed.gov/fulltext/ED535608.pdf

Sanchez, C. (2017). *5 million voices—English language learners: How your state is doing.* NPR Education. Retrieved from https://www.npr.org/sections/ed/2017/02/23/512451228/5-million-english-language-learners-a-vast-pool-of-talent-at-risk

Schmidt, N. (2017, March 16). *Humanizing online teaching and learning: The quest for authenticity.* EDUCAUSE Review. Retrieved November 20, 2018, from https://er.educause.edu/blogs/2017/3/humanizing-online-teaching-and-learning-the-quest-for-authenticity

Schunk, D. H., & Rice, J. M. (1991). Learning goals and progress feedback during reading comprehension instruction. *Journal of Reading Behavior, 23*(3), 351–364. https://doi.org/10.1080/10862969109547746

Serravallo, J. (2015). *The reading strategies book: Your everything guide to developing skilled readers.* Portsmouth, NH: Heinemann.

Slavin, R., Hurley, E., & Chamberlain, A. (2003). Cooperative learning and achievement: Theory and research. In W. M. Reynolds & G. E. Miller, *Handbook of psychology* (vol. 7, pp. 177–198). Hoboken, NJ: John Wiley & Sons.

Soroten, R. (2016). *A summer study of a student-owned goal setting and reflection tool on growth mindset, empowerment and academic behaviors* [White paper]. Retrieved from https://s3-us-west-1.amazonaws.com/sown-to-grow/step-summer-sown-to-grow-whitepaper.pdf

Spencer, J., & Juliani, A. J. (2017). *Empower: What happens when students own their learning.* San Diego, CA: IMpress.

Sterner, T. M. (2012). *The practicing mind: Developing focus and discipline in your life.* Novato, CA: New World Library.

Stiggins, R. J. (2014). *Revolutionize assessment: Empower students, inspire learning.* Thousand Oaks, CA: Corwin.

Stiggins, R. (2015, October). *The role of student growth in teacher evaluation.* Keynote address at the Teaching, Learning, Coaching Conference, Denver, CO.

Tanner, Kimberly D. (2012). Promoting student metacognition. *CBE—Life Sciences Education, 11,* 113–120.

Texas Education Agency. (2012). *Texas essential knowledge and skills for mathematics, Subchapter A: Elementary.* Retrieved from http://ritter.tea.state.tx.us/rules/tac/chapter111/ch111a.html

Timperley, H., Kaser, L., & Halbert, J. (2014). *A framework for transforming learning in schools and the spiral of inquiry* (Seminar series paper 204). East Melbourne, VIC, NZ: Centre for Strategic Education.

Wiggins, G. (2010, March 27). What is transfer? *Big Ideas.* http://www.authenticeducation.org/ae_bigideas/article.lasso?artid=60

Wiggins, G., & J. McTighe. (2005). *Understanding by design.* Alexandria, Virginia: ASCD.

Wiliam, D. (2011). *Embedded formative assessment.* Bloomington, IN: Solution Tree Press.

Wiliam, D. (2018). *Embedded formative assessment.* Bloomington, IN: Solution Tree Press.

Zimmerman, B. J., & Kitsantas, A. (1999). Acquiring writing revision skill: Shifting from process to outcome self-regulatory goals. *Journal of Educational Psychology, 91,* 241–250. doi:10.1037/0022-0663.91.2.241

Index

activism, methods for, 263–266
add-on versus infusion concept, 26
advanced organizers, 86
Affinity Diagraming, 23
Allensworth, E., 96–97
Ambrose, S. A., 81
analysis of student work. *See* success
    criteria
anchor charts, 117
annotation, 41
anxiety, 116–118
assessment for learning culture, 5–6
assessment revolution, need for, 4–6
assumptions, 228
attainment versus capability, 25–26

Beechum, N. O., 96–97
behaviors, defined, 125
Black, Paul, 7, 30
Bloomberg, P., 242
Brandner, Melissa, 167
Bray, Barbara, 14–15
Bridges, M. W., 81
Brookhart, S. M., 139

call to action, 263–266
capability versus attainment, 25–26
CCSS. *See* standards
challenges, 70. *See also* goals and goal
    setting

checklists, 34–36, 46. *See also* rubrics
clarity
    English Language Learners and,
        109–112
    in reading, 124–126
    success criteria co-construction
        increasing, 40, 173–176
    teaching of, 166–167
Clarke, Shirley, 30, 68
Claxton, Guy, 16, 22
CLEAR goal-setting process, 52–53
coaches, 30, 68, 198–199. *See also* peer
    review
Cohen, Melissa, 54
collaboration, 93. *See also* Impact Teams
collaborative conversations, 151–159
collaborative projects, application of
    success criteria and, 42
collective teacher efficacy (CTE), 27,
    239, 242, 259
communication, trust and, 243–247
communication of role to students,
    17–18
communities of learners, learner
    dispositions and, 26–27
compliance, 138–139, 152
conferences, student-led, 75–76
conscious activism, 263–264
continuums, 141–143

contribution to learning, 16–20

cooperative learning principles, 30

The Core Collaborative Learning Network, 6–7

Costa, Art, 16, 21

critical eye development, 50

Csikszentmihalyi, Mihaly, 15

CTE (collective teacher efficacy), 27, 239, 242, 259

cultural issues, English Language Learners and, 110

culture of efficacy, 259

democracy peer review
  overview, 189–191
  envisioning success for, 202
  feedback, 197–198
  Google Docs for, 198–199
  reflection and, 198
  scavenger hunts and, 199–200
  Socratic Seminars and, 192–197
  of the teacher, 200–201
  trust building, 191–192

demonstrations, need for, 33. *See also* exemplars; modeling

design, Impact Teams and, 255–257

Dewey, John, 190–191

Di Capua, Danielle, 54

dialogue, trust and, 243–247

DiPietro, M., 81

discussion mapping, 198

diversity. *See* English Language Learners (ELL)

Donath, Melissa, 169

driving questions for Impact Teams, 252–253

Dweck, Carol, 118

Eells, R., 250

efficacy, culture of, 259

ELL. *See* English Language Learners (ELL)

emotional intelligence, metacognition and, 80

Empower: What Happens When Students Own Their Learning (Spencer & Juliani), 16–17

empowerment of students, 15–16, 59, 137–140

engagement, 13–15

English Language Learners (ELL)
  assessment and, 108–109
  clarity about, 109–112
  envisioning success for, 120
  peer review for, 116–120
  practice as essential for, 119–120
  standards and, 112–113
  success criteria for, 114–116

Essential Questions of the Year, 191

Eureka moments, 165

evidence, sources of, 255–257

exemplars, 36–37, 146, 156, 201

Farrington, C. A., 96–97

feedback. *See also specific content areas*
  collaborative conversations and, 158
  Ladder of Feedback, 158, 179
  language of, 44, 66–69
  in the moment, 198–199
  to move towards goal, 168–170
  reading and, 131–133, 135
  reflection and, 102–103
  rubrics for, 179–181
  self-efficacy and, 61–63, 65
  specifically teaching, 228

feedback on feedback, 47, 222–223

Feedback Stems and Frames, 69

Ferris Bueller's Day off, 13–15

fishbowl strategy, 39, 45

fixed mindset, 24

Flip Grid, 47

formative assessment, 7, 107–108

Fountas, I. C., 128

Fountas and Pinnell Literacy Continuum: A Tool for Assessment, Planning, and Teaching (Fountas & Pinnell), 128

framed discussions for relational trust, 245–247

Gibbs, A., 146

Glow and Grow protocol, 43

goals and goal setting. *See also* feedback
  overview, 51–55
  best practices to implement, 101–103
  defined, 125
  Impact Teams and, 254
  importance of, 70
  for literacy, 145–147
  progress and, 69–73
  promotion strategies, 54–55
  for reading, 123–124, 132–134
  for science, 183–184
  Socratic Seminars and, 194–197
  success criteria co-construction for, 71–72

Google Docs, 47, 198–199

grades, 62, 66–67

gradual release framework, 124

graduation rate, for English Language Learners, 108

graphic organizers, 199–200

growth mindset, 24

guided reading, 127

habits of mind, 191–192

Halbert, J., 251

Hattie, John
  collective teacher efficacy, 27, 239
  cooperative learning principles, 30
  impact and, 19
  metacognition, 80–81
  success criteria and, 68
  Visible Learning, 27, 108, 251

help seeking, 36, 85

history peer review
  overview, 205–206
  feedback on feedback, 222–223
  goal setting and, 223–226
  lessons learned with, 226–229
  modeling of peer-to-peer feedback, 219–221
  standards and, 206–207
  strategic revision and, 217–219, 223–226
  success criteria co-construction for, 212–217
  success criteria for, 207–211

How Learning Works (Ambrose et. al), 81–82

ideation, Impact Teams and, 253–255

Impact Team Evidence Walks, 255

Impact Teams
  components of, 238–240
  design and, 255–257
  ideation by, 253–255
  inquiry and, 249–259
  purpose and importance of, 235–238
  relational trust and, 241–247
  student-led, 201
  success envisioned by, 258–259

In the Moment coaching, 198–199

infusion versus add-on concept, 26

inquiry, need for, 163

"Inside the Black Box" (Black & Wiliam), 7

intellectuals, recruitment of, 7–9

Johnson, D. W., 96–97

Juliani, A. J., 16

Kallick, B., 16

Kaser, L., 251

Keyes, T. S., 96–97

King, Martin Luther, Jr., 5

labels, 57–58
Ladder of Feedback, 158, 179
language of feedback, 44, 66–69
language of learning, 23
Leading Impact Teams (Bloomberg & Pitchford), 242
learner dispositions, 21, 24–27
learner profiles, 21–24
learning, teacher's role in, 16–18
learning coaches, 68
learning culture, 5–6
learning goals, 51–55
learning networks, 244. *See also* Impact Teams
The Learning Pit video, 165
learning strategies. *See* goals and goal setting; metacognition; reflection
learning versus thinking, 25
listening to others, 19–20
literacy. *See also* reading
　continuums and, 141–143
　goals for, 145–147
　partnerships with teachers and, 139–140
　student interview about, 148–149
　student ownership, pathways for, 140–143
　theme rubrics, 147–148
　transferable tasks for, 143–145
lockstep learning, 138–139
Lovett, M. C., 81

mastery moments
　overview, 59–60
　building on, 63–64, 76–77
　of goal setting, 146
　practices for, 65
mathematics, 161–170
Mead, Margaret, 266
"messy" portfolios, 74
metacognition. *See also* reflection

activating cycle of, 81–89
defined, 79–80
emotional intelligence and, 80
importance of, 80–81, 89–90
Meyer, C. A., 73
Miller, Kelly, 255
mini-progressions, 130–131
modeling
　application of success criteria, 41, 166–167
　for English Language Learners, 116–117
　goal setting and, 146
　history peer review and, 219–221
　peer assessment, 44–45
　self-efficacy and, 60–61, 65
　shared reading and, 126–127
　strategic revision and, 48–49
　success criteria co-construction using, 38
　teacher buy-in reflected in, 184–185
Moss, C. M., 139
motivation. *See also* progress
　goals and reflection and, 103
　labels and, 57–58
　self-efficacy and, 59–66
"My Pedagogical Creed" (Dewey), 190–191

Nagaoka, J., 96–97
Nameless Voice, 144
Never Again MSD, 4
NGSS. *See* standards
non-examples, 38, 156
Norman, M. K., 81
Nottingham, James, 165
Nuthall, Graham, 62

observation data, 256
One Drive, 47
Orange Slice, 47
outcome goals, 51

partnerships with teachers, 139–140

Paulson, F. L., 73

Paulson, P. R., 73

peer coaches, power of, 30. *See also* peer
    review

peer power conferences, 46

Peer Power Feedback Framework
    overview, 30–32
    application of success criteria, 41–42
    feedback on feedback, 45–48
    learning goals and, 51–55, 101–103
    modeling of peer-to-peer feedback,
        43–45
    strategic revision in, 48–51
    success criteria co-construction,
        33–40

peer review. *See also* democracy peer
    review; history peer review; science
    peer review; *specific content areas*
    for academic writing, 9–10
    anonymity in, 179
    for English Language Learners,
        116–120
    pitfalls of, 118–120
    as worth time spent on, 228–229

#PeerPower Manifesto, 265–266

performance labels, 57–58

personal inventories of strengths and
    weaknesses, 84–85

Pinnell, G. S., 128

Pitchford, Barb, 242

portfolios, 73–75

PQP (Praise, Question, Polish)
    technique, 220–221

practice, for English Language Learners,
    119–120

Primary Reading Progression Tool,
    129–130, 133–134

problem solving, in math, 161–170

process observers, 46–47

process-oriented goals, 51–52

productive struggle, 5

progress. *See also* mastery moments
    goals and, 69–73
    language of feedback and, 66–69
    motivation increased by, 58
    portfolios and, 73–75
    self-efficacy and, 59–66
    student-led conferences and, 75–76

Project Aristotle, 237

psychological safety. *See* trust and safety

reading. *See also* literacy
    clarity about, 124–126
    goal setting and, 132–134
    importance of, 123–124
    self-assessment of, 128–134
    strategies for, 126–127

recruitment of activists, 6–7, 265

Reed, D. K., 146

reflection
    best practices to implement, 101–103
    characteristics of, 98–99
    discussion mapping and, 198
    examples of, 103–104, 182
    impact of, 100–101
    importance of, 95–97
    reading and, 134–135
    Socratic Seminars and, 196–197

relational trust, 241–247

respect, 184

reviews, as everywhere, 10

revision, 48. *See also* strategic revision

revision mindset, 49

re-voice rubrics, success criteria co-
    construction using, 40

revolutionary leaders, 3–4, 6–7

Revolutionize Assessment (Stiggins), 4–5,
    108

Ritchhart, Ron, 16, 21

Rockstar Teams. *See* Impact Teams

Roderick, M., 96–97

Rolheiser, C., 31
Ross, J. A., 31
routines, 101
rubrics
    creation based on success criteria
        co-construction, 34–36
    re-voice rubrics, 40
    science rubrics, 176–181
    stoplight rubrics, 36, 85
    theme rubrics, 147–148
rules, focus on, 18

safety. *See* trust and safety
samples, 33, 256. *See also* exemplars;
    non-examples
scavenger hunts, 199–200
school culture, 5–6, 259
science peer review
    overview, 171–173
    background information about
        scientists for, 174–176
    feedback rubrics, 179–181
    goal setting, 183–184
    lessons learned with, 184–185
    measurement of success, 185–186
    reflection and, 182
    rubric creation, 176–178
    starting, 178–181
self- and peer assessment. *See also* peer
    review
    benefits of, 8–9
    checklist for, 46
    importance of, 29, 30–31
    personal inventories of strengths and
        weaknesses and, 84–85
    phases of, 30–31
    as real world learning, 9–10
self-awareness, 79. *See also* metacognition
self-efficacy, 59–66, 169
sentence stems and frames, 69, 111–112,
    117–118

shared reading, 126–127
skills, defined, 125
SMART goals, 98
social media, 10–11, 264–265
social studies. *See* democracy peer review;
    history peer review
Socratic Seminars. *See* democracy peer
    review
Sown to Grow, 47, 182–183
Spencer, John, 16
standards
    chemistry and, 172
    collaborative conversations and, 153
    democracy peer review and, 195
    English Language Learners and,
        112–113
    history and, 206–207
    math and, 161–162
    student choice and ownership and,
        140–142, 168
Stiggins, Rick, 4, 108
stoplight rubrics, 36, 85
strategic revision
    history peer review, 223–226
    in Peer Power Feedback Framework,
        31, 48–51
    reading and, 134
    of success criteria, 217–219
strategies, defined, 125
strategy banks, 104
strengths and weaknesses inventories,
    84–85
struggle, benefits of, 163, 165
student expertise, success criteria co-
    construction using, 38–39
student-led conferences, 75–76
Student-Led Impact Teams, 201
students
    competencies needed by, 5
    contribution to learning, 19–20
    empowerment of, 15–16

as revolutionary leaders, 4
voice and, 256
success criteria
    application of, 41–42
    changing as lessons progress, 167–168
    clarity increased by, 40, 173–176
    co-construction of, generally, 33–40
    for collaborative conversations, 154, 156–158
    for English Language Learners, 114–116
    for history, 207–217
    for literacy, 144–145
    for math, 164–166
    for reading, 128–129
    reflection and, 98
    for science, 174–176
    strategic revision and, 50
success criteria detectives, 42
success stories, 146

TAG protocol, 43, 117–118
task demands, 82–84
teacher teams, 34. *See also* Impact Teams
teachers, 15–16, 256–257
technology, 47, 137–138
theme rubrics, 147–148
think-alouds
    application of success criteria, 41, 166–167
    revision and, 48–49
    shared reading and, 126
    success criteria co-construction using, 38
thinking versus learning, 25

tiers of support as stifling learning, 138–139
Timperley, H., 251
top down management, 240, 251
traiangulated evidence, 255–256
transfer of learning, 143–145
trust and safety
    English Language Learners and, 116–118
    Impact Teams and, 238, 241–247
    peer review and, 184, 191–192

upward spiral, 63–66

varied samples, success criteria co-construction using, 37
vicarious experiences, 60–61, 65
video observation, 40, 45, 146
video-based evidence, 256
Visible Learning, 27, 87, 251
Visible Learning Feedback (Hattie & Clarke), 68
Visible Learning (Hattie), 80–81, 108
visual cues, for English Language Learners, 117
visual icons, success criteria co-construction using, 40
voice, 256–257
vulnerability, 243–244

Wiliam, Dylan, 7, 30, 34, 90
winning streaks, 63–64
worked examples, success criteria co-construction using, 39

Yale Mood Meter, 83